Quality in early childhood services

Quality in early childhood services

An international perspective

Helen Penn

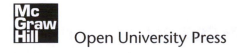

Open University Press

Open University Press
McGraw-Hill Education
McGraw-Hill House
Shoppenhangers Road
Maidenhead
Berkshire
England
SL6 2QL

email: enquiries@openup.co.uk
world wide web: www.openup.co.uk

and Two Penn Plaza, New York, NY 10121-2289, USA

First published 2011

A catalogue record of this book is available from the British Library

ISBN-13: 978-0-33-522878-2 (pb) 978-0-33-522877-5 (hb)
ISBN-10: 033522878X (pb) 0335228771 (hb)

Library of Congress Cataloging-in-Publication Data
CIP data applied for

Typeset by RefineCatch Limited, Bungay, Suffolk
Printed by Bell & Bain Ltd, Glasgow

Fictitious names of companies, products, people, characters and/or data that may
be used herein (in case studies or in examples) are not intended to represent any
real individual, company, product or event.

Mixed Sources
Product group from well-managed
forests and other controlled sources
www.fsc.org   Cert no. TT-COC-002769
© 1996 Forest Stewardship Council

FSC

The **McGraw·Hill** Companies

Contents

Figures and tables

Figures

Tables

Acknowledgements

I am especially grateful to my colleagues Eva Lloyd and Jean Murray at the University of East London who supported me in writing this book, tolerating my absences and inefficiencies. I am also grateful for the discussions with many Australian, Canadian and South African friends, and with my colleagues on the recent EU projects, especially John Bennett and Marta Korintus. Like any academic I do the rounds of conferences and workshops, and I've had lots of stimulating exchanges, feedback and strings of comments from so many people, too many to mention by name, but thank you, you are in here in the footnotes. Stephanie Frosch and Fiona Richman from Open University Press were as always very patient and supportive, even as the book completely changed its shape and timespan. Finally, thanks to my partner Tom Snow. He has mastered the art of interrupting but at the same time he has a stream of offbeat ideas and is always buying books, so there are compensations.

Preface

At the time when I began this book, my granddaughter, then aged 4 years, was living with us. Most weekdays I walked with her in the morning through the park to her nursery class. It took us about 20 minutes and she liked to talk as we went. She recited snatches of nursery rhymes and stories. She provided a running account of the state of the park; which trees still have leaves in winter, what the ducks and geese in the pond were doing; how the Christmas decorations in the café sparkled; whether we would hear the robin, or see the wagtails again. She consulted the big map of the park at the entrance gate to point out where we were going. She merged fiction with her facts. She insisted that on a walk through the park with her mother she saw two green guinea fowl in the bushes. The sight of a large Dalmation dog caused her to remember Bottomly Potts, a large spotted dog from Lynley Dodd's children's book *Hairy Maclary from Donaldson's Dairy*, a favourite bedtime reading. The changes in the weather perplexed her since she comes from a country where cold weather is rare. Will footprints show up on the hoary grass? (Try it and see, I answered.) Can you walk on the ice on the pond? (Don't ever try it out, I cautioned.) My hands are cold inside my gloves. (You need a warmer coat, we'll have to get you one, I said anxiously.) She referred backwards to other trips we have had through the park and forwards to the trips we might have next time. She was a perfect audience for my jokes and observations. Disconcertingly, she remembered most of what I had to say!

I was asked to comment in a meeting once on the topic of listening to children. I said, from my perspective as a grandparent, it was impossible not to listen. I might tune out some of my granddaughter's chatter as we go through the park, but it is impossible not to respond to her lively way of describing what she sees and what she is doing, or to be unimpressed by her vivid interest. Ignoring her questions is pointless since she usually persists in asking them until the answer satisfies her.

Most conversations between children and their mothers or other close relatives arise out of everyday activities like this and are deeply contextualized. Studies of caring, and of mothering in particular, suggest that mothers focus on the material and emotional welfare of their children, that they pursue a different 'ethic of care' from that of teachers. Mothers' knowledge and relationship to their children is not scientific and generalized, but anecdotal, subjective, ad hoc, and continuous – developing and changing over time within a specific context and intensely reciprocal. Mothers (and grandmothers) inhabit the same spaces as their children, and the time they spend with them is elastic, based on their needs and demands. Teachers and professionals on the other hand tend to hold more abstract, norm-related knowledge and expectations of children, unrelated to context. Professionals hold themselves back from intense personal relationships with children and make judgements about what they think is appropriate behaviour for themselves and for the children they are with. There are temporal, spatial as well as emotional limitations in their work with children. They are not swayed by the storms of the moment, by ecstatic joy, or temper tantrums or shades in between. They limit physical care (nursery education formally begins in almost all countries at age 2+ when children are no longer incontinent). They are more professional and detached. In a classic study, carried out some time ago now, Barbara Tizard tape recorded the conversations of 3-year-old girls at home with their mothers and compared those conversations with those they had at nursery school.[1] She found that whatever the background of the child, working class or middle class, and however limited the conversation, the talk at home was richer, more extended, and drew on a much wider range of events, and showed more evidence of logical thinking and sequential thought than any talk that took place in the nursery school. Although the book was at pains to say that nursery education provision complemented provision at home, and offered new experiences to children, it argued that professionals cannot respond like mothers and other intimate carers in cueing into the contexts of children's speech and language.

And yet, what I take as normal in my dealings with my grandchildren, our conversation, its familiarity and its continuity; and what social scientists take as a legitimate area for study, the relationships between adults and young children most often exclude the realities that exist for the majority of the world's children and families. The intensity, primacy and verbosity of the mother–child relationship which is taken as a sine qua non of upbringing in the global North simply does not exist in the same way, nor is it considered so important in many of the families in the global South. The anthropologist Robert LeVine suggests that by comparison with many young children's experiences in Africa, we inflate the egos of our children to (relatively) monstrous proportions by our intense focus upon them.[2] My conversations with my granddaughter in the park are a particular product of time and place, rather than a universal phenomenon. This is a very disconcerting thought when what I was doing seemed so natural and instinctive and good for both of us. Thinking about my actions and my conversation in the park in this relative way doesn't at all negate what I believe and feel to be right. But it does suggest that understanding of young children can be broadened and enlivened by knowing more about what goes on in the world, and by thinking about the very different conceptions of childhood that exist and how they overlap and how they differ.

This book is an exploration of what we *believe* is natural and normal in regards to young children, and how we institutionalize those beliefs in different places and contexts. It explores some of the assumptions and practices in our understanding and ways of relating to young children. It deals with the question of how the idea of good practice is derived, who then carries out the practice, and how the work of practitioners is in turn assessed. In thinking about 'quality', that is how we provide the best environments for bringing up young children, I explore to what extent ideas about quality are informed and tempered by very different kinds of circumstances and broader societal arrangements. In the process of writing the book, I've come to the conclusion that, even if it is apparently far removed from my daily experience taking my granddaughter to her nursery school, those societal arrangements are crucial. The nursery class wouldn't exist without them.

It is very unlikely that anyone working with young children would willingly admit that what they are doing is poor practice. But many, many young children spend their time with others in some kind of institutional setting, and are relatively powerless within it. Supposing someone from the outside – a professional visitor, a parent or a researcher or even a neighbour – judges that the quality of what is going on in a nursery is poor, what happens next? Who is responsible and what can be done about it? Does it help if there are agreed criteria for quality and the nursery or centre or kindergarten can be shown to be in breach of what is acceptable? Or does the existence of such quality criteria – particularly if they are fairly basic and in place just to avert the worst conditions – then serve to depress standards? Are there alternative ways of looking after and caring for children? In various guises as a parent and then a grandparent, as an administrator in a variety of places, and as a researcher working in some outlandish places, I've had to ask all these questions.

But the answers are elusive. Given my present trade as a Professor of Early Childhood I've had to think again about the notion of quality and how it is defined, measured, enacted and enforced in early childhood. At various times, I have researched and written about quality, at length and for many different audiences. I have explored the quality frameworks in place in a number of countries and contributed to international symposia and agreements. I have been asked to comment about quality in meetings in countries as far apart and as different as Kazakhstan and South Africa. I've worked in countries which are so resource poor that the most basic criteria for quality were rarely met, and in countries that are so resource rich that for a lot of the time I felt like a poor relation. I've changed my mind about quality a number of times (a privilege of growing older). It is such a well-worn theoretical path, that perhaps I am being optimistic in thinking I can contribute any more to it.

But even if the topic of quality is overdone in innumerable books and pamphlets and governmental guides, even if the word quality has become a mantra, a short cut for saying 'don't bother, we've got it right', even if quality assurance is more about assurance than quality, even if it has become a hackneyed debate, I would argue that the concept of quality still needs reworking.

The theories, as theories in the social sciences tend to do, present us with alternative pictures. Put crudely, on the one hand there is a view that quality is necessary and needs to be defined, and defining it is a straightforward empirical exercise of identifying relevant variables. At the other extreme, there is a view that quality is a meaningless concept, given the relative nature of people's perceptions of one another, and the need always to be negotiating the terms and conditions of one's relationships. There is another theoretical continuum about the relative importance of macro-level explanations (policies and rationales) and micro-level explanations (what happens today in – and on the way to – the nursery class). I've tried to travel up and down these theoretical tramlines.

Although I've tried to present an analysis of quality that deals with the topic from many angles, it is also, in one sense, a jackdaw collection of ideas culled from many sources. Whatever the reading equivalent of an alcoholic is, I am one. I read widely, and some of the areas in which I am interested are not directly related to early childhood at all. But if ideas are useful, and metaphors illuminating to my arguments, then I've tried to use them even so. With the kind agreement of the publisher, I have provided citations in end-notes, because I think it is both more comprehensive and less intrusive than putting publication dates in the text, and a reference list at the end.

I hope then, to provide an international perspective on quality, examining how certain ideas in early childhood have become powerful, how practices persist, and how ideas and practices have been transported around the globe. It must also be obvious by now that although ideas are being tossed about, and practices critiqued, what the book doesn't do and can't do is offer a foolproof guide to quality. To suppose there is one is to search for fool's gold.

Notes

1 Tizard, B. (1984) *Young Children Learning: Talking and Thinking at Home and at School*. London: Fontana.
2 LeVine, R. (2003) *Childhood Socialization: Comparative Studies of Parenting, Learning and Educational Change*. Hong Kong: Comparative Education Research Centre.

1 A brief introduction

The American socio-biologist Sarah Hrdy describes the phenomena of nurseries in this way:

> grouping infants together – like bats in a communal nursery – for a certain number of hours everyday under the supervision of *paid* alloparents (substitute parents) who are not kin, but who are expected to act as if they are, is an evolutionary novelty, completely experimental.[1]

Explanations of quality

This book is concerned with one particular aspect of early childhood: that is the societal arrangements that are made for the care and education of young children. It enquires what rationales are being put forward to justify them, and how they are judged in providing a service. What does quality mean in these circumstances, and who arbitrates? As Hrdy's quotation colourfully indicates, nurseries offer a relatively new way of bringing up children. In a few countries, such as Belgium and France, full-time nursery education for children aged 3–5 was well established over a hundred years ago. Day nurseries, by which I mean the communal housing of very young infants, are more recent and more controversial. But the regular and widespread use of nursery education and day nurseries in most countries has only really happened in the last 25–50 years, or less. In some countries it hasn't happened systematically at all.

In Chapters 2 and 3, I explore the kinds of policy rationales, sometimes overlapping and sometimes used in separate ways that are used as a justification for developing early childhood services. Currently there are two main rationales in use, sometimes used in tandem, sometimes used without acknowledgement or understanding of what the other involves. The first is that women/parents need to reconcile family and work obligations, and childcare is a necessary support in order for women to work. Second, early education interventions are an essential foundation for subsequent learning and schooling. There are various versions of these rationales, plus some additional rationales, which I will try to detail.

These rationales are often historic. In fact in all countries there has been a complicated policy history in introducing early education and care services, which reflects wider national concerns and dilemmas that may have very little to do with early childhood per se. These origins may be long since forgotten, yet they nevertheless continue to influence current provision, in what is sometimes called 'path dependency' or 'policy stickiness'. Current research and theory is usually dominated by relatively short-term policy perspectives, but policy rationales almost always have roots in the past. Rationales for policy are important because they determine the issues around which discussions of quality take place. The frame for quality is set by governments, by intent and by default, even if the learning and development that occurs among children in nurseries may depend in the last resort on an individual relationship between an adult and a child.

In Chapters 4, 5, and 6 I discuss quality at a systemic level. In each country early childhood education and care (ECEC) encompasses a different spectrum of services. In each country the auspices differ, that is nursery provision may be organized at a national or at a local level, financed in different kinds of ways, or be delivered by the state itself or by a variety of providers. In each country too, there is more or less education, more or less care, more or less training of those who work in the sector, more or less attention to social circumstances.

In the view of a number of international organizations who have taken an international overview of early education and care services – OECD (Organization for Economic Cooperation and Development), Unicef, Unesco and the EU – the extent to which the system is coherent and extensive critically determines quality. Unicef for example gives 10 indicators of quality. Some of these indicators, for example levels of poverty or child health, are not directly concerned with early childhood services but critically affect the effectiveness of such services. When children experience conditions of acute poverty and inequality then it is an uphill battle for early childhood services to compensate for these disadvantages. I focus on the work of these international organizations, and the discussions they have had about quality in Chapter 4.

In Chapter 5 I discuss the role of the market and the attempts to regulate it. A major new concern in the development of early childhood services has been the growth of private for-profit provision for those who can pay for it. In the USA, as I indicate below, the childcare sector has always been predicated on the private market. But this has not been the case in other developed or rich countries. In the UK there has been a startling turnaround and from having a mainly government funded and delivered system, there has been a substantial growth of the private sector. For-profit programmes, run as small businesses or as corporate endeavours, may present particular problems of quality.

Understandings of quality have become closely linked to the ideas of choice and value for money. I explore the evidence about the way the growth of the private market has changed people's perceptions of services, and in turn reshaped the notion of quality. Adult–child ratios, curricula, levels of training, and space requirements may all be subject to regulation, but the person (or company) who runs the private provision may embody a particular ethos in which profit, accumulating income, is of paramount importance, over and above other considerations of child learning or parent well-being.

In Chapter 6 I discuss issues of curriculum and training and explore how they vary internationally. What children should be learning and how they should be learning have led to some very public battles. In the early childhood sector, where training is not consistent or mandatory within or across countries, many research findings suggest that the level of training, initial and in-service, is the most important single factor in achieving high quality services. I review some of the evidence about how training is conceptualized and carried out across different countries. A key issue here is gender, and I include reflections on the traditional notions of gender and caring and how they are linked.

After considering more general issues, I explore quality at programme and practice levels. There is less variation and less bad practice where services are well funded and systematically organized, but of course there is good and bad in every system. So what makes a difference between those projects which are described as 'high quality' and those which are not?

In Chapter 7, working spaces, I explore space and design for adults and children. Space and design seem to me to be very neglected areas of quality, partly because in the UK, and in some other countries, children's physical activities and aesthetic feelings are completely under-rated as an aspect of their well-being and as an underpinning of their learning. I think working spaces matter, for children as well as for adults. The practical spatial organization of early education and care work raises some fundamental issues.

In Chapter 8, I consider ideas about working practices. There is a literature about co-operative management (although less so in the field of early years), which suggests that worker participation and decision-making may be more productive of quality than hierarchical management. Leadership and good resource management are clearly important in any sector, and there is a substantial literature about leadership in the early years, but does ownership and participative or collegial practice matter too? I review the evidence and make some suggestions about management and leadership.

In Chapter 9 I discuss the kinds of relationships teachers and practitioners forge with individual children, and the way in which children's learning is encouraged. Individual relationships matter enormously although what is valued is also highly cultural. As Bruner has famously said 'perhaps even more than with most cultural matters, childrearing practices and beliefs reflect local conceptions of how the world is and how the child should be readied for living it'.[2]

The intimacy, continuity and contextual nature of familial relationships and the cultural understandings they draw upon cannot easily – if at all – be replicated in an institutional setting, where unrelated groups of children and adults must rub along together. Hence Sarah Hrdy's remark about the unfamiliarity and strangeness of the idea of nursery provision. Ideas and understandings about how adults should conduct themselves and what they should be doing in nurseries are often treated as straightforward when they are not. Many practitioners working in the field are trained at a basic and vocational level, especially those caring for very young children, and their didactic training does not equip them to deal with abstract ideas and challenging issues. Some theories of practice do push these boundaries, especially those labelled as 'postmodern' and I discuss them in this chapter.

For slightly older children, the emphasis switches to learning and how practitioners (or teachers) can encourage learning. I have met practitioners who have a joie de vivre and a gift for inspiration who can captivate the attention of any group of children they work with. One of my most vivid memories is of a teacher with a very large (50 or so) group of children passing round a large onion and talking about its taste, texture, smell and preparation. She managed to hold the attention of the children despite the size of the group and the inappropriateness of the surroundings – a large hall. When knowledge is regarded as something to transmit – or where circumstances are difficult – teaching is valued as performance. In this sense a good teacher is like an entrancing magician, with a repertoire of activities, constantly refreshed, maintained and polished. But if knowledge is regarded as participative and co-constructed, additional or different skills are required. Being ingenious and inspiring in finding topics and projects and resources in working with children is only half the story. The other half of course is to be able to relate to the children themselves, to be able to listen, to enable them to voice their situations and enlarge their understanding.

Children's learning in the early years is phenomenal, but it is also subject to considerable interpretation by adults. Practitioners and professionals are taught to draw on a normative idea of childhood, an understanding derived from the field of child development, of children's capabilities and needs. In very diverse situations, where children come from a wide range of backgrounds and may exhibit a wide range of behaviours, then such norms – essentially derived from a white Anglo-American view of early childhood – are insufficient preparations for practice. Learning to deal with diversity, of race, class, language and health, presents many challenges for practice. In writing about quality, I necessarily deal with issues of diversity. These issues are especially pertinent in poorer countries, where the resources available to children are very meagre. I focus on the attempts made in poor countries to introduce early education and care – and on the attempts of rich countries to influence them – in Chapter 10.

Each level in the account of what quality means raises questions of analysis, measurement and accountability. There are various standardized tools for measuring quality in early childhood, mostly at a programme and a practice level, and I discuss the use of some of these measures. But as I have indicated, the matter is not simple. To use the word 'quality' implies that children are being well cared for and educated, and we are doing the best for them that we can. In reality 'quality' is a layered concept which reflects a range of assumptions about childhood, and about provision for and practice with young children.

At an international comparative level – the comparisons made by such bodies as OECD, the EU and Unicef – measurement may include an overview of the tools and frameworks which are in place in a country for assuring quality – legal frameworks, codes of practice, training requirements, voluntary codes of practice etc. Or it might encompass issues of service accessibility, sustainability of services and working conditions of frontline staff; or a specification of the skills of the workers involved.

At a programme level it may include the degree of involvement of users and workers in the implementation of the service; or advice, complaints and redress procedures; or cyclical processes such as participatory review mechanisms. Or it may just focus on child outcomes; or the extent to which the service contributes to maternal employment. Or it may try to measure children's well-being. I was at a conference where a childcare consultant said her criterion for quality was 'Are the children happy?' This is a nice approach, and no doubt genuine, but it is not the full story. All the other aspects of nursery provision cannot simply be waived away.

Ideas and priorities about quality differ from country to country, and within countries. Standard measurements undoubtedly have their uses as a comparative tool, as a means of obtaining a systematic overview of a particular situation. But such tools are only good for what they set out to measure. Using a centimetre ruler, even when it is subdivided into millimetres, is not going to help you measure the volume of sound on a radio. Using an instrument such as the Early Childhood Environmental Rating Scale will tell you little about the organization or cohesion of the early education and care system, or the political claims which are being made for it – although you might legitimately infer that, given the lower end of the scale, what is being measured may sometimes be dire.

So although standard measurements may be useful in highlighting broad variations across programmes or practice, they offer relatively limited information, which somebody else (a politician?) has to interpret if changes are to be made. The extent to which policy is evidence based – or as the cynics put it, the extent to which evidence is policy driven – is something of a sore point in the voluminous literature on the relationship between policy and research. On the other hand more or less everyone acknowledges the need for accountability, to the taxpayers, to parents, and increasingly to the children who experience the service. How necessary is it for parents and children to voice their views on services? How might it be undertaken? Although questions of measurement arise throughout the book, I deal with measurement specifically in Chapter 11.

In Chapter 12, I try to sum up the many arguments I have raised. As Sarah Hrdy suggests, we are still experimenting. We engage in many novel evolutionary behaviours but Hrdy's comments raise the question about how one can understand 'quality' in the light of something that may be 'unnatural' or counter-instinctual in the first place, especially when there is such a variety of understandings of what constitutes good care and education. I conclude that it might be more appropriate to think of quality not as a noun but as a verb. Quality might be best viewed as a search for improvement, a search to provide the best we can for the young children who are being educated and cared for by people other than their parents, but it is a search where the topics, the strategies and methodologies still require much elaboration.

Internationalism

In this book I take an international perspective on quality in early childhood services. I do this partly because there are similarities as well as differences in the way in which people educate and care for young children in various places, and making sense of these similarities and differences broadens and deepens any discussion about quality. In addition, what others see from their various perspectives of history and geography may help us overcome our own parochialism, in whichever country we reside. Quality is nothing if not relative, and there are no magic formulae, only many adjustments to suit each set of circumstances.

I argue that history and geography cannot be ignored. As well as enlarging our horizons, they help us to combat the parochialism that is very often the enemy of quality. My own claims to have an international perspective arise from the work I have undertaken for international agencies, including the OECD, and most recently for an EU project comparing early education and care services, regulation and quality across Europe, which I discuss in Chapter 4. While somewhat ashamed of my carbon footprint, nevertheless I am very grateful for the exceptional opportunities that I have had to discuss issues of quality in so many places.

Countries like Canada, Australia and New Zealand are to an extent chips off the old block and reflect the particular political and policy dilemmas of an English liberal heritage. A lot of development work in the field of early childhood has taken place in each of these countries, through dedicated advocacy and research, and offers useful lessons on quality which I try to include.

But I have been particularly fortunate in that some of the international work I have done has taken me to some extraordinary places in Africa and Asia, and there the challenges to conventional understanding about what quality means are much greater. Jones writing about early childhood in Peru, as part of the *Young Lives* project, suggests:

> it is critical to unpack culturally specific understandings of core cultural concepts . . . (such as 'children', 'family' and 'work') and how these are subject to competing interpretations and reinterpretations in societies undergoing rapid social, political, economic and demographic transitions.[3]

Cultural unpacking is necessarily part of the account in this book.

Working in these countries confronts us with issues of knowledge transfer. Many of the ideas and understandings about early childhood have been articulated and published in the global North, in rich countries, and are applied willy-nilly to poor countries in the global South whether they are relevant and appropriate or not – a phenomenon I have described elsewhere as 'Travelling policies and global buzzwords'.[4] In writing about quality, I also hope to be able to question the way in which ideas about quality in early childhood services are so blithely and inappropriately exported from one country to another, especially from rich countries to poorer ones.

The process of knowledge transfer is nowhere more pronounced than in the USA. Some of the most gifted writers, some of the most interesting research, and some of the most innovative practice in the field of early childhood come from the USA. Yet in terms of the range and quality of its early childhood services, the USA ranks near or at the bottom of every league table. It is utterly in hock to the for-profit sector, and increasingly, to the corporate sector. Research on early childhood from the USA infrequently acknowledges that this is the case, taking what is exceptional in every other country as too ordinary for comment. The USA also has one of the greatest inequality (or gini) ratings among developed nations and is weak in providing the redistributive services, such as health care and other social benefits, which in other countries are used to counter inequality. This degree of inequality and social segregation skews understandings about what might be expected or achieved in the delivery of early childhood services. I am at pains to state this so clearly because the USA is held up so often as a model. The World Bank, which funds early education and care programmes in poor countries throughout the world, uses little or no other evidence in support of the programmes it promotes other than the evidence from the USA. Human capital theory, widely cited by economists as a rationale for investing in early childhood, relies heavily on evidence from the USA. And so on. It is a distortion to regard the extreme circumstances of the USA as anything other than as exceptional, and therefore parochial.

In discussing the concept of quality it is important to understand the strengths, but also the limitations, sometimes the grave limitations, of the evidence available. These questions of international understanding underwrite the book.

Notes

1   Hrdy, S.B. (1999) *Mother Nature: Maternal Instincts and How They Shape the Human Species*. New York: Ballantine. The quotation is from p. 506.
2   Bruner, J. (2000) 'Foreword.' In J. DeLoache and A. Gottleib (eds) *A World of Babies: Imagined Childcare Guides for Seven Societies*. Cambridge: Cambridge University Press, p. xi.
3   Jones, N. with Villar, E. (2008) 'Situating children in international development policy: Challenges involved in successful evidence-informed policy-making.' *Evidence and Policy* 4(1): 31–51. The quotation is from p. 45.
4   Penn, H. (2010) 'Travelling policies and global buzzwords: How INGOs and charities spread the word about early childhood.' *Childhood* forthcoming.

2   Sticky policies and path dependencies

> Culture and history have to be the basic frames within which one's attempts to understand and explain are set . . . no educational policy can be properly understood except by reference to the web of inherited ideas and values, habits and customs, institutions and world views which make one, or one region, or one group distinct from one another.[1]

In this chapter and the subsequent one, I explore – in a potted version – the rationales that have led to setting up of early childhood education and care services in a number of different countries. Rationales are important; they are the justification for the policy decisions which are made. They may be explicit or not, but it is ultimately on these rationales that any judgement of quality rests. For instance, if the rationale for providing services is to improve children's education performance at school, then discussions about quality will focus on children's learning. Even so, it is rarely simple or straightforward to measure quality even when the rationales are laid bare. I deal with issues of measurement in the final section of this book.

I have visited or worked in all of the countries I describe, and know their histories, although I present an eclectic selection in no particular order, rather than a systematic overview. My criterion for writing about them is that they represent a spread of policy options. They offer an illustration of the possible routes in the development of ideas about the purposes and functions of early childhood education and care. I have not included a contextual account of Nordic countries, which also represent another policy direction, partly because I do not have the in-depth knowledge of them that I have of other countries, and partly because they are widely written about. But it doesn't constitute an important omission because this chapter is not a review of international policy development in early childhood. Instead it is intended to demonstrate the context and the continuity of policies over time, and how these affect definitions of quality. Since I know the UK best, as probably many readers will, I have provided a particularly detailed account of it, a blow by blow legislative history. But in each case the rationales I discuss have roots in the past – this is partly a history chapter.

The notion of time is of course relative, and in the introductory chapter, I cited Sarah Hrdy's contention that nurseries are, evolutionarily speaking, a new thing. However, in speaking about the history of policy-making in early childhood, and its roots, we are not considering the deep time of evolutionists, but about a span of around 150 years, sometimes a much briefer span. The point is there are rarely new starts; everything builds to an extent on what has gone before.

A book by Karen Schweie and Harry Willekens uses the history of early childhood institutions in a variety of European countries to argue that current research and theory is dominated by relatively short-term policy perspectives, but that policy always has roots in the past. They explore the notion that

> preschool organizations have their roots in different national traditions, themselves having their origins in different eras of social and economic development. These traditions have been crystallized in different institutions, in socially and legally structured ways of doing things which tend to facilitate the introduction of some innovations and to stand in the way of others. To understand the development of public childcare and preschool organizations and the range of accessible solutions for contemporary social policy issues it is imperative to see how these institutions create openings at the same time as being obstacles for certain kinds of solutions.[2]

The authors use the phrase 'path dependency' to illustrate how decisions made long ago in the past still influence decisions in the present,[3] and 'policy stickiness' to describe a situation where policy stagnates partly because efforts to change it fail to recognize what really needs to be changed. The examples in this chapter suggest at the very least it requires a very concerted policy momentum to recognize path dependency and to deal with it. Policies appear to unaccountably stagnate at the same time as they are being advanced. This chapter explores why this might be so.

UK

The UK education system illustrates the long arm of the past. The school starting age of 5 in the UK is an accident of history, rather than a considered pedagogic choice. In fact children typically start school in the year in which they become 5; most 4 year olds are in reception classes. The age of admission to school in the UK was a footnote to legislation passed in 1870. It was originally going to be age 6, but on the spur of the moment elderly male politicians voted for age 5, because of a perceived rivalry with the Austrian empire, where school started at age 6. But once the decision became law, it has become justified in all manner of ways by professionals and played out in the UK curriculum, inspections and testing. As Robin Alexander has pointed out, the decision to make education universal and compulsory was not a generous one.[4] The education system was devised as a 'Gradgrinder' system, in which the poor were to be drilled in the three Rs to make the working classes more employable in the manufacturing industries.[5] Echoing this first arbitrary decision, and reflecting the legacy of a punitive attitude towards the poor, the UK still expects a performance and outcome level for children aged 5 which by European standards might be considered absurd. This is an example of policy stickiness and path dependency – an ad-hoc accidental decision made long ago, and a class divisiveness, which determine the shape of provision now. The origins of these UK policies are long since forgotten, although their effects endure. The current national curriculum in England as well as the patterning of early childhood services are in part a reflection of these decisions made long ago.

Nursery education was (and is) defined as an extension to the education system for children aged 3–4, provided in schools. To begin with nursery education was generally provided only in urban areas, and on a limited basis of 12.5 hours per week. Only in 1972 was there a belated acceptance (by Margaret Thatcher) that nursery education was a good idea for all children. It took another 30 years to try to implement it.

While schooling exerted a downward pressure, what one expert has called 'the schoolification of early childhood',[6] welfare has been another, separate matter, warranting a different kind of intervention. The behaviour of poor children and their feckless parents has been criticized for centuries, and is a major concern still.[7] The middle classes by contrast have been able to buy their way out of trouble, and evade scrutiny, by employing servants and nannies and using public (private) boarding schools. The dominant feature in the history of day nursery provision and other forms of family welfare has been social class, and philanthropic concern about what to do about the poor. It has been about corralling the poor, about targeting and rationing; defining and maintaining the boundaries of who is entitled to provision and who is not.

Traditionally (for over 100 years) in the UK 'childcare' has been seen as a service providing alternative care for mothers who were unable to provide for their children aged 0–5 for reasons of poverty or inadequacy. A small number of day nurseries were provided during and after the Second World War by health authorities. In 1974 the responsibility for day nurseries was transferred to social services. The remit of these local authority nurseries was to provide daycare for poor or feckless mothers whose children would otherwise be taken away and placed into local authority care. Local authority social service departments varied considerably in the number of places they provided in nurseries, urban areas providing the most provision. Overall less than 1 per cent of children aged 0–5 attended day nurseries.

Generally mothers with young children were strongly encouraged to stay at home with their young children. For a long period, up to the 1980s, less than 5 per cent of mothers of young children were in full-time work, although many more worked part-time. Working mothers were so unusual that they were an object of interest and concern in the psychological and sociological literature.[8] Working mothers were expected to make the arrangements and meet the costs themselves, the local authority role being limited to minimal regulation. Most local authorities interpreted the 1974 legislation and subsequent government guidance notes to local authorities as forbidding the use of day nurseries for children under 3 years for psychological reasons. The government promoted childminding (family daycare) instead, so there were very few day nurseries in existence other than social service nurseries. From 1974 also local authority social service departments were responsible for registering and inspecting childminding and any other form of childcare. Nannies, as an in-house arrangement, was exempt from any kind of inspection.

From the late 1970s there was a movement, led mainly by feminists, to open co-operative or community day nurseries for working parents. These were funded directly by progressive local authorities, with small fee charges, usually on a means tested basis. The playgroup movement also began in the 1970s as an attempt to compensate for the lack of nursery education and to provide self-funded low key informal group experiences for children aged 3–5 on a sessional basis for 5–10 hours a week. The playgroup movement, which was widespread, also endorsed a policy of encouraging mothers to stay at home. More children attended playgroups than nursery education.

In 1989 the Child Care Act explicitly permitted babies and children under 3 years to be accommodated in nurseries. As a result, there was a slow growth of private for-profit self-funded nurseries. In addition local authority social services nurseries began to admit children aged 0–3 of working mothers on a full-cost or partly subsidized basis, and the numbers of community nurseries increased.

In 1997 the Labour Government came to power with a mandate to encourage and enable women's workforce participation. It also promised to expand nursery education to reach all children, although still on a part-time basis of 12.5 hours per week for 33 weeks a year. The position in 1997 was:

- Publicly funded, publicly provided local authority day nurseries for approximately 1 per cent of children 0–5, mostly children 'in need', mostly in urban areas.
- Part-time publicly funded publicly provided (maintained) nursery education for about 33 per cent of children aged 3–4, mostly in urban areas, and mostly in the form of nursery classes attached to primary

schools. There were a small percentage of free-standing nursery schools.

- A regulated voluntary non-profit self-help playgroup movement offering informal group care for about 30 per cent of children aged 3–4, relying mainly on volunteer staffing and rented accommodation.
- Regulated childminders (family daycare) offering provision for approximately 10 per cent of children under 5 years.
- A small for-profit private regulated childcare sector, catering for about 5 per cent of children.
- A small number of regulated co-operative or community nurseries, mainly in urban areas, offering childcare for children 0–5.

Although the Labour party rhetoric was to support working mothers, the government inherited a fragmented system, with private and public stakeholders with a vested interest in preserving the particular format of services endorsed by their own organization. Reconciling the interests of the many stakeholders was problematic. The childcare and education policies were first of all administered separately, with little reference to each other, even although the age groups overlapped. Childcare continued to be for children 0–5 (soon extended to cover out-of-school care for children 5–12) and nursery education for children 3–4.

In 2000 the government transferred responsibility for childcare from social services to education, at a local and a national level, and all provision, whether designated as childcare or as nursery education, has been administered through the Department for Education (DfE, which was known as the Department for Children, Schools and Families (DCSF) between 2007 and 2010).[9] There is now a common curricular framework for all childcare and education provision for children aged 0–5. Responsibility for registering and inspection has been taken away from local authorities and is carried out centrally by Ofsted (the Office for Standards in Education, Children's Services and Skills).

Despite the administrative transfer, and various initiatives on the ground to bring different stakeholders together to discuss common interests, the separate traditions of childcare and education have continued within the DfE. The childcare workforce, for example, is regulated as part of a wider low-skilled social service workforce, with mainly low-level vocational courses, while the teaching workforce is separately regulated, requiring skilled postgraduate qualifications. Similarly the Ofsted standards required for schools are significantly more stringent than those required for childcare. Most importantly funding mechanisms for childcare and education differ. The former is almost entirely through demand side funding (funding parental choice) whereas nursery education is funded through supply side funding directly to the institution (see below).

Policies have been promoted through a series of strategy papers leading up to legislation, subsequent and guidance notes for local authorities. At time of writing, the two most recent key strategy papers were *Five Year Strategy for Children and Learners* (2004), which stressed educational outcomes, and *Choice for Parents: The Best Start for Children – A Ten Year Strategy for Childcare* (2004), which stressed the importance of parental choice and market flexibility. In response to a series of scandals about abused children, a government booklet *Every Child Matters* was issued in 2006, setting out government priorities for children, including the promotion of their health and safety and well-being. Any inherent contradictions between the positions put forward in these various documents have not been explored. The government view, although only indirectly stated in *Choice for Parents*, was that the private for-profit market was the best means of expanding services quickly for working parents, given the low starting point.

Moreover, many of the policies have been implemented not through gradual expansion of universal provision, but through special government-led short-term initiatives such as Sure Start, Neighbourhood Nurseries and Early Years Development and Childcare Partnerships (EYDCP). These special initiatives were intended partly to expand provision, and partly to try to reconcile the interests of the many public and private stakeholders. They have proved short-lived. The current initiative Sure Start Children's Centres are mainly attached to schools. The Sure Start Children's Centres first of all had a brief to include childcare for working mothers, but in the most recent government guidance, in 2009, this requirement has been dropped.

The most important changes carried out by the Labour Government since 1997 have been concerned with funding. In 1998 Childcare Tax Credit was introduced. This provides government funding for tax credits to enable parents to choose and pay for childcare. This led to the rapid growth of the for-profit childcare sector, and the emergence of corporate for-profit childcare businesses as smaller businesses consolidated. In 2006, the Childcare Act removed powers from local authorities to fund or provide childcare directly, and legislated for 'childcare market management'. The job of local authorities is now mainly to manage and co-ordinate supply and demand for childcare by providing local information for parents about the local childcare market and other services for children, and to stimulate the creation of local for-profit providers to meet demand. Many local authorities now have 'childcare business managers'. All childcare is expected to be self-funding or 'sustainable'.

Since 2002, the private for-profit market has grown by 70 per cent; 85 per cent of childcare is now provided by the private for-profit market.[10] Over half the market is provided by companies (defined as owning 5 or more businesses). Of the 20 largest for-profit companies, 19 are corporate companies answering to shareholders. The Childcare Act 2006 also permitted private for-profit nurseries to offer nursery education for children aged 3–4, providing the business met with curricular and staffing regulations (less than those required for formal nursery education). In those areas where there was insufficient nursery education for all children, rather than education authorities creating new provision, the private for-profit sector or voluntary sector were expected to offer it instead and the local authority would have to recompense them at a standard rate. At the time of writing, private for-profit and non-profit nurseries are arguing that the recompense for providing nursery education is insufficient and does not match that received by the maintained or publicly funded sector. In response to these complaints, the DCSF issued a paper in July 2009 *Implementing an Early Years Single Funding Formula: Practice Guidance*, suggesting that the private sector and publicly provided (maintained) nursery education be funded at the same rate, but this has been temporarily waived for further consideration, in the light of objections from the publicly funded or maintained sector, where standards are higher because of the employment of more highly qualified staff than in other sectors.

Since 1997 therefore, there has been a tranche of legislation and guidance concerning childcare and nursery education. This is now codified in the 2008 *Statutory Guidance on the Early Years Foundation Stage*, which constitutes the quality framework for all discussions about early years provision. Although nowhere stated as an explicit policy, the main beneficiary of these policies has been the private for-profit sector. Despite government efforts, the number of women working full-time has not significantly increased since 1997, partly because of the high cost of for-profit childcare, and because of the difficulties of reconciling childcare and education (as well as limited maternity/paternity and parental leave arrangements). Although provision has increased, and there is now over 95 per cent coverage of nursery education for 3–4-year-old children, there is still considerable policy overlap and confusion.

In the UK especially, the latest guidance note or policy document from the government is almost always a compromise of some kind, but tends to be treated as a revelation. The extreme hype and extravagant claims for the much vaunted Sure Start programme – the Labour party's flagship programme to address child poverty – is a case in point.[11] This arrogance about the relevance of the past was epitomized for me by a very young Treasury official in the UK. He was compiling a report on the training of early childhood workers, and he told me that he had 15 minutes in which to 'download' my brain! This is a comical example (especially to me) but there are many instances of efforts to deal with the question of quality as if it can be addressed in a policy vacuum. On the contrary, the past is ever-present – indeed how could it not be, especially for those of us who have lived through a generation of changes. The history of the UK is unique and its policy discourses on early childhood and its various conceptions of quality have their own especial flavour (a quixotic one).

Now there is a new government in the UK, and a scare about public finances. Another round of changes is likely to be introduced. But it is something of a certainty that it will be more variations on the same tune; policies in this area have stuck more firmly in the UK than in many other countries.

Belgium

In Belgium, the state provided nursery schools for 49 per cent of children aged 3–5 in 1900 (long before the *first* state nursery school was opened in the UK). School begins in the year in which the child reaches the age of 6 years. By 1961 91 per cent of children attended. When the first attempt was made in the UK in 1972 to seriously expand nursery education on a part-time basis, *over 95 per cent* of Belgian children were in state-run nursery schools full-time. Harry Willekens points out that the growth of nursery schooling in Belgium had nothing to do with working women because the numbers of women in the workforce have fluctuated up and down according to economic circumstances irrespective of whether nurseries were provided. Nor was it anything to do with family policy or a pro-natalist stance, as in France, where there was also a very early start to nursery education. The Belgians by contrast were rather backward about many family policy and welfare issues. It was not even particularly related to a revolutionary pedagogy, as in the Soviet Union, where children were being deliberately weaned from their families. The only explanation appears to be the rivalry between the Catholic Church and the state in the late 1880s, both of whom vied to recruit young children, either as Catholic or as secular citizens. Catholic and non-Catholic organizations opened nurseries in competition with one another. But once established, the nurseries were favourably received by the population and just went on expanding until they reached all children. Like policy in the UK, it was another accident of history:

> The more it [nursery education] became settled, the more effort would have been required to turn it from its course; but since the relevant social actors had an interest in its perpetuation, there was nobody to make such an effort.[12]

Belgium is in effect two separate countries, Flanders (Dutch speaking) and Wallonia (French speaking), and the histories of the two parts do differ.[13] But overall, the history is similar and the policies follow similar trajectories.

Former Soviet Union and its satellites

Perhaps the prime example of the way government has shaped pedagogical understanding was in the former Soviet Union and its satellites. In the Soviet era childhood and early childhood education achieved an iconic status – there were innumerable posters of Lenin and Stalin surrounded by rosy, alert, admiring young children, as if to exonerate the ruthlessness of the communist regime.[14] The extent of early childhood education and care in the Soviet Union, even in its most remote and backward corners, in the steppes and in the desert, was astonishing. It emphasized the importance of the collective group nature of early education and care and the importance of providing an alternative to claustrophobic family life. The kindergarten was the place where the new generation of Soviet citizens was to be created. Some of the pedagogic methods adopted were originally at least, in the 1920s, liberal not to say anarchic. Over time the system solidified, and anarchy and self-expression were replaced by expectations of extreme conformism. Yet the coherence of the system and the level of investment in facilities for young children were unmatched in any other non-communist country. Kindergartens were developed with meticulous detail. The pedagogy was continuously worked on with academics, and implemented within the schools by especially trained 'methodologists'. Kindergartens were designed to be holistic – to provide good background medical surveillance, opportunities for regular and vigorous exercise, nutritious food – as well as a pedagogy which valued systematic and positive learning experiences, and also tried to alert children to the community and the world of work to which their families belonged.[15]

Many of the kindergartens had – by Western standards – an amazing range of facilities, including dance halls, swimming pools and medical suites. This represented an unparalleled societal investment in early childhood. It was good enough to impress distinguished visitors from the USA in the 1960s such as the highly respected Urie Bronfenbrenner.[16] Bronfenbrenner had Russian parents and spoke Russian, so his insights into the system should have been perspicacious, although he minimized the oppressiveness and dreariness of the Soviet regime that other commentators had shuddered over.[17] Bronfenbrenner argued that Soviet kindergartens had much to teach the USA in the way they used group goals and group pressures with younger children rather than promoting individualism.

> Perhaps we have reached the point of diminishing returns in allowing excessive autonomy and in failing to use the constructive potential of the peer group in developing social responsibility and consideration for others.[18]

After transition and the fall of communism, these kindergartens were said – by those consultants sent in to reform them – to represent all that was wrong with communism: didacticism, a pressure to conform instead of an emphasis on individuality, a rigid hierarchy, stagnation, and a profligate level of expenditure which could not be sustained, and worse still, corruption, and routine distortion of data. Most of the Western advisers who were brought in, especially economic advisers, simply regarded the kindergarten system as unsustainable, and recommended closure. Education specialists – for example those employed by the Soros Foundation – considered that the conformity which they saw as the hallmark of the communist system had to be radically changed in favour of an individualized approach to learning. Yet there was tremendous resistance by teachers – and parents – to these changes. They were viewed by them as a diminution of acceptable standards.[19] Definitions of quality swung around, depending on who wielded influence, and who provided money. Robin Alexander who carried out a comparative study of Russian education in the 1990s still found very positive aspects of the education system, which he considered as thoughtful and well worked out. He coruscated the Western advisers who had tried to write off the system and change it.[20]

After 1990, kindergartens were closed down throughout the Soviet Union, and in former communist countries, although this was partly because many of them were attached to state industries as workplace nurseries. When the industries were dismantled so were the kindergartens. In Kazakhstan for example before 1990, 50 per cent of children aged 3–5 attended kindergarten – a very high percentage given the remoteness of the Kazakh steppe – and then numbers fell to 11 per cent. The Unicef Innocenti Research Centre (IRC) set a special monitoring project (MONEE) to try to record the very disadvantageous changes in children's lives as a result of the fall of communism, which makes bleak reading, although more recently there have been some improvements.[21]

In the former Soviet Union macro-level and micro-level initiatives influenced and fed into one another and neither could be considered without the other or without a sense of history. It is an especial irony that Lev Vygotsky, the Soviet theorist of early childhood, whose work was a reflection of and a response to the Soviet attempt to shape children as the collective citizens of the future, is now seen as a developmental psychologist only concerned with micro-level questions of pedagogy and learning for individual children.

The Soviet Union serves as a particularly vivid illustration of the complexities of policy-making and the importance of context. Even now, former communist countries tend to have good provision,[22] although the system has become very vulnerable to cutbacks. For example when I visited Bulgaria in the late 1990s, over 90 per cent of the children in the capital Sofia attended full-time kindergarten, and most of these kindergartens had their own swimming pools and dance halls, as well as a suite of rooms for health professionals. But by then, upkeep had become impossible, teachers' salaries had fallen, and most of the kindergartens were falling into disrepair. By failing to recognize the effort that had gone into setting up the kindergarten system, across the Soviet Union, the baby was being thrown out with the bathwater. Very little was viewed as worth keeping. As one parent said to me bitterly, 'Everything communist is regarded as bad. Everything Western is good.'[23]

Italy

In each European country there have been particular policy discourses which have shaped provision. In Italy,[24] for example, some of the earliest nurseries were in Reggio Emilia, founded between 1910 and 1920 in response to local working conditions. Similarly during and after the Second World War, Reggio Emilia again took the lead in founding 24-hour nurseries, supported by the Resistance movement and the Italian Women's organization Unione Donne Italiane. Building on the local tradition of support for childcare, the communist mayor of Reggio Emilia in the 1960s supported the development of municipal nurseries, which have since become very famous because of their innovative pedagogical direction. At the same time, because of tensions with the Catholic Church, and between left and right political parties in Italy, it was very difficult to legislate nationally about education, to establish preschool institutions or to promote the training of teachers. In 1968 a controversy over the expansion of nurseries even brought the Italian Government down. So municipalities like Reggio Emilia had to act independently if the municipal nursery schools were to continue and they had to undertake their own in-service or continuous training to make up for the dearth of training nationally. Nursery education has now been extended to cover most Italian children, but the type of provision varies considerably across the country. Even today in Reggio Emilia the famous municipal nurseries exist side by side in the city with Catholic and state nurseries, with relatively little in the way of shared goals or activities. Conceptions of quality differ even in one small, famous, Italian city.

Another account of the culture and tradition of early childhood services is provided by Susan Mantovani.[25] She describes the strong municipal traditions, dating back to the city states of the Middle Ages. This presence of the past, in the very architecture and the local and communal cultural traditions, makes an overwhelming impression on visitors to Italy. So it is not surprising that Mantovani points to the almost insuperable difficulties of arriving at national policies, given the disparity between municipalities and between regions across Italy.

New Zealand

Australia, Canada and New Zealand are all English-speaking former colonies where the indigenous populations have been disregarded, to a greater or lesser extent, and English traditions prevail (except of course in Quebec in Canada, where the French language and traditions prevail). I write about New Zealand here, rather than Australia or Canada, for two reasons. First, the history of early childhood services in New Zealand has been particularly well documented by

Helen May, in a series of books.[26] Second, despite the weight of English neo-liberal traditions, there has been a particularly concerted attempt in New Zealand to understand and address policy issues. The role of indigenous peoples has been especially important in this process. It has also been made easier by the fact New Zealand is a small country, and not riven by the federal disputes which make policy change more difficult in Australia or Canada.

Helen May points to the parallels with the UK in conceptualizing early childhood within the field of child development. Young children were objects of scrutiny by psychologists, who tried to derive norms and standards based on their systematic observations of children's behaviour and patriarchal views about the family. Bowlby and Piaget in particular provided goalposts. But New Zealand was a settler society, concerned with fairness. In 1947, the government issued the *Report of the Consultative Committee on Preschool Education Services*, known as the Bailey Report, after its chairman, Colin Bailey. This argued for state-funded early education, on the grounds that the 'voluntary principle is generally repugnant in that it carries overtones of charity'. But although the principle of kindergartens for 3 and 4 year olds was accepted relatively early on, action was erratic. Kindergarten teachers were trained and paid for by the government. But governments changed, there were economic crises, and as in the UK, voluntary playgroups or playcentres were opened to try to make up the shortfall. In 1971, there was the *Report of the Consultative Committee on Pre-school Education*. This time there were criticisms that preschool education was already too narrow a focus: childcare should have also been included in the report, and some recognition given to the 300 or so childcare centres that were now in existence. As in the UK too, the playcentre movement was annoyed at being left out of the official reckoning. 'God forbid that we should sell our inheritance of real democracy, parent self-education, family enrichment, vitality, stimulating diversity, cross-cultural success.'[27] Various coalitions of unionists, feminists, childcare activists, and Maoris all argued for a more fundamental rethink of early education and care services, although from differing perspectives.

In 1998 a third report *Education to be More* was published. It was supported by the radical Labour Prime Minister David Lange, who then issued his own action plan *Before Five*. This plan attracted international attention, partly because of its determined attempt to reconcile care and education, within an education framework, and partly because of the unprecedented attention it gave to the needs of the Maori minority in the *Te Kohanga Reo* (Maori run centres). Working groups were set up to consider the implications for training, curricula, regulation, funding, and quality was tied to a charter for community/parental participation. As ever politics intervened. The radical developments in all these areas were curtailed. Lange resigned, and a conservative government was returned. Kindergartens were told that they were too expensive and too part-time, and had to raise money or suffer the consequences. There was a lot of agitation, but to no avail. The curriculum developments, perhaps the most radical innovation remaining, were worked on by Maori as well as white academics and activists, and codified into a national curriculum *Te Whariki* (a woven mat). This took as its central principles well-being, belonging, contribution, communication and exploration – a move away from the traditional English curricula of physical, intellectual, emotional and social skills. Margaret Carr, who had been involved in developing *Te Whakiri*, also developed an approach to assessment called *Learning Stories*, also widely cited as an alternative to more conventional assessment tests or views of quality.[28]

But despite these radical initiatives and good intentions, New Zealand has not in the end changed as much as some had hoped.[29] Once different providers have set up shop, it is difficult to systematize what exists without protest from one vested interest or another. The innovative curriculum is centralized, and there is a substantial and integrated training programme for early childhood workers. But there has also been a move to demand-led funding – in this case a standard per capita funding formula subsidy – a given amount depending on the age of the child and the quality rating of the centre. There are many different kinds of provision including increasing numbers of private for-profit and corporate providers, who have taken advantage of these funding arrangements.

USA

Sonya Michel has attempted to write a history of day nurseries in the USA.[30] This history focuses on the tension between women's need to work – especially poor women – and maternalist attitudes about the rightful place of women in the home. Like any historical research on US social issues, it is an especially fraught enterprise because of the sheer size and federal nature of the USA. Nevertheless, she argues on the basis of her very detailed historical research that maternalism – a view that mothers were in every way responsible for the upbringing of their children – was such a powerful ideology that until relatively recently no public group, not even well-known feminists, were prepared to contradict it. Maternalism and a refusal to see poverty as anything other than a personal misfortune or failing (rather than as an injustice to be addressed) combined to prevent any kind of national intervention in childcare. Philanthropists stepped into fill the gap, but on their own terms and for their own glory.

The need for childcare was great even at the beginning of the twentieth century, and many poor mothers, especially black mothers, were compelled to work. But the very few nurseries that existed were founded by upper-class women do-gooders. The National Federation of Day Nurseries (NFDN) was led for over 40 years by the upper-class Josephine Dodge and her committee of equally well-to-do ladies, who were self-styled advocates for childcare, and who dominated discourse about nursery provision. These women were extremely matriarchal and condescending towards the mothers whose children were admitted to the nurseries – and indeed to the exploited staff who worked in them. NFDN was so wedded to the idea that mothers *ought* to look after their children that the policy of the nurseries was to offer only temporary care, so as not to be seen to endorse working mothers. Dodge even campaigned *against* opening new nurseries to serve factories during and in the aftermath of the First World War. Leading feminist and social campaigners, such as Jane Addams, chose to argue for 'a mother's wage' rather than countenance mothers at work.

The number of working mothers in the USA rose steadily throughout the twentieth century, but even though the statistics were available, there was little public acknowledgement of the circumstances. By 1940 there were an estimated 4.6 million working mothers, but nursery places for only 23,000 children. As a result mothers made arrangements for their children that were often unsatisfactory. During the Second World War childcare provision increased slightly, but all the federal organizations involved in childcare – the US Children's Bureau, the US Women's Bureau and others – continued to have what Michel called 'tunnel vision' about working mothers. This disjuncture between what was actually happening and what experts and do-gooders felt ought to happen, was even more marked in black communities, where many more mothers worked, often in servitude to white families.

By the 1950s there was nearly full employment and labour shortages in many fields, including nursing and teaching. Yet *still* working mothers were seen as aberrations. There were debates in Congress about tax allowances, and grudgingly tax credits were offered. After 1976 the dependent care tax credit constituted the single greatest federal expenditure for childcare. Such tax legislation deliberately did not address the supply, distribution, affordability or quality of childcare – a situation which continues to prevail. By 1991 60 per cent of mothers with children under 6 (school starting age) were in the labour force, but the childcare was as erratic and as unregulated as ever. President Reagan had increased tax allowances for middle-class mothers, while paring down any kind of federal support for poor families. Emilie Stoltzfus, another historian writing about the two decades after the war, comments:

> the dramatic expansion in private commercial centres was encour-
> aged by the dearth of publicly supported childcare in a period when a
> rapidly rising number of mothers engaged in paid labour … the
> emergence of private associations of childcare proprietors helped to
> ensure the full consideration of market issues in the drafting of child-
> care licensing standards and so to solidify an enduring definition
> of publicly subsidized childcare as provision only for the very poor.
> Private owners sought to ensure their business interests by insisting

that they should play a role in writing the regulations and that publicly supported childcare must not compete with them for paying customers.[31]

The Childcare and Development Fund (CCDF) is one of a number of financial programmes aimed to support low-income mothers in returning to work. It is mostly used in the form of vouchers. It is firmly located as a welfare programme, and categorizes working women as welfare recipients, with all the conceptual and practical difficulties that implies.

The one federal initiative that did catch on was Head Start. This began in 1964 as part of President Lyndon Johnson's 'War on Poverty'. Edward Zigler, who can rightly be called the father of the Head Start programme, was its principal adviser for much of the time, and has documented its progress since its inception in 1964.[32] Head Start began as a fund for part-time local education initiatives aimed at children aged 3–6 in poor communities. Local groups were invited to apply for funds, which were administered in a 'frenzied distribution' without any regard to quality.

Although in the beginning it was overseen by the familiar committee of upper-class women, Head Start did at least have professional administrators. Zigler himself was then an expert in 'mental retardation'. As he admits in retrospect, poor children were generally assumed to be deficient intellectually and socially, and Head Start was supposed to address these deficiencies.

Head Start has continued for 40 years, but has never become mainstream. There have been other linked initiatives, such as Early Head Start for younger children, and most recently attempts to co-ordinate the programme with childcare.[33] But despite efforts by Zigler and others to talk it up and develop it as part of the education system,[34] it is still funded under the auspices of the Temporary Assistance of Needy Families (TANF) welfare programme. For some more recent commentators Head Start has become an obstacle to further progress, a welfare cul-de-sac, rather than the basis for a federally funded universal system.[35]

The USA, not surprisingly, had a critical report from the OECD, when a review team visited it in 1999.[36] They described 'a patchwork of services, regulations and funding sources leading to confusion, uneven quality and inequality of access'. Access issues were of 'serious concern' for children from black and ethnic minority families. Regulation standards in many states were set 'far too low, even for health and safety issues'. The report recommended 'a more proactive stance toward child poverty and diversity'. Even the *Early Childhood Education: An International Encyclopedia* (which devotes three volumes to the USA and one to the rest of the world) comments:

> the generally mediocre quality of U.S. early care and education programs has been identified as an enduring problem, that approaches

the level of a national crisis, especially when accompanied by concerns about the lack of equity.[37]

Now that a majority of mothers of young children are in the workforce, the ideology of maternalism is less apparent. But its legacy still lives: a refusal to see federal financial support as anything other than an unwelcome welfare necessity and an assumption that mothers, however poor, should buy their own childcare; with the result that there is very unequal access to the mostly private services that exist.

South Africa

South Africa represents another policy route altogether, one dominated by the attempt to try to undo apartheid. In our booklet, Trisha Maynard and I describe some of these policy initiatives.[38] Linda Biersteker presents a slightly earlier account.[39] In South Africa early childhood is referred to more comprehensively as Early Childhood Development (ECD). Its definition is ambitious: 'the processes by which children from birth to 9 years grow and thrive, physically, mentally, emotionally, morally and socially'. Early Childhood Development is concerned with the health, well-being and education of 8.3 million children in South Africa who fall within this age range, of whom 5.5 million are aged 0–5. In practice the Early Childhood Development range of 0–9 is subdivided into 0–5 years and 5–6 years, with different departments carrying responsibility for different aspects of ECD. School begins in the year in which the child is 7. The Department of Education has the job of trying to co-ordinate provision across the sectors.

There was no regular auditing of Early Childhood Development provision (although this situation is now changing). The most recent data, from the 2006 household survey, suggests that there are now around 25,000 preschool centres in South Africa, catering for about 16 per cent of eligible children. The poorest communities have least access where approximately 8 per cent of eligible children attend. These figures date very rapidly, but are indicative of trends.[40] Recent investment in Early Childhood Development means that the figure is likely to have risen since the last audit, but the same problems arise out of the collection of data from non-registered centres, or centres where the registers of children are not reliably kept and the figures are still guestimates. Many centres are not registered and turnover is high.

However the government has been steadily increasing the number of children aged 5–6 who attend accredited grade R classes, most often attached to primary schools.[41] In 2007 62 per cent of children aged 5–6 attended grade R classes in schools, with an additional number attending community-based grade R classes, for whom accurate data are not available. The Education White Paper 5 aimed to provide grade R classes for all 5–6 year olds by 2010.[42]

In order to try to develop its broad Early Childhood Development agenda for so many children, from a very low base the South African Government has to work across education, social development (welfare) and health. Co-ordinated plans such as these have to work not only at governmental level, but at regional and district level too – vertically as well as horizontally. There are now nine provinces in South Africa, and they each have considerable delegated powers, including budgeting.

Under the apartheid government, there was a complex pattern of government and administration according to the colour of the inhabitants. In the Transvaal for example (the white administered part of what is now Gauteng province) there was a history of free-standing nursery schools in white areas. These nursery schools, run along European lines, had very generous space and facilities and were staffed by trained teachers. They were built to serve Afrikaner and English children although by the time the new integrated administration of Gauteng was created, many if not most of them had a majority of black children, bussed in from the townships. They operated on a full day basis and employed black staff. Other provinces had created rather different patterns of nursery schooling, so there was considerable variation across the country.

The provision in the townships and rural areas themselves mainly consisted of private crèches and nursery centres, catering primarily for the children of working women, staffed by barely qualified and poorly paid women, ill equipped, in mostly unregistered premises. Some were supported or run by non-governmental organizations.

The new South African Government decided that this dual system, in which a relatively privileged minority received the biggest slice of funding, albeit in some cases providing an excellent service, was at root an unequal one. Instead it sought ways to invest in, promote and support the systems of early education and childcare that could best support poor children, whether in the townships or in rural areas and it removed direct funding from the nursery schools. This meant that many ex-nursery schools located in wealthier areas by default became fee-paying nurseries, in order to survive, and others closed altogether.

Since 1998 new policies and programmes have aimed to support young children, including free primary health care and the phasing in of a reception year of schooling. In 2004, the Cabinet mandated the social sector cluster (social development, health and education) to develop an integrated plan for Early Childhood Development. This is known as the National Integrated Plan for Early Childhood Development for Children 0–4 Years 2005–2010 (NIP). It aims to:

- create environments in which children, particularly vulnerable children can thrive

- increase the opportunities for young children to prepare for entering schooling
- provide support for adults who care for young children
- reduce the adverse developmental effects of poverty.

The aim is to scale up existing provision for Early Childhood Development by improving access and quality through a programme of legislative changes and targeted subsidies.

The Child Care Act 1983, which regulated the standards of childcare, was replaced by a new Children's Act 2008 with revised guidelines to Early Childhood Development services. This focuses on level 3 of the National Integrated Plan and deals with formal services. There are no national guidelines on the first two interventions yet and no support framework for household and community programmes, although discussion is taking place.

The government has instituted a system of per capita grants for children from low income households to attend centre-based Early Childhood Development provision. These subsidies are given directly to the centre, providing the centre is non-profit. They have to be spent directly on services for the children and cannot be used for staffing or other running costs. The amount of the grant is discretionary and decided at a provincial level, and from 2008 varies from a minimum of R9 to R18 per child per day (about £1). Around 20 per cent of centres receive these grants. The process of administration for the grants is very complex, involving several tiers of government and several departments. There are also child support grants for vulnerable households with children up to 14 years old. These grants are paid directly to carers, and appear to have been effective as a strategy in poverty relief although there is also variation and discussion at a local level as to whether these grants can or should also be used to pay childcare fees.

The centrally determined budget is allocated to provinces at national level, but has to be reallocated and spent at provincial and local level. There is evidence from recent case studies to suggest that much of the money allocated to Early Childhood Development at provincial level is unspent or redirected to other areas, because of lack of capacity at provincial level. Most provision is in the non-governmental organization and private sectors and so requires considerable administration and liaison to operate the subsidy programme.

The support and monitoring is limited although the legislation just passed will require annual checks on those centres receiving subsidies. Monitoring and obtaining accurate data on the operation of services is essential for planning but monitoring and support was an activity previously undertaken mainly by non-governmental organizations on an ad hoc basis. The grants to non-government organizations to provide and monitor services, both from external donors and from government, have largely dried up in favour of the

National Integrated Plan. However, this role has not yet been taken on in any significant way by the provinces.

There is an additional programme sponsored by the Department of Public Works to train women from poor communities as early childhood workers, as part of an employment initiative. The trainees receive a stipend while they are training. But this raises the question of pay and career opportunities in the early childhood education and care sector. Pay is very low as most provision is self-funded, and there are very few career opportunities. There is some evidence to suggest that better trained and more ambitious staff move out of the sector as soon as they can – either to schools or to more upmarket private centres in more prosperous areas.

The government has set up an accreditation system for Early Childhood Development under the South African Qualifications Authority. The National Qualifications Framework for Early Childhood Development seeks to regularize training, and credit prior learning where possible. The training is vocational and pitched at a basic level, with options of progressing to levels 4 and 5.

The development of the National Qualifications Framework has gone alongside development of the curriculum. Initial ambitious attempts to reframe the school curriculum for children 5–15 were considerably modified. Language policy is also constantly under consideration. South Africa has 11 national languages, and multilingualism, especially among the black African, Indian and coloured communities, is common. The language of instruction, especially for young children, is a deeply politicized issue. The National Early Learning Development Standards for children under 5 are still being developed, but appear to draw heavily upon the conventional USA models of 'Ages and Stages'.

South Africa, then, is a country with very ambitious policies on early childhood rapidly being developed. But there are many hurdles to overcome besides poverty and the health catastrophe of HIV/AIDs. There are many new ideas, many initiatives, and many capable and committed people at all levels. Many of the interventions, especially in rural areas, are family and community based, trying to 'motivate' local people to look after children well, in the absence of any other facilities. There is nowhere near enough money to address the severe problems of child poverty and the gross inequalities and family disruption produced by a racist past. The Head of Early Childhood Development in the Department of Education told us: 'I'm sick of international indicators where we always come at the bottom. I want to find ways of celebrating our unique African contribution.'[43] But the reality is that Euro-American definitions of standards and quality are very powerful, and require considerable resources to implement. Finding a counterweight to policies shaped in Europe or North America is, to say the least, difficult. South Africa is strategically important. Many African countries look to South Africa as a beacon for policy development in this field, yet its internal policies are inevitably problematic.

Sticky policies?

Policy in the field of early education and care tends to focus on the present or near present. But policy decisions that are shaped by an unacknowledged past go on to shape standards and guidelines in the present. Ostensibly these are a response to the particular needs and circumstances of a community or society at a particular time, for example in the UK, the concerns about child safety in the wake of child abuse cases. But invariably the criteria which inform such standards and guidelines are paraded as universal and contextless, and described as what is 'best' for children and families. Anyone delving into the archives hears the voices of the past booming down into the present. The past need not imprison us but acknowledging what has gone before would seem to be a sensible starting point. Yet guidelines about 'quality' are issued and pronounce on the question of what is best for young children and what constitutes quality without much thought as to starting points, or context, or the complexity or evolution of ideas.

The very different policy histories recounted here have led to different assumptions about quality, about what is valued in early childhood services and why. Policy-making, then, especially in a minor area (in policy terms) like early childhood, is rarely rational and considered, but a circular process whereby a government reacts to the immediate crises of the present, by inadvertently drawing on the past. And once a government has put its stamp on, or given its backing to a particular approach, it becomes the accepted 'truth' to those concerned, parents, teachers, other professionals, and society at large. Academics chew over these policy decisions and, wisely or not, depending on the context, bend over backwards to explain and elaborate policies which would not make sense if they were carried out in another country, and probably would not make sense at any other time, except the time of writing!

This very brief overview of policy history in the field of early childhood services serves to make the point that first of all policy-making is a confused and confusing process. It is fairly widely accepted that policy-making in whatever field is a somewhat arbitrary process. Except in a few exceptional instances, politicians do not make decisions rationally on the basis of existing evidence, but *necessarily* take decisions based on what they perceive they can sell to the public at the time. To say this is not to be cynical or dismissive about the political process, or to stand back from it, but in order to be realistic about how it operates.

But even if the business of policy-making is in thrall to rapidly changing events and the manipulation of public opinion, and cast in the framework of an unacknowledged past, the job of academics and intellectuals – and students – is to try to step back a little and to analyse policies and their underpinning rationales, to be sceptical. This is particularly necessary in a relatively new and emerging field of endeavour like early childhood services. There is great pressure to take government policies for granted, to follow them blindly because of their prestigious source. Taking a broad view of history suggests that this is a mistake, although it may be unavoidable at the time. It only leads to more blind alleys.

Notes

1 Alexander, R. (2000) *Culture and Pedagogy: International Comparisons in Primary Education*. Oxford: Blackwell. The quotation is from p. 5.
2 Schweie, K. and Willekens, H. (eds) (2009) *Child Care and Preschool Development in Europe: Institutional Perspectives*. Basingstoke: Palgrave Macmillan. This interdisciplinary book edited by two academic lawyers considers how systems have developed in a number of European countries. The quotation is from p. 2.
3 Popularized by the American political scientist Paul Pierson in 2000 in a much cited article: Pierson, P. (2000) 'Increasing returns, path dependence and the study of politics.' *American Political Science Review* 94: 251–277.
4 Alexander, *Culture and Pedagogy*. He compared France, India, Russia, the UK and USA.
5 Alexander, *Culture and Pedagogy*.
6 Bennett, J. (2006) 'Schoolifying early childhood education and care? Reflections on a perennial challenge.' Paper given at a conference to launch the OECD report *Starting Strong* at a conference given at the Institute of Education, University of London, 10 May.
7 Cunningham, H. (1991) *Children of the Poor: Representations of Childhood since the 17th Century*. Oxford: Blackwell.
8 There was a series of books about the exceptional nature of women who wanted to work. One of the most influential was Myrdal, A. and Klein, V. (1946) *Women's Two Roles: Home and Work*. London: Routledge & Kegan Paul, updated in a second edition in 1968. The feminist publisher Virago issued a number of books on the topic, including a history book, Black, C. (ed.) (1983) *Married Women's Work*. London: Virago, and a series of personal accounts in Gieve, K. (ed.) (1989) *Balancing Acts: On Being a Mother*. London: Virago.
9 Full details of all the UK legislation mentioned can be found on the Department for Education website: www.education.gov.uk
10 Since 2002 Ofsted has changed its categorization and no longer provides information on the types of services available other than that between 'domestic' and 'non-domestic' premises. The information on private sector provision comes from private sector analysts: see Laing & Buisson (2009) *Children's Nurseries: UK Market Report 2009. Eighth Edition*. London: Laing & Buisson.
11 The eminent psychiatrist and epidemiologist Michael Rutter has highlighted some of the simplistic assumptions of the Sure Start programme. He

acknowledges that it was well intentioned, but criticizes its naive assumptions about poverty reduction and community intervention. See Rutter, M. (2007) 'Sure Start local programmes: An outsider's perspective.' In J. Belsky, J. Barnes and E. Melhuish (eds) *The National Evaluation of Sure Start*. Bristol: Policy Press. See also description in Chapter 3.

12 See H. Willekens (2009) 'How and why Belgium became a pioneer of preschool development.' In K. Schweie and H. Willekens (eds) (2009) *Child Care and Preschool Development in Europe: Institutional Perspectives*. Basingstoke: Palgrave Macmillan, pp. 43–56. The quotation is from p. 55. I was also rapporteur for the OECD in Flemish Belgium, and wrote an account for the OECD. See OECD (2001) *Starting Strong: Early Education and Care*. Paris: OECD.

13 The OECD report *Starting Strong* had to treat Belgium as two separate countries and issue two separate reports on the status of early education and care services.

14 The history of childhood in Russia is dealt with in detail by Kelly, C. (2007) *Children's World: Growing Up in Russia 1890–1991*. New Haven, CT: Yale University Press. An account of the development of kindergartens in the Bolshevik era is provided by Kirschenbaum, L. (2001) *Small Comrades: Revolutionizing Childhood in Soviet Russia, 1917–1932*. New York: RoutledgeFalmer.

15 For a more detailed account, see Penn, H. (2010) 'Swimming pools in the steppes and pianos in the desert.' *Global Childhoods* 1(1) forthcoming.

16 Uri Bronfenbrenner led an American Psychological Association inquiry into childcare in the Soviet Union, which was published as Bronfenbrenner, U. (1974) *Two Worlds of Childhood: US and USSR*. Harmondsworth: Penguin Education.

17 One of the most depressing accounts of the Soviet Union is *Imperium* (1993) by the Polish journalist Ryszard Kapuściński. The paperback translation is Kapuściński, R. (2007) *Imperium*. London: Granta. This is an unrelenting account of the corruption, oppression and misery experienced by many millions of Soviet citizens, especially in the now disbanded Soviet Empire.

18 Bronfenbrenner, *Two Worlds of Childhood*, p. 166.

19 See my account of kindergartens in Khazakhstan: Penn, H. (2005) *Unequal Childhoods*. London: Routledge.

20 Alexander, *Culture and Pedagogy*.

21 The MONEE reports are online at www.unicef-irc.org.

22 OECD's *Starting Strong II* contains accounts of the Czech Republic, the former German Democratic Republic and Hungary. See OECD (2006) *Starting Strong II: Early Childhood Education and Care*. Paris: OECD.

23 See Penn, *Unequal Childhoods*, p. 102.

24 The information in this account comes primarily from Hohnerlein, E.M. (2009) 'The paradox of public preschools in a familist welfare regime: The Italian case.' In K. Schweie and H. Willekens (eds) *Child Care and Preschool Development in Europe: Institutional Perspectives*. Basingstoke: Palgrave Macmillan, pp. 88–105. The work of Loris Malaguzzi, the psychologist who was seen as the pioneer of

the Reggio Emilia tradition, is portrayed in dozens of books about Reggio Emilia. My own work in Italy is described in Penn, H. (1997) *Comparing Nurseries: Staff and Children in Italy, Spain and the UK.* London: Paul Chapman. I investigated nurseries in three Italian municipalities, all of which had similar practices to Reggio Emilia, but drew their inspiration from a very different philosophical source, that of the Hungarian psychologist Emmi Pickler, whose theories were known as the Loczy model (for a fuller account of Emmi Pickler, see Petrie, S. and Owen, S. (2005) *Authentic Relationships in Group Care for Infants and Toddlers.* London: Jessica Kingsley). The commonalities of the Italian nursery practices would seem to owe something to a wider Italian tradition of discussion and participation, not just to early years pedagogy.

25 Mantovani, S. (2007) 'Italy.' In R. New and M. Cochran (eds) *Early Childhood Education: An International Encyclopedia,* vol. 4. Westport, CT: Greenwood.

26 May, H. (1997) *The Discovery of Childhood.* Auckland, NZ: Auckland University Press. May, H. (2001) *Politics in the Playground: The World of Early Childhood in Postwar New Zealand.* Wellington, NZ: Bridget Williams Books.

27 *NZ Play Centre Journal,* cited in May, *Politics in the Playground,* p. 111.

28 Carr, M. (2001) *Assessment in Early Childhood: Learning Stories.* London: Sage.

29 May, H. and Mitchell, L. (2009). *Strengthening Community-based Early Childhood Education in Aotearoa New Zealand.* Wellington: NZEI Te Riu Roa.

30 Michel, S. (1999) *Children's Interests/Mothers' Rights.* New Haven, CT: Yale University Press.

31 Stoltzfus, E. (2003) *Citizen, Mother, Worker.* Chapel Hill, NC: University of North Carolina Press, p. 236.

32 Edward Zigler records that the launch party for Head Start at the White House was a glitzy affair, and he was startled to find himself next to the busty Italian actress Gina Lollobrigida!

33 Goffin, S. and Washington, V. (2007) 'History of US early childhood care and education.' In R. New and M. Cochran (eds) *Early Childhood Education: An International Encyclopedia.* Westport, CT: Greenwood, vol. 4, pp. 417–423.

34 Finn-Stevenson, M. and Zigler, E. (1999) *Schools of the 21st Century: Linking Child Care and Education.* Boulder, CO: Westview.

35 Zigler, E. and Muenchow, S. (1992) *Head Start: The Inside Story of America's Most Successful Educational Experiment.* New York: Basic Books.
Zigler, E. and Styfco, S. (2004) *The Head Start Debates.* Baltimore, MD. Paul H. Brookes.

36 OECD (2001) *Starting Strong: Early Childhood Education and Care.* Paris: OECD, p. 184.

37 New, R. and Cochran, M. (eds) (2007) *Early Childhood Education: An International Encyclopedia.* Westport, CT: Greenwood, vol. 1, p. xxxii.

38 For an account of South Africa, see Penn, H. and Maynard, T. (2010) *Siyabonana: We All See Each Other. Building Better Childhoods in South Africa.* Edinburgh: Children in Scotland.

39 Biersteker, L. (2007) 'South Africa.' In R. New and M. Cochran (eds) *Early Childhood Education: An International Encyclopedia*. Westport, CT: Greenwood, vol. 4, pp. 1194–1239. Linda Biersker also kindly directed us to the contemporary sources of statistics we draw on in *Siyabonana*.

40 Department of Education (2001a) *Nationwide Audit of ECD Provisioning in South Africa*. Pretoria: Department of Education.

41 School starting age in South Africa is the year in which children become 7 years of age. The South African Government has introduced a 'grade R' or Reception year for children aged 5–6.

42 Department of Education (2001b) *Whiter Paper 5 – Early Childhood Development*. Pretoria: Early Childhood Development (ECD) Directorate.

43 Penn and Maynard, *Siyabonana*, p. 15.

3   Rationales and oxymorons

This chapter is mainly drawn from a paper I wrote for the Network of Experts of Social Scientists in Education (NESSE) which was commissioned by the European Commission Directorate of Education and Culture to inform member states of the research underpinning policy initiatives in early education and care. It therefore focuses on European provision rather than having a broader international focus. Although the examples come mainly from Europe, the arguments are more general.[1]

In Chapter 2 I reviewed how policy rationales for early childhood services have developed in particular countries. I argued that the historical roots of policies were often unacknowledged, and policy-making and discussions about quality tended to be less coherent as a result. In this chapter I approach the issue of policy rationales from another perspective. I explore the range of rationales that are put forward to justify expenditure on early childhood services, the research evidence they typically draw upon, and the policy conclusions they lead to. One set of rationales is to do with early education or some other kind of early intervention and its perceived benefits for children. A second set of rationales is to do with the position of mothers and their roles in relation to their children. But there is also a relatively new set of rationales, to do with the rights of the child.

The rationales which justify expenditure on early childhood are not permanently fixed. On the contrary they change often, as politicians adopt new causes. Because we are mostly fixated on the present, it is hard to recognize what went before, or to predict the direction of future change. The discourse on child rights, for example, seems a likely arena for change in many countries. But before discussing these rationales for early childhood, I point to two contemporary general trends which are also influencing conceptions of early childhood services: the increasingly global, interdisciplinary and contentious nature of academic discussion, and the reach of economics.

Changing theories, changing disciplines

The theoretical ideas and research which inform policy rationales for ECEC, and the academic disciplines from which they are drawn, are shifting. Academic discourses in general are more global, more wide-ranging and more contentious. The discussion of early childhood is based on current perceptions of the needs and interests of young children but while this has most often been viewed from a child development perspective, new fields of study have emerged giving a somewhat different picture of how children's interests are best described and served. Most research in the field of child development for example has been derived from a narrow population of children (mainly from North America and Europe) and may well not be easily generalizable beyond its original catchments.[2] There is a small body of evidence, mainly from anthropologists which radically challenges or extends some of the standard assumptions of parenting and child development which underpin discussions about early childhood.[3] This points to the need for an interdisciplinary approach to interpreting evidence about early childhood. One study on alloparenting (care other than by parents) draws on socio-biological, physiological, demographical and anthropological material to build up a complex picture of the impact of alternative care on young children's lives.[4]

As an example I have just been asked to contribute a chapter to a new book on childhood. The aim of this book, the authors write, is:

> to demonstrate how over time there have been various movements to impose a particular conception of childhood on certain groups of children within Western European or North American countries or on children in 'non-Western countries' through colonial social welfare programmes, missionary education and more recently, through the work of international agencies such as the UN, the World Bank and international law etc. However, we want to show that people do not passively imbibe these notions of childhood. Instead, they may reject such notions of childhood and continue their local practices or they may seek to accommodate it creating a situation whereby modern conceptions of childhood may co-exist with more traditional conceptions. Therefore, we are interested in this coming together of global and local and the implications it poses for how we understand and talk about childhoods today.[5]

The writers who have been asked to contribute to this book come from every continent, and from very different backgrounds. I often get requests along these lines, asking me to situate my work in a global context (although global often means just the industrialized or rich world). Increasingly there are international comparisons, international encyclopedias, and international journals. As importantly, most of these books and journals are interdisciplinary and try to take a global perspective. A new awareness of the interdisciplinarity and potential contentiousness of interpretations of childhood is reshaping rationales and justifications for promoting early education and care.

Economics and marketization

A second important trend influencing thinking and decision-making in early childhood is the increasing importance of economic rationalization. Almost anything can be a fit object of scrutiny for economists. Economics is a quantitative, empirical, scientific (or pseudo-scientific) way of describing financial transactions between people, and predicting wealth and poverty on a national and international scale. Barbara Coyle, in her prizewinning book on economics *The Soulful Science*,[6] claims that empirical economists are charting the economy and society in what is 'a golden age of discovery.' There are dissenters from this view, who are sometimes referred to as 'post-autistic' economists,[7] economists who regard the claims of traditional economists as bizarre and out of touch with the everyday world. One of the most notable critics of traditional or classical economists is the Harvard political scientist, Michael Sandel.[8] He argues that the idea that economics offers sufficient explanation of society is crude and undermines human solidarity and collective action. But whichever economic viewpoint you accept (and I'm definitely in the Sandel camp) economic explanations now have a very powerful impact.

Many economists, then, regard money transactions as a non-moral issue. Perhaps this is what has enabled for-profit childcare to gain such a hold. On one level making a profit out of children (like making a profit out of old and frail people) is morally repugnant. It is an exploitation of vulnerability and need. Yet if you look at the company reports or market analysis of banks and private equity companies investing in childcare, the discussion is primarily about the company's anticipated profits from caring for children, with no mention of the children themselves. For-profit childcare is increasingly the main form of childcare in the UK, and in other English-speaking countries, although much less so within the European Union. Much of the research from the USA, which is widely cited in the child development literature, fails to take account of the context of marketization and the distortions this produces in access and equity.[9] The narrow definitions of quality that are often adopted can be applied even when a for-profit entrepreneur is making money hand over fist, and exploits not only the parents paying for the service but the workers delivering it.[10]

So there are many competing, intersecting and overlapping arguments and perspectives involved in defining and providing rationales for ECEC provision. I set out some of the most well-known rationales, the kind of research evidence they draw upon, and the policy conclusions they lead to in Table 3.1. As I have stressed, not all these perspectives are compatible; indeed, they may sit alongside one another without the contradictions being addressed. I have also tried to highlight the policy implications of these various rationales – although, as I have also stressed, policy development and implementation are rarely straightforward or coherent, particularly when early education and care spans several policy areas. Then I discuss these rationales in more detail.

Table 3.1   Rationales for ECEC provision

Rationale	Research perspective	Policy focus and quality implications
Early intervention is a good investment in that it mitigates the expense of remedial action in primary and secondary schooling and results in subsequent adult productivity, and in the relative absence of antisocial behaviour	Economics, human capital theory, long-term societal benefits: draws on large-scale longitudinal aggregated data sets and cost–benefit studies of early childhood interventions	Provide targeted services for the most vulnerable children. Quality includes appropriateness of targeting mechanisms and degree of take-up by the most vulnerable families; and good long-term social outcomes
Early education (and care) is a good investment only if it is of high quality. Poor care may do more harm than good for the most vulnerable children	Child development research that suggests good child–staff ratios, staff training and good programmes are essential aspects of quality	Provide targeted early education services with emphasis on defining and monitoring quality
Early education benefits *all* young children, enhances dispositions for learning and socializes them for starting school, especially children from poor and migrant families	Child development research about children's leaning processes and teachers' pedagogic practices	Provide universal early education as part of an education system to ensure access and support for the most vulnerable. Quality includes sensitivity to special educational needs and subsequent school outcomes
Education and lifelong learning are essential to a competitive knowledge economy. Education promotes social mobility	Education research and comparative education data from OECD and other transnational sources	Provide universal early education as part of education system. Quality includes subsequent school outcomes

Women are essential contributors to a dynamic economy	Economics, cost-benefit studies of labour market participation, gender studies	Remove disincentives to women's participation by the provision of full-time childcare (Barcelona targets). Quality includes levels of provision and women's workforce participation
Working mothers contribute to tax revenues and lessen the need for social security payments; they make an important contribution to family income	Welfare economics, emphasis on workplace participation of single parents and other parents who would otherwise be dependent on state benefits	Maternity, paternity and parental leave and provision of full-time childcare, work support schemes. Quality measured by mother's (and father's) well-being and levels of provision
Mothers need to be involved with their children; parents are a child's first educators	Child development research which stresses critical early period and importance of family environment and mother–child attachments	Home visiting schemes, parenting classes, mothers as volunteers. Quality measured by improved nature of mother–child interactions
Low birth rates below the level of replacement are a societal problem	Demography, social welfare studies of population growth	Pro-natalist policies, child benefit, maternity and paternity leave, childcare. Quality measured by mother's well-being and rise in birth rate
Children, including young children, are rights bearers and *all* children have a right to protection, provision and participation	Legal requirements of Human Rights and Child Rights legislation. Legal and sociological studies investigating children's experiences and well-being in the here and now, and children's agency	Broad approach, including reduction of child poverty, health and welfare support; defining provision from children's perspective. Quality measured by children's reported well-being
Child poverty impacts severely on children's educational performance, their sense of self-worth and their subsequent societal contributions	Social welfare research on the impact of poverty on families	Redistribution of taxes and benefits and other social policies to mitigate child poverty; labour market legislation such as minimum wage. Quality measured by reduction in child poverty

Rationale 1: *Early intervention is a good investment in that it mitigates the expense of remedial action in primary and secondary schooling and results in subsequent adult productivity, and in the relative absence of antisocial behaviour*

This rationale is derived from human capital theory, which focuses on the economic productivity of individuals over time, and the conditions which enhance it. Human capital theory has undoubtedly contributed to a rethinking of macro-economic policies and how they are applied. Investing in people, especially investing in educating them, brings substantial pay-offs. James Heckman, a Nobel Prize winner and a leading theorist of human capital theory argues that investment in early childhood brings greater returns than investment in any other stage of education.[11]

This economic evidence usually gets a starring role in the literature of international development organizations such as the World Bank, Unicef or the Bernard van Leer Organization.[12] American liberal think tanks such as the Rand Corporation and the Brookings Institution recycle this interpretation of human capital theory again and again.[13,14] There is now a small sub-industry around the use of economic and business arguments for early childhood. As Sabo comments, in the USA 'business men and women committed to early childhood education have become a hot commodity on the legislative briefing and advocacy luncheon circuit.'[15]

But the evidence Heckman and his acolytes draw upon is problematic in a number of ways.[16] The promotion of the economic evidence in this way by all these bodies reflects American angst about failure to develop a coherent policy, or to spend money on early childhood services. Where there are entrenched views about the need for taxation and the role of the state in paying for services, as in the USA and Canada, even economic arguments about the utility of early childhood interventions may cut little ice. Jerome Kagan, for example, an eminent Harvard psychologist, argues that the claims for long-term benefits arising from early interventions exist because the alternative, the recognition of deep inequalities in the USA, is so painful. In addition using taxation to pay for services is so politically unacceptable.[17] The fixation on a particular kind of economic evidence may be pragmatic in the USA but is less appropriate for those countries (an overwhelming majority of those in the rich world and many of those in poorer countries) who have already accepted the need for a decent tax base to pay for services. Even if the use of economic development rationales is flavour of the month for child advocates in the USA, progress towards a fair and rational system of early childhood services is still very slow or non-existent in that country.

Human capital theory has highlighted early childhood intervention as a particularly effective *economic* investment. Improbable as it might seem (but so are a number of economic theories) a well-directed early intervention enhances the productivity of individuals in adulthood. The evidence is derived from controlled trials of centre-based early intervention with long-term follow-up, that is for at least 15 years, following a young child into early adulthood. As such studies are very expensive and time consuming to carry out, there are not many of them; in fact there are only three, whose findings are endlessly recycled in the literature. A systematic review of longitudinal cost-benefit studies of early interventions identified only three studies:[18] Perry High Scope,[19] the Abecedarian,[20] and the Chicago Child-Parent Centres.[21] These interventions took place in the 1960s, 1970s and 1980s and were carried out in ghettoized areas in the USA. The populations investigated were overwhelmingly Black African and Hispanic. The Abecedarian study investigated a particularly deprived population. The first two were randomized controlled trials – although some queries have been raised about the randomization of the Perry study – and the third used a control group. Each of the three intervention studies has spawned a series of publications over decades.

The three interventions differed from each other in their aims, the age ranges of the children, the length of time of the intervention, the role played by mothers, the outreach facilities available, and in various other ways. The cost-benefit calculations based on the studies follow broadly similar and acceptable economic procedures. These are, however, reliant on specific local school models for their costings (repeat years, nature of remedial assistance) and use US databases to make other financial projections, for instance on juvenile offending rates and crime compensation.

Each study reported significant longitudinal outcomes for the intervention group. All three studies reported an improvement in school performance for the control group, with less repetition and remedial assistance rates. The Abecedarian study reported a marginally significant difference in the education rates of teenage mothers of participants, and a marginally significant difference in the type of employment of all mothers. The major finding was that the Perry High Scope and the Chicago study reported a significant difference in juvenile crime rates between the intervention and control groups, although at the minimal level of significance. The Abecedarian intervention group showed no difference. Crime reduction in the intervention group forms the major part of the saving in the Perry High Scope and Chicago studies. However, costs of crime in the USA are very considerable. The three strikes law means that levels of incarceration in the USA are particularly high. Victim compensation is also uniquely costly in the USA because of the significant incidence of gun-related crime.[22] It is unlikely that savings of the order reported from early intervention in these two studies would accrue in any other country.

Each study made an overall estimate of the ratio of dollars spent to dollars saved, taking long-term projections of benefits into account. The Perry High Scope study claimed an overall ratio of $7.16 saved for every dollar spent; the Chicago Child Parent Centres study $7.14 saved per dollar spent, and the Abecedarian $3.78 saved for every dollar spent. The size of the effect varies considerably according to the instruments used, and the attribute being measured. The figures are open to interpretation although unsurprisingly, the most favourable figures are generally used as a basis for extrapolation.

There are many questions to be asked about the application of the findings beyond the communities in the USA where the investigations were undertaken, or indeed about the wisdom of generalizing from prevention programmes which focus exclusively on micro-level interventions. For example the possibility that racism may have distorted the interpretation of these longitudinal studies, is only marginally addressed by the Abecedarian study and is not raised by the other studies. However, other authors, especially black authors writing about this period of American history, describe the racism as overwhelming.[23] Some psychologists too have claimed that in general, as well as in these longitudinal studies, the importance of context is invariably downplayed and that research has largely ignored or misunderstood the position of poor blacks and Hispanics in the USA.[24] Definitions of 'poor and vulnerable' are problematic and overlap with race and class. For example the Perry High Scope intervention referred originally to its sample of children as 'functionally retarded, culturally deprived, Negro, preschool children',[25] a description that has been carefully modified over time to 'low-income-children'.

In fact, there is now some kind of consensus among economists that longitudinal intervention studies are too costly and the information they provide is both limited and dated – the questions which prompt the study are out of date 20 years later when the study is completed.[26] Instead economists and social commentators are focusing on large data sets followed over time. The Millennium cohort study in the UK is following up 19,000 children who were born in 2000, and asking a range of questions about family circumstances, childcare use, and educational progress. The EU-SILC (European Union Statistics on Income and Living Conditions) data in particular are likely to be a fruitful source of information.[27] They are household panel surveys, first commissioned in 2003, and undertaken every four years, and co-ordinated across the European Union. They provide cross-sectional data on a range of variables including income, poverty, employment and social exclusion. They offer important comparative information about how families use the services that are available to them. A longitudinal picture will also emerge, as families are tracked over time, but the cross-sectional data are also important. So the obsession with the particular kind of restricted data offered in Heckman's iconic studies is outdated.

But even if the evidence on which Heckman relies is parochial, does targeting in early childhood make sense? If there is not enough money to provide services for all children, should services for some children be prioritized? The policy focus of much of the economic work on ECEC is to suggest that targeted interventions are the most cost-effective in producing better outcomes. All governments must ration resources and prioritize, and targeting the children who can benefit most is a useful strategy. The American economist Gary Becker, another Nobel Prize winner, has forcefully argued that investment in early childhood interventions is cost-effective only for vulnerable children. He discounts all other arguments for state investment. For a majority of children state investment is not deemed necessary, since it is much more efficient to have better-off families buy childcare services in a private competitive market than to spend tax revenue on preschool government-run programmes for the children of these families. For those who would benefit from interventions, a demand-led system (giving parents tax credits or vouchers) is better than a supply-side system (direct subsidy to the provider of services). The subsidies for poor families take the form of vouchers which poor families can spend on any approved private daycare. In his view the market will ensure a sufficient and adequate supply of provision, and competition would ensure sufficient quality, for all types of demand. This approach is informed above all by the view that the state has a minimalist role and more tax is always bad.[28]

The OECD report *Starting Strong II* on the contrary suggests that targeting vulnerable children has significant drawbacks. The report cites the adage 'a service for the poor is a poor service.' This is for a number of reasons. Targeted provision is more likely to be located in poor areas, and to be poorly staffed and staff may have lower aspirations for children. Targeting is associated with stigmatization and may be unpopular with the very families for whom it is designed, so that take-up is low. The social segregation involved in targeting at a preschool level is likely to continue into primary schooling, in so far as the targeted provision is attached to a primary school. The problems of boundary maintenance between the poor and non-poor are considerable and the administrative resources needed to decide on eligibility for scarce places may be inefficient. Targeted programmes for vulnerable children may have only short-term funding and be vulnerable to political trends. Finally, as the US Head Start programme suggests, targeted programmes get sidelined and do not feed into the mainstream. One leading academic involved with the UK Sure Start programme has argued that it should be regarded as a step towards universalism, a 'targeted universalism'. But 'targeted universalism' is an oxymoron. A programme is either targeted *or* universal. It is hard, if not impossible, to find a targeted programme that has transmogrified into a universal one. As Chapter 2 suggests, this is a naive view of policy-making.

It may be useful to use the much vaunted multimillion pound Sure Start targeted early intervention programme in England as an example, because it is so well documented (as have been all Labour government sponsored early childhood initiatives). It was inspired by the Head Start programme in the USA – and by the newer economic rationales for intervening in disadvantage, again from the USA. Sure Start has not lived up to its aim of reducing child poverty and improving child outcomes, partly – although not only – because of targeting and implementation difficulties. The programme targeted 'communities' rather than individuals, in an attempt to avoid stigmatization (which raised even bigger kinds of measurement problems in defining communities). But some communities, especially in cosmopolitan London, are socially mixed, the very rich living in the same streets as the very poor, even if social contact is limited. In these areas, it was the rich 'yummy mummies' who tended to monopolize some of the Sure Start programmes, rather than the poor. Conversely, many poor families do not live in poor areas, especially those who live in rural areas, and had no access to any Sure Start programme. In the very poorest areas, large social housing estates on the periphery of big cities, the Sure Start programme, like so many other welfare interventions, did carry an aura of stigma, and attendance was pitifully low. Yet ironically, Sure Start was supposed to be giving women in local communities – downtrodden women – a voice, support in making their decisions and using their time. In that sense at least it did, on paper, try to reject the old philanthropic paternalism.

The programmes were meant to be multidisciplinary, but health, social work, education and voluntary agencies did not easily work together. There were also squabbles between staff.[29] Sure Start was viewed as separate from existing structures of nursery education or day nurseries or health services. As a self-proclaimed new departure it was always unclear how Sure Start would link with these existing services. So boundary maintenance problems – among users, among staff and between different kinds of services – dogged Sure Start. As the implementation report on Sure Start noted, they were also uncosted. On average, individual projects took more than twice as long as expected to get going, and the delays soaked up funds.[30] Yet politicians still cite it as a flagship programme, as an illustration of government commitment to early childhood education and care. It was in British terms an outstanding initiative, but the bar was not high.

If the services in the UK were to expand, an alternative strategy would have been to extend what was commonly acknowledged to offer the highest standard of provision for children, the free-standing nursery schools (kindergartens). There were about 500 of these in 1997. They were mostly in poor urban areas. They were generously equipped, with good outdoor space, and with highly trained staff. They were usually very popular with parents, and viewed as non-stigmatizing. As nursery schools they were part of a universal education system. But they were a costly option, and firmly rooted in an educational tradition. Instead, Sure Start was firmly located in the British welfarist tradition, although it claimed to be starting afresh and forging its own community traditions.

Overall Sure Start, however well intentioned, was wildly overambitious and foolish in its claims to change lives and reduce poverty.[31,32] The example of Head Start in the USA that influenced UK politicians was a limited success and produced very uneven outcomes; and the theory that influenced the UK Treasury – that same human capital theory – was based on flawed evidence. Very few of the predicted outcomes were achieved for Sure Start. As a targeted intervention, by its own criteria, it was a costly failure, but because it was trumpeted as the linchpin of the government's effort to reduce child poverty, its critics got short shrift. The supporters of the programme still lamely claim that even if there are no obvious – or indeed any – benefits now, the results will begin to show in adulthood, and the longitudinal effects will be similar to those reported in the iconic US longitudinal studies.

The rationale for targeted early interventions then is much less robust than it might appear. Other rationales appear much stronger.

Rationale 2: *Early education (and care) is a good investment only if it is of high quality. Poor care may do more harm than good especially for the most vulnerable children*

Two reviews by Paul Leseman[33] suggest that although there are well-known basic criteria to ensure minimum quality including generous adult–child ratios, well-trained adults and a stimulating cognitive environment (see below), the policy challenge is to

> '*(re)build (current) systems of ECEC to meet crucial design features*' to provide quality ECEC services for *all* children that are '*integrated and attractive and affordable to all families regardless of social class or minority status*', yet sensitive to differing educational needs.[34]

There is a consensus across a wide range of child development research in several countries that good quality ECEC provision produces good outcomes, and conversely poor provision leads to worrying outcomes. Children who have experienced poor care may behave in negative or aggressive ways. Their language development may be impaired. This is especially the case for very young children. These findings are very troublesome. What they leave out is pretty troublesome too. There is no mention of child happiness or physical well-being, or maternal anxiety at encountering poor quality care. There is no mention of the job satisfaction of those working in good environments or sheer fed-upness and boredom of working in poor environments. But what exactly do we mean by poor quality and good quality?

The National Institute of Child Health and Human Development (NICHD) study in the USA collected a vast array of longitudinal information about demographic, family, and childcare characteristics and children's behaviour and development during the first three years of life for a diverse sample of

1364 children and their families – although excluding the poorest communities.[35] It concluded that the most important factors for ensuring quality are good adult–child ratios, well-trained staff, and good pedagogic programmes. The Effective Provision of Pre-School Education (EPPE) project in the UK, similarly large scale, has highlighted the importance of good pedagogical practice for children's outcomes and conversely signalled the adverse impact of poor practices.[36]

The contentious issue is to arrive at a satisfactory and culturally relevant definition of 'quality' and ways to monitor it. The Anglo-American literature stresses the importance of staff–child ratios and staff training, and good pedagogic programmes. For young children, empathetic sensitive caregiving is regarded as important. These attributes are monitored and evaluated by standardized measuring instruments such as the Early Childhood Environment Rating Scale, and by testing children on their subsequent education performance. These quality factors are deemed to operate whatever the auspices or the provider, that is who runs and delivers the service, in care or education, in public or private for-profit or non-profit settings. A range of auspices is taken for granted, so much so that monitoring and research does not consider it important enough to distinguish between them. In other countries, auspices may matter greatly and is scrutinized much more carefully. In those countries influenced by child rights debates (see below) these general criteria of quality are insufficient, and evaluation is regarded as a complex interactive process.

Services which are promoted through demand-side rather than supply-side funding (mainly English-speaking countries) and which rely heavily on the market and private for-profit entrepreneurs have encountered problems in maintaining quality and/or in maintaining access for poor and vulnerable children. Studies in a number of countries suggest that for-profit care is usually of lower quality than either non-profit care or state-provided care. Joelle Noailly and Sabine Visser suggest that the introduction of a free market and demand-led subsidies in childcare in the Netherlands has led to a shift away from non-profit provision in poorer areas to for-profit provision in high-income urban areas.[37] Gordon Cleveland and his colleagues reanalysed large-scale Canadian data sets and came up with an estimate of the difference in quality between for-profit and non-profit care to be between 7.5 per cent and 22 per cent.[38] Using the NICDH data, Laura Sosinsky and her colleagues from the Zigler Centre at Yale University examined the relationship between childcare quality, cost and type of provision;[39] they concluded that for-profit care, especially corporate care, was likely to have more poorly trained staff, to pay them less, and to be rated lower for quality than non-profit provision. These findings and others are considered in more detail in Chapter 6.

Quality issues in countries where services have been privatized have raised real concerns. But mainstreamed state services are certainly not exempt from criticism either. There is discussion in the OECD report of the *schoolification* of early education and care.[40] Where ECEC services are regarded as a downward extension of the school system, rather than as a system specifically designed to meet the needs of young children, provision may be inappropriate – formalized teaching of large groups over-relying on didactic approaches, an overemphasis on targets and testing, and rigid regimes taking place in unsuitable spaces. This criticism has been levelled for instance at both the French system,[41,42,43] and at the English system, where there is currently considerable opposition to the implementation of the new Early Years Foundation Stage Curriculum, dubbed the *nappy curriculum* by the campaign group Open EYE, not least because of the 69 targets it sets for children 0–6.[44]

There is also concern in a number of countries about the relevance of ECEC services for migrant families, and the extent to which universal services can be socially inclusive. It is a common finding across countries that ethnic minority children are less likely than other children to use existing ECEC services.[45] ECEC is used as a strategy for assimilating migrant families, for language teaching and for cultural assimilation.[46] In 2008 a European Commission report on education and migration also put emphasis on the role of schools in supporting *assimilation*.[47] But is assimilation the right strategy?

Immigrant communities differ considerably in background and outlook, and in many cases have better long-term education outcomes than indigenous communities. In the UK, for example, white working-class boys have consistently poorer outcomes than most immigrant groups.[48] Many activists and researchers argue that racism and structural inequality are key issues for migrant families and need to be addressed as well as any changes in provision itself.[49,50]

Because very young children are completely dependent on their families and ECEC services may provide their first experiences away from those families, issues of inclusion, diversity and respect should be paramount in the agenda of services.[51] The Bernard van Leer Foundation supports the Diversity in Early Childhood and Training European Network (DECET). Based in Belgium, and particularly active in Belgium, the Netherlands and Germany, DECET has produced a variety of resources and training materials to promote diversity. Its mission, shared by many other early childhood advocacy groups, is that inclusiveness and respect for diversity are essential ingredients of quality provision.[52] Accepting difference rather than promoting similarity is better for young children, but more difficult to do.

In former communist European countries universal health care was closely tied in with crèche and kindergarten provision. In some countries, most notably France, health ministries still control services for children under 3 years. Child health screening and nutrition are regarded by the World Bank for example as part of the definition of 'holistic ECEC services' and an integral aspect of quality. Conversely from a health point of view, monitoring and screening of young children is essential, and close links with ECEC services offer a means of achieving better coverage of child health.

Rationale 3: *Early education benefits all young children, enhances dispositions for learning and socializes them for starting school, especially children from poor and migrant families*

There is more or less unanimous agreement in the child development literature that children's earliest experiences and learning form the basis for subsequent learning. 'Skills beget skills', and infancy and early childhood are critical periods for learning. There is widespread agreement that early learning is extensive and important as a basis for subsequent dispositions for learning; for language, cognition, numeracy and emotion regulation, although theoretical conceptions of the processes involved may differ. The evidence from the field of child development has been very adequately reviewed by Paul Leseman.[53] He comes up with the same holy grail of integrated services, an optimal arrangement that in practice, has been so very hard for most countries to achieve:

> The ideal early education system is both integrated and differentiated, ensuring both common developmental and educational goals, yet is adaptive to individual needs and preferences, and works both in a child centred and family centred way. The system joins up the different kinds of care, education and support that are provided and is marked by equivalent quality regulations for all systems.[54]

Some commentators have felt it necessary to try to use neuroscientific evidence to underpin arguments for early education.[55] The argument has been used by Unicef-IRC, for example, in its 2008 report card on ECEC.[56] It is fairly well established that the brain shows remarkable plasticity and adaptivity and grows extremely rapidly in the first few years. The stimulation of the brain through 'appropriate' caregiving (that is by the carer talking, singing and reading to very young children) is said to develop neural networks and promote brain growth. But these claims have been pumped up by the media. There is *no direct* neuroscientific evidence to back up the claim that teaching mothers and carers how to stimulate their children makes a significant difference to long-term outcomes. Critical periods are exceptional, rather than typical in brain development, brain development is lifelong but above all the study of the human brain is in its conceptual infancy. Most neuroscientists point to the extreme complexity of the brain and caution against such extrapolation.[57]

Max Bennett and Peter Hacker, a neuroscientist and a philosopher working together, go still further and argue that the concept of 'mind' cannot be mapped onto the brain. The processes of consciousness and learning require a different order of definition and explanation. In their view, correlations and comparisons are logically meaningless.[58] In other words those who use the claims derived from neuroscience to advocate early childhood interventions are badly overstepping the mark.

Whatever the ins and outs of the arguments, there is a widespread consensus that *quality* early education benefits *all* children, and extends and enhances the learning that is naturally taking place, especially in the domains of cognition and in emotional regulation. Most European countries have accepted this argument and offer an entitlement to nursery education for all children from 3 or 4 years old.

However, there is not a consensus about how much nursery education should be provided, at what age it should be provided or what the content of it should be, or indeed how teachers might be trained to deliver it. The nature of the entitlement varies considerably across countries, by type of provision and number of hours of entitlement. Preschool and childcare are used interchangeably in the literature but in practice they may refer to many different kinds of arrangements. Nursery education is by definition located within an education system in which explicit (national) curricular goals are set, and in which the educational performance of the child is measured according to national expectations and standards. The staff usually have pay and working conditions which are negotiated with teacher unions and are nationally set in line with the hours and holidays offered by primary and secondary schools, but which preclude the more flexible arrangements that care services offer.[59]

To be more precise, countries may differ in their offer of nursery education in the following ways:

- The age nursery education begins and ends
- The hours per day it is available
- The years spent in nursery education before primary school
- The range of activities or social interactions that promote cognitive development
- The space in which it takes place
- The size and age range of the group
- The adult–child ratios
- The training of teachers.

The extreme variation in provision is outlined in Table 3.2, using four comparator countries. This comparison is indicative only and does not include information such as policies towards parents or children from immigrant families who do not speak the language of the host country or about new policies on child rights and participation. Eurostat figures on nursery education in all EU countries are available and published in the Eurydice 2009 report.[60] However the *education* data collected across Europe by Eurydice are formal education data only and do not include hybrid or care arrangements of any kind so this is a limitation of the evidence. Table 3.2 tries to capture some of the variation

Table 3.2 Comparison of nursery education in four selected EU countries

Types of service and service provider	Auspices	Take-up	Space	Staffing: training and % primary teacher salary	Child–adult ratio	Hours available	School start age	Continuity of care	Entitlement	Cost to parent
Czech Repub. Public: Kindergarten 3–5	Education	98%	Purpose built, generous inside and outside space	Kindergarten: specialized 3 years tertiary pedagogy 75% salary	1:12	Full day 8–10 hours	6	3 years	None, but places widely available	Free
Finland Public day care centre + preschool education for children 6–7	Social welfare Education	70% 97%	Purpose built, generous inside and outside space	1/3 of staff: Bachelor or Master of Education 3 year tertiary pedagogy Bachelor or Master of Social Sciences 3 year tertiary (with pedagogical training) 81% salary (not sure) 2/3 of staff: secondary level in social welfare and health care	1:7	Full day 8–10 hours Preschool ~4 hours daily (700 hours annually)	7	7 years	Entitlement to all ECEC services Out-of-school services widely provided for first and second graders, and for all children with special needs	Fee paying as % of household income Preschool education free

France	Public: Ecoles maternelles 2 yr olds Ecoles maternelles 3–5 yr olds	Education 35% 99%	Mostly purpose built, some in converted primary school space	Specialized. Bac. plus 2 years pedagogy	2:27 teacher plus helper	Full day 8 hours	6	3–4 years	Entitlement Free
UK–England	Public and private: Nursery classes, 3–4 yrs, increasingly with private providers Reception year in primary school at 4	Education 99% 100%	Mostly converted premises attached to primary schools, no mandatory outside space for private sector	Non-specialized. Degree any subject plus 1 yr teacher training; Nursery nurse, 2 yrs secondary. New training being introduced 100% salary in public sector for teachers but not for non-teachers. Private sector very variable	2:26 teacher plus nursery nurse (1:10 in non-public education premises)	12.5 hrs per week, 33 weeks per year 6 hours 33 weeks per year	5	1–2 years	Entitlement for all 3–4 year olds on part-time basis Free but part time. Out-of-school care from private providers at commercial rates

Note: The figures given are approximations, adapted from OECD data. Direct comparisons are always difficult between highly specific systems across countries. Even in the most comprehensive systems there is hybridity and continuous experimentation so that such information becomes quickly dated. The Finnish system, for example, is comprehensive and universal but also in the process of changing and there are many complications as the table (which was revised by the Finnish STAKES correspondent)[61] demonstrates.

The research literature is not clear about the relative effects of these organizational factors, not least because they are closely interlinked and they differ considerably between countries. Table 3.2 raises the point about the importance of local contexts and the need for more detailed comparative work, but comparative data are difficult to obtain, when systems are so different. In the broadest sense, early education confers benefits, but the devil is in the detail. This is a matter for policy as well as for research; the research can only comment on the efficacy of the policy once it has been enacted, and when there is a basis for comparison. Costing such diverse systems is especially difficult, although there is an attempt to do so in the Eurydice report.

In all countries take-up of nursery education is very high and has increased in recent years as more provision has become available.[62] It is a clearly popular service, not least because it is free and is seen as a useful preparation for school. Parents see it as being a valuable service for their children, and there is almost 100 per cent take-up in those countries where it is offered.

Rationale 4: *Education and lifelong learning are essential to a competitive knowledge economy. Education promotes social mobility*

Across the EU there is concern about the competitiveness of the economy, and the role that education has to play in providing and updating individuals with the skills they need in order to be productive citizens, and in order to promote inclusiveness. Jane Jenson refers to the overarching precepts of human capital theory, which has been the driver for recent EU reforms.[63] Human capital theory essentially values *individual* economic productivity as a critical indicator in calculating economic competitiveness – as opposed for example to previous social welfarist approaches which emphasized the family as unit within the labour market. Children are viewed as potentially productive individuals, whose most important contribution lies in the future, hence the emphasis on preparing them for their productive future through appropriate education reforms. Conversely, it is important to avoid lack of productivity, and to ensure that children are not excluded from these ambitious futures, or take paths that undermine the future of others – such as crime. Social inclusion policies aim to ensure that all children are involved in the drive towards productivity.

Children have different endowments at birth; genetically, environmentally, and in their opportunities for family life and material support. If equity is considered as an important goal for education, that is providing all children with equal opportunities to benefit from their educational experiences, then early education is doubly important. As Gøsta Esping-Andersen, in a much cited article, succinctly puts it: 'If the race is already halfway run even before children begin school then we clearly need to examine what happens in the earliest years'.[64]

One of the difficulties in providing an inclusive education system and predicting its outcomes is that an estimated one in six children has some kind of disability or problem that may temporarily or permanently disrupt their learning. These learning problems are spread right across the social spectrum, but poor families have the least resources to deal with them.[65] Social inclusion policies mean that services have to orientate themselves to deal with a very wide range of children's needs. It may be that some types of service are particularly ill suited to do this, for example in a for-profit market system. One of the disadvantages of the private sector is that children with special needs frequently require some kind of specialized support, which the private sector is unable to provide without it affecting profitability (see the next section for a fuller discussion of this point).

The question remains then about the conditions under which social mobility can be promoted.[66] In some countries, despite significant recent investment in early years, social mobility appears to have decreased. The evidence strongly suggests that poverty and vulnerability are multicausal. Education, including early education, may make an important contribution but cannot redress wider inequalities or produce social mobility per se. As the eminent psychologist Jerome Kagan has famously commented, ECEC appears to offer a promise of change, and is overemphasized as a solution to social mobility because the alternative of tackling redistribution and inequality through economic and social measures is much more challenging:

> So many people believe in infant determinism [because] it ignores the power of social class membership. A child's social class is the best predictor of future vocation, academic accomplishments and mental health.[67]

This is not to deny the role ECEC might play in a variety of situations, but to highlight the need to avoid rhetoric and simple solutions.

Rationale 5: *Women are essential contributors to a dynamic economy*

In 2000, the Lisbon Summit stressed the need for the EU to retain a competitive edge and recognized the employment of women made an indispensable contribution to the economy. In this context, the Barcelona targets of 2002 stressed that

> Member states should remove disincentives to female labour force participation and strive, taking into account the demand for childcare facilities, and in line with national patterns of provision, to provide childcare by 2010 to at least 90 per cent of children between 3 years old and mandatory school age and at least 33 per cent of children under three years of age.[68]

The targets have been criticized by many social policy activists for regarding children as an impediment to women's working life, and regarding childcare as a kind of child parking, rather than as an important service for children alongside or co-terminus with early education. The *Eurochild* press release on the occasion of their seminar at the European Parliament in April 2008 made the following points:

> The Barcelona targets overlook many of the essential qualitative elements of a sound early childhood policy, for example:
>
> - the need to regard young children as citizens with rights to protection, infant health care and early education and care services
> - the need to adopt an inclusive concept of services in particular from pre-natal to 3 years
> - the need to give attention to the training, pay and working conditions of staff, particularly in the childcare sector.[69]

Ruth Lister[70] and Jane Jenson[71] have provided overviews of the gradual adoption of human capital theory over previous social welfare models not only in the UK and Europe, but also across the world. In particular they have explored some of the implications for women and children of this shift from family welfare concerns to competitive individualism. With some fury, Jenson argues that human capital theory in its emphasis on lifelong learning, and on the economic contribution of successful and productive individuals, by default ignores or downplays the particular conditions and circumstances of women and children – which are not the same as those of men. Structural issues are of less importance in human capital theory than is the encouragement of individual striving. But women have legitimate concerns – for example care for the very young and for elderly people – which may appear to be at odds with the demands of a competitive economy:

> as decades of feminist analyses and whole libraries of publications have shown, gender inequalities are NOT the result of women's

inadequate preparation, education or lack of ambition. They are due to the systematic and structural blockages to equal opportunities, either through direct discrimination or through the working of indirect mechanisms.[72]

As Jenson points out, it is not enough to focus on childcare in order to support women. In order to enable women to participate fully in the workforce other measures are necessary too – work and family life have to be reconciled. Sheila Kamerman and Peter Moss have reviewed maternity and paternity leave, and parental leave across a range of countries.[73] They argue that perhaps even good parental leave policies are not enough to enable mothers to reconcile family and work and contribute to child well-being. Since families are so diverse, and needs so variable at different periods, perhaps leave should be conceived of as a block of paid time to be taken over the course of a lifetime, for both men and women. Working patterns as well as leave patterns need to be rethought.

Maternity leave and parental leave arrangements have to dovetail with care and education, in order for mothers to hold down jobs. There is a broad consensus that rather than provide care for the very youngest children, it may be better in the interests of the child as well as in the interests of the mother to offer mothers and fathers maternity/paternity leave to cover up to the first year of life. Some countries offer considerably more than this, up to three years. At a minimum, the leave policies need to relate to the availability – and perceived desirability of – formal childcare. In most countries the majority of very young children (under 3 years) with working mothers are cared for informally. Many mothers are heavily reliant on the assistance of their family, sharing care with husbands or partners or with grandparents or other family members, as an alternative or as a supplement to the institutional care that is available. (As a grandmother this is a very familiar and enjoyable arrangement to me.)

However, as children reach the age when they can begin nursery education, mothers face another set of difficulties about fitting in with school hours. In countries like the UK, the nursery education is very short, around 12–15 hours a week, and mothers must sort out the care they need around the nursery education – not an easy task. In other countries like France, nursery education is routinely offered for 28 hours a week, with out-of-school provision. In the Nordic countries, the care incorporates nursery education and is offered on a full day basis.

These leave arrangements of course apply only to those countries where work is regulated. Within the EU there have been many directives about working conditions, in order that one country does not have an unfair advantage over another. Even so in most, if not all, countries there is an informal economy, by its very nature unrecorded, where wages are paid in cash, no questions asked. Women – mothers – take up these jobs in catering, in hospitality, in care work, in cleaning and in agriculture. Often these jobs are done by migrants. Several writers have identified what is called 'the care chain' whereby mothers from poor countries such as the Philippines or the Caribbean islands leave their families behind, and come to rich countries to look after other people's children and elderly relatives.[74] Mothers can buy in nannies and au pairs, and go out to work, but they may do so at the expense of other women who have left their families a continent away. This is a common phenomenon in middle-class families in the UK and USA, and in the richer countries of the Middle East.

In poor countries, there is a great deal of migration from rural to urban areas. In these situations mothers leave their rural communities, and struggle to survive in townships or favelas. They work very long hours as domestic servants or as market traders. Nurseries have mushroomed rapidly in urban centres to cater for them but are usually of very poor quality. About 30 per cent of young children are simply left at home to fend for themselves.[75] So in rich countries, and in Europe, there are some privileges for mothers at work; but other mothers are conveniently overlooked. For mothers in poor countries gender equality may appear unrealizable.

Within Europe however, leave arrangements of some kind mostly exist. An indicative table for four European countries is presented below which gives some idea of the complexities of the situation and the difficulties in making generalizations across the EU. Again the situation is rapidly changing as some countries are increasing their provision, while others – for instance the Czech Republic – are shutting down crèches and promoting instead benefits to mothers who stay at home.

Table 3.3 compares four countries, to illustrate the range and types of parental leave and other support. The nature of the offer varies considerably.

A comprehensive review of the inter-relationships between childcare and leave arrangements in Europe is provided by Janneke Plantenga and Chantal Remy from the European Commission's Expert group on Gender and Employment Issues.[76] Mothers are more willing to work if they have flexible employment conditions, if they have adequate maternity, paternity and parental arrangements, and if they are satisfied with the childcare available to them – its affordability, availability and quality. In France, for example, there are clear correlations between parental leave, the provision of childcare and mothers' workforce participation.[77] But there are also countries which have a very high level of participation of mothers with young children, and do not have either the childcare or the leave arrangements – most notably the USA and Canada. Because mothers work despite the absence of these arrangements, some economists take it as a sign that they are not necessary. Aggregate figures of mothers' workforce participation on which such judgements are often based conceal substantial variation within and across countries and obscure the dilemmas expressed by mothers, and the problematic circumstances of children who attend poor quality childcare provision.

Table 3.3 Spectrum of support for mothers and fathers

	Employment rate for mothers of children under 3	Maternity leave	% of salary	Parental leave entitlement	% of salary	Supplemental leave	Daycare for young children	Cost
Czec Repub.	14.2%	28 weeks	69%	Up to age 4	Flat rate		Most crèches closed since transition; only 67 remain	Fee paying; supply side funding
Finland	66.4%	18 weeks	~66%	26 weeks	~66% of earned income (gross)	Paternity 1–3/5 weeks Homecare leave until youngest child turns 3 (when not in municipal daycare) Partial leave for 0–second grade primary, allowance under 3+ first and second grade primary Leave for sick children	Family daycare and daycare centres cover 38.9% children under 2, 65% 3 yr olds (these are statistics 2006, including public and private)	Fee paying as % of household income; supply side funding

(Continued)

Table 3.3 (continued)

	Employment rate for mothers of children under 3	Maternity leave	% of salary	Parental leave entitlement	% of salary	Supplemental leave	Daycare for young children	Cost
France	49.2%	16 weeks	84% with upper limit	Until age 3	€485 per month flat rate, income tested	Paternity 14 days	Crèches and family daycare cover 36% of children under 2 Ecoles maternelles for 35% of children 2–3	Fee paying, with subsidies; supply side funding
UK–England	55% of mothers of children under 5, 40% part-time	26 weeks plus further 28 weeks unpaid if employed for 26 weeks with same employer	6 weeks at 90%, 20 weeks at flat rate of £100 or 26% at 90% of wage, whichever is lower	13 weeks; 18 weeks if disability	Unpaid	Paternity 1–2 weeks, £100 per week or 90% of wage, whichever is lower	Mainly private for-profit nurseries, diminishing number of childminders	Commercial costs, average £300+ per week in central London; demand side funding; tax credits to parents (mostly claimed by middle income parents; low take-up by poorest families)

From the children's point of view, if not that of the mothers, the provision needs to be of good quality. Yet much of the debate about women's workforce participation ignores this aspect. The OECD in its *Babies and Bosses* reports argues that far from quality being a given, there is a necessary trade-off between quantity and quality in the provision of childcare for young children. Policy-makers may well choose to sacrifice quality in order to increase provision, but whether mothers would agree is another matter.[78]

Rationale 6: *Working mothers contribute to tax revenues and lessen the need for social security payments; they make an important contribution to family income*

One reason for encouraging mothers into the labour market is that social security payments to single mothers and mothers in low income households are regarded as a drain on the national economy, but once in work, such mothers contribute instead of taking from tax revenues. There is then a net benefit to the Treasury. Another reason for encouraging mothers of young children to work is that the poorest households tend to be workless households and wages critically augment family income. Evidence from diverse countries suggests that governments have an interest in encouraging mothers to work, and in providing childcare to facilitate their entry into the workforce.[79,80]

Mothers are more likely to work if they have flexible employment conditions, good parental leave and good childcare. But the local job market is also likely to be a critical factor. Work is more difficult for mothers if they have to add travelling time to their working day, and they are more dependent on the local job market. If there is only factory work or shift work or some other kind of low-paid inflexible employment mothers may be better off, financially and emotionally, by not working officially (although they may have cash in hand jobs).[81] The ratio of costs and benefits in individual households may not be sufficient to entice women to work. Immigrant women may have particular difficulties in obtaining employment.[82]

So although policy-makers have homed in on mothers' waged work, especially single mothers and mothers from low income families, and this forms part of standard economic reasoning about women's workforce participation,[83] the evidence is contradictory. The participation of mothers in the workforce differs considerably within and across countries; without the spectrum of support mothers are less likely to work. For example, the Sure Start programme in England had as one of its aims to encourage mothers back into work, in order to limit benefit payments and increase tax revenues by offering mothers life-skills training and support into work. Despite considerable government investment in the programme, it failed to change rates of mothers in the workforce significantly, although there was a slight rise in the numbers of single mothers who worked. Childcare tax credits, which subsidized the costs of private day-care, were also not claimed by the poorest groups partly because of the bureaucratic difficulties of making claims.[84] In addition, childcare in the UK is heavily privatized, of very variable quality and expensive, and poorer mothers have shown some reluctance to use it.[85]

Countries where the spectrum of support *is* available tend to have very high mothers' labour force participation rates, assuming that the job market is available. In many former communist countries work was *compulsory*, but the leave and childcare arrangements were also mostly in place. The labour market for women shrank after transition and so did the childcare. So unless there is 'joined-up thinking' and these different policy rationales are considered together, for example between quality provision and mothers' workforce participation, policies are likely to be ineffective.

Rationale 7: *Mothers need to be involved with their children; parents are a child's first educators*

One rationale that is often put forward, in apparent contradistinction to efforts to persuade mothers of young children to work, is that mothers have an important job to do in bringing up children. Caring for others is a task which involves commitment and reciprocity.[86] Caring for children in particular is time consuming and physical. Time use studies on the impact of children on adult time suggest that mothers are overwhelmingly preoccupied by their young children; fathers much less so. Employed mothers typically work what is called 'the double shift', and have to undertake their caring role alongside their paid work, frequently at personal cost such as the loss of leisure and the loss of sleep.[87] The use of the word 'parent' blurs this gender inequity in the distribution of childcare and household tasks.

Studies of mothering suggest that mothers focus on the material and emotional welfare of their children, that they pursue a different 'ethic of care' from that of teachers. Mothers' knowledge and relationship to their children is not scientific and generalized, but anecdotal, subjective, ad hoc, and continuous – developing and changing over time within a specific context. Mothers usually love and protect their children; they have intense and intimate relationships with their children, especially when they are very young, and they dream about their futures. Teachers and professionals, on the other hand, tend to hold more abstract, norm-related knowledge and expectations of children, unrelated to context, and without expectations of reciprocity or continuity. Young children in turn develop rapidly but are dependent physically and emotionally on their mothers and other carers. Those commentators who have attempted to extrapolate from neuroscientific studies of the brain argue that the mother's role is a key one in stimulating cognitive growth and developing the brain (although others are considerably more sceptical about the use of such studies in justifying particular approaches to parenting).

The evidence suggests that mothers from poor homes do worse in preparing their children for the specific requirements of school, irrespective of ethnicity or any other variables. A mother's educational level and social class are strongly correlated with child outcomes. The differences in the willingness or capabilities of families to take advantage of educational opportunities exacerbate social class differences and limit actual equality of opportunity.[88] John Ermisch, an economist, has analysed the Millennium cohort data in the UK, and concluded that differences in cognitive ability and behavioural development at age three are correlated with parental income. The lower the parental income, the poorer the scores are on standard cognitive and behavioural tests. Using a production function framework, he argues that these differences can be partly explained by parenting styles, low-income parents demonstrating less interest in cognitive-promoting activities like reading.[89] Kathy Sylva and her colleagues reach a similar conclusion in their EPPE study, arguing that parental style is a more powerful determinant of subsequent child outcomes than any educational intervention, although early education interventions also do make a difference to outcomes.[90]

The importance of the home environment, and in particular the vulnerability of children from dysfunctional homes, has led some countries to invest in home visiting and parental education programmes. If the role the mother plays is crucial in determining a child's initial progress and subsequent readiness for school, so it makes sense to focus on the home environment and home–school relationships in the early years. The literature on parental involvement however tends not to disaggregate gender, and makes assumptions about the availability of mother's time and willingness to engage in such programmes. In addition recent evidence suggests that home visiting and parent education do not significantly affect children's outcomes, although they may in some cases alter parental behaviour.[91,92]

But it is also a global experience that families are more diverse. There are more parents choosing not to marry; more divorce, more single parents; more role reversals between men and women, with men choosing to stay at home, and women choosing to work; more older mothers, more mobility within and across countries, and so on.[93] So it is sensible to explore and make explicit the assumptions about family life that are being used as a basis for early childhood intervention.

'Parental involvement' often has a narrow meaning for professionals, who may hold a traditional, or unexplored, view of family life. From this perspective a parent's role (not disaggregated by gender) is to be a loyal supporter of the activities of the nursery or school, to fund-raise, join in school outings etc. An alternative view put forward in some services, most notably in the nurseries of Northern Italy, is that parents – men and women- are rightful partners in the joint enterprise of care and education.[94,95] The many experiments and projects across the EU to involve parents, detailed by various advocacy groups such as DECET, Children in Europe and Eurochild argue for ECEC provision to be seen as a 'democratic space', a place where fruitful debate can take place about the wider implications of bringing up children in society in diverse communities.

Given the pressures that mothers encounter, the challenge for ECEC services is how to support mothers, not only those living in vulnerable circumstances, but also working mothers, by recognizing the hours women work inside and outside the home, and by acknowledging their rights as parents. Both the Unicef-IRC report and the OECD *Starting Strong II* report argue that services should ideally recognize mothers' and fathers' *rights* within services; their right to be informed, to comment, and to participate in key decisions concerning their child.

Rationale 8: *Low birth rates below the level of replacement are a societal problem*

There is yet another rationale which has prompted countries to invest in ECEC services, this time a demographic one. Almost all rich countries are facing falling birth rates. This fall in birth rates is especially acute in post-transition countries such as the Czech Republic. (The exceptions are among migrant groups from outside the EU, whose birth rates tend to be much higher.) This is a serious problem because of demographic forecasts about the capacity of some countries to ensure future labour supply and maintain present economic growth. In these countries, parental leave policies tend to be longer and stronger, to support mothers at home.[96]

Family patterns are changing, with educated women choosing to have families later or not at all. A combination of employment, family and ECEC measures to facilitate families in bringing up children undoubtedly supports women's labour force participation, although, as this chapter has been at pains to point out, the picture is a complex one. Although those countries with the best packages (France and the Nordic countries) tend to have the highest birth rates, so do Ireland and the UK, which do not have good packages. This lack of a clear correlation between compensatory measures and birth rates has led commentators like Gary Becker[97] to claim that such compensatory packages are economically wasteful, even if mothers strongly welcome them. They require state expenditure yet there are no direct economic benefits or predicable outcomes (well-being of mothers and children not being counted as an economic benefit). In addition mothers have an important role in bringing up children. Fortunately his position is regarded as an extreme one.

The falling birth rates have led some EU countries to reconsider their position about women with young children in the labour market. The 2009 Czech presidency conference *Parental Childcare and the Employment Policy* brought together demographers, family policy experts, and advocacy organizations to reconsider the issue, particularly changes in policy which might encourage mothers to stay at home with young children. The global recession is also likely to throw into question policies concerned with women's employment.[98] Some of the papers at the conference stressed the importance of 'traditional' family values and support for the family life where the man is the breadwinner, and the mother is the stay-at-home support.[99] Catherine Hakim claimed that the evidence about the willingness of mothers of young children to participate in the labour force has been grossly overestimated. Chiara Saraceno by contrast has analysed family trends in the enlarged European Union and has concluded that moves towards more supportive family policies *have* had a positive impact on both birth rates and women's emancipation.[100]

One final point is that mothers (and fathers) appear to welcome part-time employment options while their children are very young. For mothers to have some control over their working hours is beneficial to their health and well-being – but that is not the same as saying childcare arrangements should be infinitely flexible – see below.[101]

Rationale 9: *Children, including young children, are rights bearers and all children have a right to protection, provision and participation*

The approach enshrined in human capital theory views the child as a person in the making who can be shaped to meet society's needs by appropriate educational instruction and other developmental or corrective interventions; and deposited and guarded safely in ECEC arrangements if mothers are not available to care for them directly. This assumption that childcare is unproblematic also informs the Barcelona targets.

By contrast, the child rights and child well-being arguments insist on the importance of addressing present conditions and concerns. As the French sociologist Luc Boltanski has powerfully commented (in a rather different context),

> To be concerned with the present is no small matter. For over the past, ever gone by, and over the future, still non-existent, the present has an overwhelming privilege: that of being real.[102]

In other words, children's daily experiences are vivid and deeply felt, and bad or mediocre experiences while possibly not harmful in the long run may lead to considerable unhappiness. An example might be the flexible provision of childcare which, although enabling mothers to work, might mean very disjointed experiences for children, who may attend different childcare facilities on different days, and are not consistently with a peer group. Friendships are important at any age. Childcare that is contingent on a mother's working schedule, rather than on a child's own requirements for continuity and stability, is likely to undermine children's experiences. The pay-as-you-go ultra-flexible arrangements that have been sanctioned – indeed trumpeted – as increasing parental choice in the UK, could be said to breach young children's rights.

The UN Convention on the Rights of the Child (UNCRC) stresses that children are *citizens* who have rights by virtue of being members of a community. The UN Committee on the Rights of the Child meeting in 2005 issued a comprehensive comment elucidating the rights of young children. These include the following:

- *To engage in capacity building for young children*, particularly through resource allocation and provisioning.
- *To construct a positive agenda for all young children, giving, in particular, close attention to young children in need of protection*, through multisectoral approaches and ensuring an adequate standard of living and social security.
- *To recognize that young children are holders of all the rights enshrined in the Convention including the right to education*, education being defined broadly from infancy through to transition to school.
- *To construct high-quality developmentally appropriate and culturally relevant programmes*, which means defining and monitoring quality in local contexts rather than applying blanket definitions.
- *To understand central features of child-rearing and early child development*, including among other aspects, the child's rights to rest, leisure and play.

The UN Convention on the Rights of the Child has led to many new interpretations of policy and practice in ECEC services, not least the work being undertaken by international organizations. The Unesco 2007 Monitoring Report on *Education for All* focused mainly on an interpretation of UNCRC in early years. Unicef has developed benchmarks for ECEC services in rich countries in the light of UNCRC. These points are considered further in Chapter 4.

UNCRC has spawned a considerable legal and sociological literature, which it would be redundant to review here. There are now methodologies for statistical and social accounting, disaggregating and identifying the position of children in social and welfare analyses. Sociologists have attempted to conceptualize the position of children as a social group holding certain attributes in common, much as sociologists have previously distinguished race, class and gender as separate social categories worthy of study. Others have explored the notion of competency. Children, even very young children, are seen as social actors in their own right, as people with agency who make decisions about their own lives in the here and now within the constraints set by adults. Historical studies have also contributed to a broader understanding of attributes of childhood. Paula Fass,[103] for example, has provided challenging conceptualizations of the notion of 'play' and its role in children's lives and explored understandings of what constitutes play and what constitutes work or learning in various historical periods or geographical spaces.

There is increasing interest in how conceptions of childhood in poor countries may differ from or overlap with those of children in rich countries. For instance, a major longitudinal study *Young Children's Lives* is currently being undertaken in Peru, India, Ethiopia and Vietnam tracking 15,000 children over a fifteen-year period to explore the impact of poverty on their lives and the commonality of their experiences *as children*, including their experiences of ECEC.[104] A broader international understanding of the conditions under which children thrive and act will enhance more parochial understandings of children's capacities.

The implication of these approaches for ECEC services and more broadly for young children's lives has been the subject of a report card by Unicef/IRC – discussed further in Chapter 4. A child rights approach offers challenges to current futuristic economic thinking in that it focuses on and organizes effort on the experiences of children in the here and now, and solicits their participation. Early intervention is not something that is done to young children in the hope of (re)shaping their future, but a collaborative venture with them. This point of view about services is most commonly elaborated in relation to ECEC services in Northern Italy where pedagogic practices are organized on the basis of 'a pedagogy of well-being'.[105] This approach emphasizes participatory processes at various levels, with children, with parents, with staff and with the wider community. It highlights the importance of the peer group. Unlike conventional assumptions of learning which privilege adult instruction and regard the child as an individual learner, a participatory approach views learning and emotional support as critically deriving through the peer relationships of children.[106]

It is no exaggeration to say that from the perspective of children's rights, ECEC services need to be rethought. Gilles Brougère and Michel Vandenbroeck have produced an overview of new developments in ECEC in Europe, stemming from this rights based perspective.[107] Advocacy organizations also increasingly tend to espouse a child rights perspective. But greater attention is necessary to the other circumstances of children's lives, most importantly their material well-being, and the ways in which their mothers and fathers can reconcile family and work. This is the last but not least rationale for promoting ECEC.

Rationale 10:   *Child poverty impacts severely on children's educational performance, their sense of self-worth and their subsequent societal contributions*

There is a substantial literature on child poverty and this is an extremely brief summary. It is unequivocally known that child poverty adversely affects educational outcomes and that relative wealth or poverty is a crucial aspect of child well-being. The issue that concerns us here is the extent to which ECEC services are redistributive, and can combat child poverty.

Jonathon Bradshaw and his colleagues have pioneered child focused methods of estimating poverty. They argue for the following indicators of child poverty: material situation; housing; health; subjective well-being; education; children's relationships; civic participation and risk and safety.[108] The team has provided pan-European comparisons using these criteria. The detailed study of the UK shows how its performance on child poverty compares with other European countries – it is inadequate. One of their conclusions is that in the UK public attitudes towards poverty tend to be hostile; poverty is due to lack of effort rather than to structural inequalities.[109]

This attitude is held in common with other neo-liberal countries, of which the prime example is the USA. There is a culturally entrenched public view that poverty is associated with laziness and lack of striving. Wealthy individuals are seen as deserving of their income; and conversely, income inequality is not a major concern. Neo-liberal attitudes minimize the importance of inherited assets and social capital, and emphasize individual effort and competitiveness. The attitude is that everyone can make it if they try hard enough. In reality some children get off to a flying start, and others face almost insurmountable obstacles. Those born, as the saying goes, with silver spoons in their mouths, almost never relinquish them.

Esping-Andersen has attempted to provide an explicatory model according to the ways in which responsibility for social welfare is allocated between the state, the market and households. He categorizes three approaches: *residual* (liberal economy regimes), *social insurance* (conservative) and *universalist* (social democrat) welfare regimes. *Universalist* regimes have been able to significantly reduce child poverty through a spread of measures; while *liberal economy* regimes tolerate large degrees of inequality and child poverty.[110]

Total income is of less importance than inequity. The well-being of children is affected by their and society's perception between their lives and the standard of living enjoyed from more affluent backgrounds. Inequity has also been a concern of the Unesco Education for All Global Monitoring Report *Overcoming Inequality: Why Governance Matters,*[111] and of the OECD *Growing Unequal? Income Distribution and Poverty in OECD Countries.*[112] A recent analysis that has attracted a lot of attention is that of Richard Wilkinson and Kate

Pickett.[113] They explore a range of indicators including health and education outcomes. Their conclusion is that the greater the degree of inequality in society, the more adverse the outcomes for the poor.

In general, child poverty depresses expectations and aspirations. Poverty is not merely income poverty; it typically includes a cluster of adverse factors. Children in low income families are more likely to be living in poorly functioning families; more likely to be living in problem neighbourhoods where there is drug use and high unemployment rates; and more likely to encounter problems with disability – vision, hearing, sight or mobility. Parents from poor and vulnerable families are less likely to seek ECEC services, and children in poverty will have poorer educational outcomes than other children.

The *redistributive* role of ECEC services is discussed in the OECD report *Starting Strong*.[114] Those countries with universal ECEC services tend to have lower rates of child poverty, but they also tend to be the countries where there are other redistributive measures in place, for example redistributive taxation and generous benefits for families with children. Targeted early intervention approaches may enable children to gain some respite from their adverse circumstances and *may* have some gains for the small population of children who are targeted, not least some respite from their home circumstances. But family poverty continues, unless other redistributive actions are also undertaken. It is very unlikely that the distribution of wealth and income in a society will be affected, if at all, by the provision of early childhood education and care. It is an unwarrantable burden on those providing such services to expect them to cure poverty, although they can perhaps makes its effects less harsh for those they work with.

This chapter makes the point, I hope strongly, that the delivery of early childhood education and care is shaped by many considerations, some of which may not even be directly linked to practice in nurseries. Quality is not an abstraction, but a product of particular policies. To consider quality anywhere, without taking account of the policy framework and the wider society in which it is embedded, is a half-enterprise. But conversely, to consider policy without being grounded in practice, and having views about what constitutes good practice, is also a partial exercise. The trick is to move from one to the other, seamlessly.

Notes

1 European Commission/NESSE (2009) *Early Childhood Education and Care: Key Lessons from Research for Policy-Makers*. Brussels: European Commission, Education and Culture DG. Available at www.nesse.fr/nesse/nesse_top/tasks

2 LeVine, R. and New, R. (eds) (2008) *Anthropology and Child Development: A Cross-cultural Reader*. Oxford: Blackwell.

3 DeLoache, J. and Gottlieb, A. (eds) (2000) *A World of Babies: Imagined Childcare Guides for Seven Societies*. Cambridge: Cambridge University Press.

4 Bentley, R. and Mace, R. (eds) (2009) *Substitute Parenting: Alloparenting in Human Societies*. Oxford: Berghahn.

5 Afua Twom Danso, personal communication.

6 Coyle, B. (2007) *The Soulful Science: What Economists Really Do and Why it Matters*. Princeton, NJ: Princeton University Press, p. 232.

7 One of the journals which challenged orthodox economics was called *Post-Autistic Economics Review*. See www.paecon.net/HistoryPAE.htm

8 Sandel, M. (2009) *Justice: What's the Right Thing to Do?* London: Penguin.

9 Sosinky, L., Lord, H. and Zigler, E. (2007) 'For-profit/non-profit differences in center-based childcare quality: Results from the National Institute of Child Health and Human Development Study of Early Child Care and Youth Development.' *Journal of Applied Developmental Psychology* 28(5): 390–410.

10 Penn, H. (2011) 'Gambling on the market.' *Journal of Early Childhood Research* forthcoming.
Kilburn, R. and Karoly, L. (2008) *The Economics of Early Childhood Policy: What the Dismal Science Has to Say about Investing in Children*. Santa Monica, CA: Rand.

11 Heckman, J. and Masterov, D. (2004) *The Productivity Argument for Investing in Young Children*. Cambridge, MA: National Bureau of Economic Research. See http://jenni.uchicago.edu/Invest/
Heckman, J. (2008) 'The case for investing in young children.' In Brookings Foundation (2009) *Big Ideas for Children: Investing in Our Nation's Future*. Washington, DC: First Focus, Brookings Institution.

12 See Penn, H. (2011) 'Travelling policies and global buzzwords: How INGOs and charities spread the word about early childhood.' *Childhood* forthcoming.

13 Brookings Foundation (2009) *Big Ideas for Children: Investing in Our Nation's Future*. Washington, DC: First Focus, Brookings Institution.

14 The World Bank has funded the development of an 'early childhood calculator' to enable countries to calculate the profits of investment in programmes per 1000 children. See http://go.worldbank.org/KHC1NHO580

15 Sabo, J. (2007) 'Dancing the dance of capitalism: The economic rationale and the politics of kids.' *International Journal of Economic Development* 9(4): 302.

16 Sonya Michel in her history of American childcare argues that philanthropic interventions were characterized by an absence of any kind of participatory management or democracy by users or staff; the nurseries were run on an entirely top-down basis. The style of the experimental interventions described here is also characterized by a patrician view of the intervention – we are here to do good for you. There is no room for a contribution to decision-making about the projects by users or staff, who are there as objects of a well-meaning academic experiment. See Michel, S. (1999) *Children's Interests/Mothers' Rights*. New Haven, CT: Yale University Press.

17 Kagan, J. (1998) *Three Seductive Ideas*. Cambridge, MA: Harvard University Press.

18 Penn, H. et al. (2006) *Systematic Review of the Economic Impact of Long-term Centre-based Early Childhood Interventions. Research Evidence in Education Library*. London: Social Science Research Unit, Institute of Education. See www.eppi.ioe. ac.uk

19 Barnett, W.S. (1996) *Lives in the Balance: Age-27 Benefit-Cost Analysis of the High/ Scope Perry Preschool Program*. Ypsilanti, MI: High/Scope Foundation.

20 Ramey, C.T., Campbell, F.A., Burchinal, M., Skinner, M.L., Gardner, D.M. and Ramey, S.L. (2000) 'Persistent effects of early intervention on high-risk children and their mothers.' *Applied Developmental Science* 4: 2–14.

21 Reynolds, A.J. (2000) *Success in Early Intervention: The Chicago Child–Parent Centers*. Lincoln, NE: University of Nebraska Press.

22 Aos, S., Phipps, S., Barnoski, R. and Lieb, R. (2001) *The Comparative Costs and Benefits of Programs to Reduce Crime*. Olympia, WA: Washington State Institute for Public Policy.

23 Heath, S.B. (1983) *Ways with Words: Language, Life and Work in Communities and Classrooms*. Cambridge: Cambridge University Press.
Heath, S.B. (1990) 'The children of Trackton's children: Spoken and written language in social change'. In J. Stigler, R. Shweder and G. Herdt (eds) *Cultural Psychology: Essays on Comparative Human Development*. Cambridge: Cambridge University Press, pp. 496–519.
Rosaldo, R. (1993) *Culture and Truth: The Remaking of Social Analysis*. London: Routledge.
The novels of the black author Walter Mosley set in the 1950s and 1960s also portray a profoundly racist society.

24 Johnson, D., Jaeger, E., Randolph, S., Cauce, A., Ward, J. and the National Institute of Child Health and Human Development Early Child Care Research Network (2003) 'Studying the effects of early childcare experiences on the development of children of color in the United States: Towards a more inclusive research agenda.' *Child Development* 74(5): 1227–1244.

25 Weikart, D.P. (ed.) (1967) *Preschool Interventions: Preliminary Results of the Perry Preschool Project*. Ann Arbor, MI: Campus, p. 57.

26 Meadows, P. (2007) 'The methodologies for the evaluation of complex interventions: An ongoing debate.' In J. Belsky, J. Barnes and E. Melhuish (eds) *The National Evaluation of Sure Start*. Bristol: Policy Press.

27 Plantenga, J. and Remery, C. (2009) *The Provision of Childcare Service: A Comparative Review of 30 European Countries*. EU Directorate for Employment, Social Affairs and Equal Opportunities/European Commission's Expert Group on Gender and Employment Issues (EGGE). Brussels: EU. This document draws on EU-SILC data and their uses in investigating childcare use and its relationship to family variables.

28 Becker, G. (2005) *Should Governments Subsidize Childcare and Work Leaves?* Becker-Posner blog, November 2005: www.becker-posner-blog.com/

29 I visited one local programme where the social work manager pointed out as her greatest success a computer system which was compatible with the local NHS Primary Health Care Trust system.

30 Tunstill, J. and Alnock, D. (2007) 'Sure Start local programmes: An overview of the implementation process.' In J. Belsky, J. Barnes and E. Melhuish (eds) *The National Evaluation of Sure Start*. Bristol: Policy Press, pp. 79–96.

31 Belsky, J., Barnes, J. and Melhuish, E. (eds) (2007) *The National Evaluation of Sure Start*. Bristol: Policy Press.

32 National Equality Committee (2009) *An Anatomy of Economic Inequality in the UK*. London: Centre for the Analysis of Social Exclusion.

33 Leseman, P. (2002) *Early Childhood Education and Care for Children from Low Income and Minority Backgrounds*. Paris: OECD.
Leseman, P. (2009) 'The impact of high quality education and care on the development of young children.' In Eurydice (2009) *Early Education and Care in Europe: Tackling Social and Cultural Inequalities*. Brussels: Education, Audiovisual and Culture Executive Agency, pp. 17–40.

34 Leseman, P. 'The impact of high quality education and care on the development of young children', p. 39.

35 NICHD Early Child Care Research Network (2005) *Study of Early Child Care and Youth Development*. New York: Guilford Press.

36 Siraj-Blatchford, I., Sylva, K., Gilden, R. and Bell, D. (2002) *Researching Effective Pedagogy in the Early Years*. London: Department for Education and Skills.
Siraj-Blatchford, I. and Sylva, K. (2004) 'Researching pedagogy in English pre-schools.' *British Educational Research Journal* 30(5): 713–730.
Siraj-Blatchford, I., Taggart, B., Sylva, K. et al. (2008) 'Towards the transformation of practice in early childhood education: The effective provision of pre-school education (EPPE) project.' *Cambridge Journal of Education* 38(1): 23–36.

37 Noailly, J. and Visser, S. (2009) 'The impact of market forces on the provision of childcare: Insights from the 2005 Childcare Act in the Netherlands.' *Journal of Social Policy* 38(3): 477–498.

38 Cleveland, G., Forer, B., Hyatt, D., Japel, C. and Krashinsky, M. (2007) *An Economic Perspective on the Current and Future Role of Nonprofit Provision of Early Learning and Childcare Services in Canada*. Toronto: Toronto University and Human Resources and Skills Department, Canada.

39 Sosinsky, L., Lord, H. and Zigler, E. (2007) 'For-profit/non-profit differences in center-based childcare quality: Results from the National Institute of Child Health and Human Development Study of Early Child Care and Youth Development.' *Journal of Applied Developmental Psychology* 28(5): 390–410.

40 OECD (2006) *Starting Strong II: Early Childhood Education and Care*. Paris: OECD.

41 Plaisance, E. and Rayna, S. (1997) 'L'éducation préscolaire aujourd'hui: Réalités, questions et perspectives.' *Revue française de pédagogie* 119: 107–139.

42 Caille, J. and Rosenwald, F. (2006) *Les Inégalités de réussite à l'école élémentaire: Construction et évolution*. Paris: INSEE.

43 Brisset, C. and Gosle, B. (eds) (2006). *L'Ecole à 2 ans est-ce bon pour l'enfant?* Paris: Odile Jacob.

44 Open EYE Early Years Campaign (2008) *Memorandum Submitted to the Select Committee on Children, Schools and Families. Minutes of Evidence.* London: House of Commons, May. See www.parliament.the-stationery-office.co.uk

45 OECD, *Starting Strong II.*

46 Eurydice (2009) *Early Education and Care in Europe: Tackling Social and Cultural Inequalities.* Brussels: Education, Audiovisual and Culture Executive Agency.

47 European Commission (2008) *Education and Migration: Strategies for Integrating Migrant Children in European Schools and Societies. A Synthesis of Research Findings for Policy-Makers.* Report submitted to the European Commission by the NESSE network of experts, 2008.

48 Strand, S. (2008) *Minority Ethnic Pupils in the Longitudinal Study of Young People in England: Extension Report on Performance in Public Examinations at Age 16.* Research Report 029. London: Department for Children, Schools and Families.

49 Vandenbroeck, M. (2007) *Deculturalising Social Inclusion and Reculturalizing Outcomes in Promoting Social Inclusion and Respect for Diversity in the Early Years.* The Hague: Bernard van Leer Foundation.

50 Gillborn, D. (2008) *Racism and Education: Coincidence or Conspiracy.* London: Routledge.

51 Brougère, G. and Vandenbroeck, M. (eds) (2007) *Repenser l'éducation des jeunes enfants: Deuxième tirage.* Paris: PIE Peter Lang.

52 DECET (2008) *Diversity in Early Childhood and Training European Network.* See www.decet.org

53 Leseman, *Early Childhood Education and Care for Children from Low Income and Minority Backgrounds.*
Leseman, 'The impact of high quality education and care on the development of young children'.

54 Leseman, 'The impact of high quality education and care on the development of young children', p. 40.

55 Mustard, J. (2006) *Early Childhood Development and Experience-based Brain Development: The Scientific Underpinnings of the Importance of Early Child Development in a Globalized World.* Washington, DC. Brookings Institution.

56 Unicef (2007) *Child Poverty in Perspective: An Overview of Child Well-being in Rich Countries.* Innocenti Report Card 2007. Florence: Unicef/IRC.

57 Thompson, R. and Nelson, C. (2001) 'Developmental science and the media.' *American Psychologist* 56: 5–15.

58 Bennett, M. and Hacker, P. (2003) *The Philosophical Foundations of Neuroscience.* Oxford: Blackwell.

59 Educational International (2004–2008) *Worlds of Education Journal:* www.eiie.org/en/index.php

60 Eurydice, *Early Education and Care in Europe.*

61 Paivi Lindberg, personal communication.

62 Eurydice, *Early Education and Care in Europe*, Table 2:11.

63 Jenson, J. (2008) 'Writing women out, folding gender in: The European Union "modernises" social policy.' *Social Politics* 15(2): 131–153.

64 Esping-Andersen, G. (2004) 'Untying the Gordian Knot of social inheritance.' *Research in Social Stratification and Mobility* 21: 115–139. The quotation is from p. 116.

65 Feinstein, L., Hearn, B., Renton, Z. with Abrahams, C. and Macleod, M. (2007) *Reducing Inequalities: Realising the Talent of All*. London: National Children's Bureau.

66 Feinstein, L., Duckworth, K. and Sabato, R. (2008) *Education and the Family: Passing Success Across the Generations*. London: Routledge.

67 Kagan, J. (1998) *Three Seductive Ideas*. Cambridge, MA: Harvard University Press. The quotation is from p. 147.

68 Barcelona European Council (2002) *Presidency Conclusions*. Brussels: European Union. The quotation is from p. 12. Available at www.consilium.europa.eu/ueDocs/cms_Data/docs/pressData/en/ec/71025.pdf

69 See www.Eurochild.org

70 Lister, R. (2006) 'Children (but not women) first: New Labour, child welfare and gender.' *Critical Social Policy* 26(2): 315–335.

71 Jenson, 'Writing women out, folding gender in'.

72 Jenson, 'Writing women out, folding gender in', p. 149.

73 Kamerman, S. and Moss, P. (eds) (2009) *The Politics of Parental Leave Policies: Children, Parenting, Gender and the Labour Market*. Bristol: Policy Press.

74 Williams, F. and Gavanas, A. (2008) 'The intersection of childcare regimes and migration regimes: A three-country study.' In H. Lutz (ed.) *Migration and Domestic Work: A European Perspective on a Global Theme*. London: Routledge.

75 Heymann, J. (2006) *Forgotten Families: Ending the Growing Crisis Confronting Children and Working Parents in the Global Economy*. Oxford: Oxford University Press.

76 Plantenga, J. and Remery, C. (2009) *The Provision of Childcare Services: A Comparative Review of 30 European Countries*. Brussels: EC Directorate-General for Employment, Social Affairs and Equal Opportunities G1 Unit.

77 Maurin, E. and Roy, D. (2008) *L'Effet de l'obtention d'une place en crèche sur le retour a l'emploi des mères et leur perception du développement de leurs enfants*. Grenoble: Centre pour la Recherche Economique et les Applications. Paper given May 2008.

78 OECD (2002) *Babies and Bosses: Australia, Denmark and the Netherlands*, vol. 1. Paris: OECD.
OECD (2003) *Babies and Bosses: Austria, Ireland and Japan*, vol. 2. Paris: OECD.
OECD (2004) *Babies and Bosses: New Zealand, Portugal and Switzerland*, vol. 3. Paris: OECD.
These reports were produced by the Employment Division of OECD and not the Education and Training Division which produced *Starting Strong*, which takes quality as a central issue. See Chapter 4.

79 Muller Kucera, K. and Bauer, T. (2001) *Costs and Benefits of Child Care Services in Switzerland – Empirical Findings from Zurich*. Cited in OECD, *Starting Strong II*, p. 257.

80 Pricewaterhouse-Cooper (2004) *Universal Education and Care in 2020: Costs, Benefits and Funding Options*. London: Daycare Trust.

81 Dean, H. (2007) 'Tipping the balance: The problematic nature of work–life balance in a low income neighbourhood.' *Journal of Social Policy* 36(4): 519–537.

82 Mozère, L. (1999) *Travail au noir, informalité: Liberté ou sujetion?* Paris: L'Harmattan.

83 OECD, *Babies and Bosses: Australia, Denmark and the Netherlands*, vol. 1.
OECD, *Babies and Bosses: Austria, Ireland and Japan*, vol. 2.
OECD, *Babies and Bosses: New Zealand, Portugal and Switzerland*, vol. 3.

84 Brewer, M. and Shepherd, A. (2004) *Has Labour Made Work Pay?* York: Joseph Rowntree Foundation and Institute of Fiscal Studies.

85 Vincent, C., Braun, A. and Ball, S. (2008) 'Childcare, choice and social class: Caring for young children in the UK.' *Critical Social Policy* 28(1): 5–9.

86 Finch, J. (1993) 'The concept of caring: Feminist and other perspectives.' In J. Twigg (ed.) *Informal Care in Europe*. York: Social Policy Research Unit, pp. 5–22.

87 Craig, L. (2007) *Contemporary Motherhood: The Impact of Children on Adult Time*. Aldershot: Ashgate.

88 Feinstein, L., Duckworth, K. and Sabato, R. (2008) *Education and the Family: Passing Success across the Generations*. London: Routledge.

89 Ermisch, J. (2008) 'Origins of social immobility and inequality; parenting and early child development.' *National Institute Economic Review* 205. This study analyses parental style according to six key questions, including rules and rule enforcement, regularity, eating habits and time spent television watching.

90 Sylva, K., Siraj-Blatchford, I. and Taggart, B. (2006) *Assessing Quality in the Early Years: Early Childhood Environment Rating Scale Extension (ECERS-E): Four Curricular Subscales*. Stoke-on-Trent: Trentham.

91 Blok, H., Fukkin, R., Gebhardt, E. and Leseman, P. (2005) 'The relevance of delivery mode and other program characteristics for the effectiveness of early childhood interventions with disadvantaged children.' *International Journal of Behavioural Development* 29: 36–37.

92 Waldfogel, J. (2004) *Social Mobility, Life Chances and the Early Years*. CASE Paper 88. London: Centre for the Analysis of Social Inclusion.

93 Bianchi, S., Casper, L. and Berkowitz King, R. (eds) (2003) *Work, Family, Health, and Well-being*. New York: National Institute of Child Health and Human Development and Routledge.

94 Moss, P. (2007) 'Bringing politics into the nursery: Early childhood education as a democratic practice.' *European Early Childhood Education Research Journal* 15(1): 5–20.

95 Bloomer, K. and Cohen, B. (2008) *Young Children in Charge*. Edinburgh. Children in Scotland.

96 Kocourkova, J. (2009) 'Czech Republic: Normative or choice-orientated system.' In S. Kamerman and P. Moss (eds) *The Politics of Parental Leave Policies: Children, Parenting, Gender and the Labour Market.* Bristol: Policy Press, pp. 51–68.

97 Becker, *Should Governments Subsidize Childcare and Work Leaves?*

98 Conference proceedings can be found at www.mpsv.cz/en/6391

99 Dr Carlson, President of the Howard Center and Director of its Family Studies Center in Rockford, Illinois, put forward this view at the conference, as did *men* from think tanks in Germany and Austria. See www.mpsv.cz/en/6391 for list of speakers.

100 See www.mpsv.cz/en/6391

101 World Health Organization (WHO) (2003) *Global Strategy for Infant and Young Child Feeding.* Geneva: WHO.

102 Boltanski, L. (1999) *Distant Suffering: Morality, Media and Politics.* Cambridge. Cambridge University Press. The quotation is from p. 192.

103 Fass, P. (ed.) (2004) *Encyclopaedia of Children and Childhood in History and Society.* New York: Thompson/Gale.
Fass, P. (2007) *Children of a New World: Society, Culture and Globalization.* New York: New York University Press.

104 See www.younglives.org.uk

105 Mantovani, S. (2007) 'Pedagogy in early childhood in Italy.' In R. New and M. Cochran (eds) *Early Childhood Education: An International Encyclopedia.* Westport, CT: Greenwood, vol. 4, pp. 1115–1118.

106 Corsaro, W. and Molinari, L. (2008) 'Policy and practice in Italian children's transition from preschool to elementary school.' *Research in Comparative and International Education* 3(3): 250–265.

107 Brougère and Vandenbroeck, *Repenser l'éducation des jeunes enfants.*

108 Bradshaw, J., Hoelscher, P. and Richardson, D. (2007) 'An Index of Child Well-Being in the European Union 25.' *Journal of Social Indicators Research* 80: 133–177.

109 Bradshaw, J. and Bennett, F. (2007) *UK: Tackling Child Poverty and Promoting the Social Inclusion of Children: A Study of National Policies.* Brussels: European Commission (DG Employment, Social Affairs and Equal Opportunities). Web publication only: www.peer-review-social-inclusion.net/policy-assessment-activities/reports/first-semester-2007/first-semester-reports-2007/united-kingdom_1_07

110 Esping-Andersen, 'Untying the Gordian Knot of social inheritance.'

111 Unesco (2009) *Overcoming Inequality: Why Governance Matters. EFA Global Monitoring Report.* Paris: Unesco.

112 OECD (2008) *Growing Unequal? Income Distribution and Poverty in OECD Countries.* Paris: OECD.

113 Wilkinson, R. and Pickett, K. (2009) *The Spirit Level: Why More Equal Societies Almost Always Do Better.* London: Allen Lane.

114 OECD (2006) *Starting Strong II: Early Childhood Education and Care.* Paris: OECD.

4   The international consensus on ECEC

Chapters 2 and 3 dealt with rationales, the reasons governments give – or fail to acknowledge – in developing early childhood policies and services. These rationales explain why services are important enough for the government to invest in them, or not important enough to warrant expenditure. These rationales are an expression of what is valued, and how that value is to be judged. In this chapter, I explore how rationales get transformed into policy, and what conditions need to be in place for a policy to be effective. What is it that governments should do to ensure that quality services can be developed – even if they are based on differing rationales and espouse different policies?

Examining ECEC systems at the level of government is essentially a comparative exercise. It is only partly possible to judge how effective a government is by exploring the internal or national evidence alone. This dictum applies to many areas of government as well as ECEC. For example if one country consistently has much lower carbon emissions than another, are there lessons to be learnt from their success? If another country consistently has very high levels of child poverty, is there a policy lesson to be drawn from their failure in combating poverty? If educational outcomes in one country are consistently better than in another, what does this say about the efficacy of the education system?

In the field of ECEC there are now plenty of comparative data to draw on, since a number of international organizations have already undertaken this analysis of early childhood services. The OECD, Unesco, Unicef and the EU have all produced guidelines on quality system operation and development, based on comparisons and/or ratings between countries. There are a variety of reasons why debate has shifted from individual countries to the international stage. One reason is that economic analysis has become very important in a world where economies are so interdependent. Providing ECEC services has been viewed as improving the economic well-being of countries, although, as I explained in Chapter 3, this argument is a rather flawed and complicated one. But if providing ECEC gives a competitive edge, either by training young children to be active go-getting citizens, or by enabling mothers of young children to contribute to the economy, or at the very least by mitigating later expenditure on controlling social disorder, then there is good reason to promote it internationally.

These lines of reasoning have been behind OECD and EU interest in ECEC. The other main reason is the increasing prominence of child rights. All children should benefit from the wealth of nations, not just a few of them. The Unicef Innocenti Research Centre has been monitoring the progress of Young Children's Rights in rich countries for some time now. Unesco has an interest because it has a duty to promote Education for All (EFA) across rich and poor countries, and it privileges the rationale that early childhood education and care is the surest foundation for subsequent learning.

All these organizations have weighed in to advise their members, supporters and other interested partners about which are the most successful approaches to delivering and administering early childhood services. The advice may be unheeded, but it certainly exists. OECD in particular is generally seen as the world's leading knowledge generation organization. Its education data for example, summarized in its regular reports, *Education at a Glance*, are cited throughout the world as a standard. OECD offers meticulous comparative information and rankings for countries, and it would be a foolish government that ignored its findings. (Unless of course it did poorly on the international indicators, in which case it might want to downplay the results. The USA is usually the biggest culprit in this respect.) The EU has a brief only for members of the European Union, and as citizens of the UK have good cause to know, not all of its members are equally enthusiastic about its recommendations.

These organizations inevitably lean on one another, their representatives speak at each other's conferences, their personnel swop over from one organization to another, and they share their arguments and research evidence. Each of these organizations too has many internal sections, or administrative units. As in any government administration, these units or sections may have competing priorities. Round these organizations is a swirl of lobbyists, policy think tanks and others keen to join in the fray to promote their cause (or in the case of the EU, to win EU tenders to undertake work the EU wants done). Unesco, OECD and the EU work to politically appointed committees, sometimes with overlapping members. So there is considerable sharing of information and policy consensus, although these international organizations may choose to emphasize one aspect rather than another – as Unicef does for example with child rights. However, it is also the case that all these organizations, whatever their official and unofficial links, and whatever their internal dissensions, do consider government intervention in ECEC is necessary and hold similar views about how it might be structured. Very broadly speaking, in order to achieve quality early childhood services, governments should have in place some kind of legal authority to act, to set targets, to regulate and oversee services; they should make financial resources available, because early childhood is a social and educational service rather than a self-supporting business enterprise; they should allocate human resources, in particular in the training of staff who work in services and make sure those working in the services have acceptable pay, working conditions and rights at work; and they should make sure there is an adequate infrastructure for services – the capital investment for buildings and other physical resources.

Even then, as suggested in Chapter 3, the efficacy of early childhood services is dependent on the wider social and economic environment. The more poverty and inequality for example, the less likely early childhood services are to be successful in their aims. The weaker the government recognition of mothers' and fathers' need to reconcile work and family life, the more complications this causes in the delivery of services. The more preoccupied the government with the marketization of services, the less likely coherence will be achieved, and – in the view of some commentators – the more civic society will be undermined because services become so stratified and the rich use one type of service while the poor use another. ECEC services alone, however well put together, cannot solve generic problems. This is not to say government action is unnecessary – far from it.

This chapter then explores some of the priorities and rationales put forward by international bodies for achieving quality in early childhood education and care.

Unicef / IRC

Unicef has taken the broadest perspective on early childhood, because of its commitment to the well-being of all children. It has chosen to stress the impact of the wider social and economic environment in which children grow up as being of paramount importance. The UN Convention of the Rights of the Child outlines the responsibility of governments as

- 'rendering appropriate assistance to parents, legal guardians and extended families in the performance of their child-rearing responsibilities' (articles 18.2 and 18.3)
- 'including assisting parents in providing living conditions necessary for the child's development' (article 27.2)
- 'ensuring that children receive necessary protection and care' (article 3.2).

Unicef's research arm, the Innocenti Research Centre (IRC) based in Florence, has undertaken a considerable programme of work on early childhood, based on its interpretation of UNCRC. It notes that (of course) government capacities and income may differ widely between rich and poor nations, and between transitional (former Soviet countries and their allies) and Western Europe. But it considers that it is important that rich countries set an example, and demonstrate serious committment to realizing UNCRC. A booklet from IRC issued in 2008 suggests that there are four key dimensions in setting standards for ECEC:

- a national commitment to early childhood services
- access and inclusiveness
- quality of early childcare and education
- the social and economic context into which the child is born.

It then goes on to describe 10 benchmarks for ECEC services. These are illustrated in Figure 4.1.

Unicef/IRC argues that far from being a description of an ideal, the benchmarks represent no more than an initial attempt to establish minimum statistical accounting, and minimum standards that put the needs of children first while at the same time recognizing the realities facing both parents and governments in the advanced economies. 'The proposed benchmarks therefore represent a standard below which no rich nation should fall; but a standard which, over time, will need to be raised'.[1]

The advanced economies investigated were mostly those that featured in the OECD report *Starting Strong*, partly because robust data were already available for them. Predictably the Nordic countries are at the top of the report card with 8–10 points; at the bottom are the neo-liberal economies, the USA, Australia, Canada and Ireland with 1–3 points. The UK has a score of 5, a reflection of recent investment in Early Childhood Services, but falling far short of the Unicef standard on child poverty, and in ECEC expenditure overall. The league table was influential. It has attracted considerable attention and is used by campaigners to try to influence government action.

European Union

The EU is primarily an *economic union* and has a brief for the economic development of its member states. They act together as an economic bloc. The EU is concerned that economic rules should be consistent throughout the EU, so that no one country is unduly advantaged, nor socially excluded from economic success. The internal rules of the EU, which are supposed to be binding on all of its members, are intended above all to improve the economic competitiveness and the economic success of member states. Like the other international organizations, the EU has no powers of enforcement except on matters which have been enshrined in EU law, mainly to do with these business competition issues. The EU issues 'directives', communally agreed

This Report Card discusses the opportunities and risks involved in the child care transition, and proposes internationally applicable benchmarks for early childhood care and education – a set of minimum standards for protecting the rights of children in their most vulnerable and formative years.

The table below shows which countries are currently meeting the suggested standards, and summarizes this first attempt to evaluate and compare early childhood services in the 25 OECD countries in which data have been collected.

Benchmark	Number of benchmarks achieved	1 Parental leave of 1 year at 50% of salary	2 A national plan with priority for disadvantaged children	3 Subsidized and regulated child care services for 25% of children under 3	4 Subsidized and accredited early education services for 80% of 4 year olds	5 80% of all child care staff trained	6 50% of staff in accredited early education services tertiary educated with relevant qualification	7 Minimum staff-to-children ratio of 1:15 in pre-school education	8 1.0% of GDP spent on early childhood services	9 Child poverty rate less than 10%	10 Near-universal outreach of essential child health services
Sweden	10	✓	✓	✓	✓	✓	✓	✓	✓	✓	✓
Iceland	9		✓	✓	✓	✓	✓	✓	✓	✓	✓
Denmark	8	✓	✓	✓	✓		✓	✓	✓	✓	
Finland	8	✓	✓		✓	✓	✓	✓		✓	✓
France	8	✓	✓	✓	✓	✓	✓		✓	✓	
Norway	8	✓	✓		✓	✓	✓	✓		✓	✓
Belgium (Flanders)	6		✓	✓	✓	✓	✓				✓
Hungary	6		✓		✓	✓	✓			✓	✓
New Zealand	6		✓	✓	✓	✓	✓	✓			
Slovenia	6	✓	✓		✓	✓	✓			✓	
Austria	5		✓		✓		✓	✓		✓	
Netherlands	5		✓	✓	✓	✓	✓				
United Kingdom*	5		✓	✓	✓	✓	✓				
Germany	4		✓		✓		✓	✓			
Italy	4		✓		✓	✓	✓				
Japan	4		✓				✓	✓			✓
Portugal	4		✓			✓	✓	✓			
Republic of Korea	4		✓				✓	✓			✓
Mexico	3		✓			✓	✓				
Spain	3			✓		✓	✓				
Switzerland	3			✓				✓		✓	
United States	3			✓			✓	✓			
Australia	2			✓		✓					
Canada	1			✓							
Ireland	1					✓					
Total benchmarks met	126	6	19	13	15	17	20	12	6	10	8

Figure 4.1   Early childhood services – a league table.

Note: Data for the United Kingdom refer to England only.

Source: Downloaded from http://www.unicef-irc.org/publications/pdf/rc8_eng.pdf

policies to which members are generally expected to adhere, but – as is often the case with the UK – they may choose to opt out. The UK is generally wary of any directives which can be seen to curtail their own market competitiveness, such as limiting working hours, or increasing maternal/parental leave.

The EU has a curious political structure. It is in theory governed by an elected parliament, based in Strasbourg, but key decisions are made by nominated ministers from member states. There is a rotating six-month presidency. Each country takes it in turns to host the EU, using the opportunity to advance issues about which it is concerned. The EU works through a powerful, if labyrinthine secretariat, the European Commission (EC) based in Brussels. The commissioners, those who run the commission, are nominated by member states. The EC is much smaller than its caricature as a snare of red tape might imply. In fact all these arrangements might be described as painstakingly democratic, a model of federalism, even though the EU is not strictly a federation but an economic union.

The EC itself has an international workforce, recruited by open competition from across the EU. The EC is divided into directorates, who advise on EU policy and who commission a range of work from a variety of organizations and researchers and consultancy firms to try to flesh out the detail of policy and the research evidence to substantiate it. Fuller details about how the EU operates, and its institutional arrangements, are readily available from the EU website.[2]

The EU has arrived at the view, enshrined in its legislation, that the well-being of the workforce is integral to its economic success – its education and training, its workplace rights, its health, its transferability (from one member state to another) and its voice or representation in business affairs. As part of the concern with the efficiency of the workforce, it considers that the position of women is a key to productivity, since women are potentially half the workforce. So equal opportunities at work, and measures to reconcile family life and the workplace through provision of childcare and maternity, paternity and parental leave, are considered as essential measures.

From this perspective of economic well-being and competitiveness, the two directorates of the European Commission who have had most to do with ECEC (although not necessarily acting in tandem) are the Education and Culture directorate and the Employment, Social Affairs and Equal Opportunities directorate.

The Education and Culture directorate has commissioned a series of research reports, statistical reports and policy documents to do with early education.[3,4] The most recent of these was the NESSE report discussed in Chapter 3, but there are many others over time. The directorate has a stated concern with lifelong learning and with social inclusion within education, especially for the children of migrants. Most of the data used by researchers working for the directorate have been collected through *Eurostat*, and refer only or mainly to statistics obtained from education authorities. Uptil recently it has had few statistics on childcare available. The introduction of the new EU-SILC (statistics on income and living conditions – see Chapter 11 for more details) monitoring and tracking system should provide more useful information, for use by researchers with a variety of concerns including ECEC.

The Employment, Social Affairs and Equal Opportunities directorate (written hereafter as DG5) has also had a long-standing interest in ECEC, mainly from the perspective of equal opportunities for women, and the reconciliation of work and family life. In the mid 1990s, when Europe was a mere 15 countries (as opposed to 27 members now, plus others on the waiting list or peripherally attached) it commissioned the European Childcare Network to explore issues of quality in childcare. The network was made up of nominees from equal opportunities organizations in each member state, and convened by my colleague, Peter Moss. Some of the work was in turn subbed out to others – and like the NESSE report, I had an input, and have a bird's eye view of the process. The European Childcare Network produced a discussion document on quality, suggesting it had to be dealt with at the systematic level as well as at the programme level.[5] In a subsequent document these were transposed into quality targets which aimed to bring together education *and* care:

> from a service perspective it is neither necessary or desirable to treat (children with employed parents) separately from other children. The development of services for young children should be based on a policy that takes account of **all** children and carers and **all** their needs.[6]

The targets were grouped under the following headings:

- a policy framework for service provision, including co-ordination of responsibility for services
- financial targets in terms of percentage of GDP
- targets for levels and types of provision for different age groups
- education targets including a curricular framework
- targets for staff ratios
- appropriate staffing and staff conditions including training and pay
- environmental and health
- parent and community targets
- performance targets including research and monitoring.

This report (published in 1996) was translated into all the European languages, and was very widely circulated.

In some countries it was used and valued as a basis for further work on quality systems, and in others it sunk without much trace. Perhaps its most lasting influence was on the OECD, where it was cited as 'a benchmark' for the report *Starting Strong*.

The report seems to have been put in a cupboard somewhere (as is the case with so many reports) and since it predated web documents, not much more was heard of it. The next significant point in the development of ECEC services in Europe was the EU Lisbon treaty. A follow-up meeting in Barcelona specified the workforce components of the Lisbon treaty. The target for the female participation rate was a rise from an average of 51 to 60 per cent by 2010. In addition, the Barcelona targets stressed that

> Member States should remove disincentives to female labour force participation and strive, taking into account the demand for childcare facilities and in line with national patterns of provision, to provide childcare by 2010 to at least 90% of children between 3 years old and the mandatory school age and at least 33% of children under 3 years of age.[7]

Many of the lobby groups around the EU objected to these targets on the grounds they say nothing about quality or quality systems for delivery of services and do not dovetail with education.[8] Subsequently DG5 has commissioned a report on childcare from the perspective of women's rights, which omits much of the education orientated data, but shows clearly the relationships between childcare provision, women's employment, and parental leave arrangements.[9]

Most recently DG5 has commissioned work on what it calls 'social services of general interest'. The brief includes work on long-term care for elderly people, social housing, employment services, and for our purposes here, childcare. All these services have in common that, to a greater or lesser degree, they have been 'modernized', that is opened to market competition. The work is to explore the extent to which modernization has made a difference to the regulation and quality. There has been a recent legal decision in the European Court of Justice that social services which meet social needs and act as safety nets can be exempted from competition rules. Governments can legitimately make political decisions *not* to privatize services, not to allow business to make a profit from the most vulnerable. DG5 wish to know how member states are managing their modernization or privatization policies, and what the relationship is between auspices (funding), regulation and quality. The definition of quality includes ways in which the services can be monitored and updated, the extent to which there is widespread and easy access for those that need to use services and the extent to which workforce rights are protected, and workers are given a voice in the services in which they work.

The EU represents a progressive voice on early childhood care and education, and through the European Commission, has provided many summaries of the situation on early childhood services. It is a useful source and a useful forum for those involved. But it is limited by its remit, and by its administrative structure, from intervening too much or too radically.

Organization for Economic Cooperation and Development

The OECD, sometimes called the rich man's club, is based in Paris. It was founded in 1961 and represents 31 countries (soon to be 34) including the USA, Australia, Japan, Korea, Mexico, Chile and other leading world economies including a tranche of European countries. It has links with a further 70 countries. It brings together the governments of countries committed to democracy and the market economy from around the world to:

- support sustainable economic growth
- boost employment
- raise living standards
- maintain financial stability
- assist other countries' economic development
- contribute to growth in world trade.

The OECD is the leading transnational body for knowledge generation and exchange, and employs high-powered researchers. It enables governments to compare policy experiences, seek answers to common problems, identify good practice and co-ordinate domestic and international policies. It is one of the world's largest and most reliable sources of comparable statistics and economic and social data. Its 'Education at a Glance' statistics, for example, are a world benchmark. As well as collecting data, OECD monitors trends, analyses and forecasts economic developments and researches social changes or evolving patterns in education, trade, environment, agriculture, technology, taxation and other relevant areas. The OECD is 'consensus led'. It has a council of representative delegates of its members, plus one member from the European Commission. The council works through its secretariat, also subdivided into directorates. Each of the directorates reports to a committee whose members are nominated from each member country.

The two directorates that have had an input into early education and childcare services are the Directorate for Education and the Directorate for Employment, Labour and Affairs. In addition, the OECD carries out regular economic surveys of each member country, in which it makes recommendations about more efficient expenditure. The OECD criticizes expenditure on childcare in the UK for example, both because it is at a low level, and because the tax credit system is poorly harmonized with other benefits – the result being that expenditure on childcare by parents is higher than in all other OECD countries investigated with the exception of Ireland.[10,11]

Figure 4.2 gives a summary of childcare and pre-primary (nursery education) spending across OECD countries, as a percentage of GDP.

The Education Directorate has had a major project 1999–2006 reviewing early education and care across 20 countries, including the UK, USA, Canada,

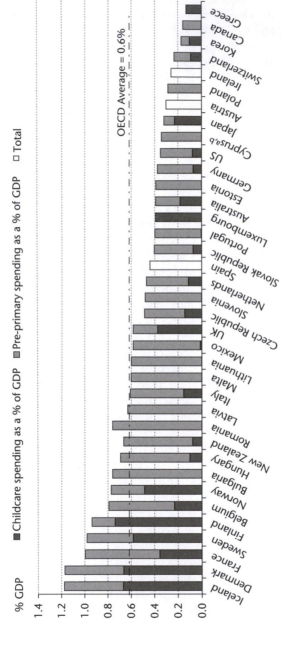

Figure 4.2 Public expenditure on childcare and early education services, per cent of GDP, 2005.

Notes: Figures for Austria, Ireland and Spain cannot be disaggregated by educational level.

a Footnote by Turkey: the information in this document with reference to 'Cyprus' relates to the southern part of the island. There is no single authority representing both Turkish and Greek Cypriot people on the island. Turkey recognizes the Turkish Republic of Northern Cyprus (TRNC). Until a lasting and equitable solution is found within the context of United Nations, Turkey shall preserve its position concerning the 'Cyprus issue'.

b Footnote by all the European Union Member States of the OECD and the European Commission: the Republic of Cyprus is recognized by all members of the United Nations with the exception of Turkey. The information in this document relates to the area under the effective control of the Government of the Republic of Cyprus.

Source: Social Expenditure database 1980–2005; OECD Education database; Eurostat.

Australia, Korea, Mexico, the Nordic countries, the Czech Republic, France, Germany, Hungary, Ireland, Italy, the Netherlands and Portugal. It culminated in a landmark study setting out principles for the development of early education and care services *Starting Strong II: Early Childhood Education and Care* – which should be, if it isn't already, a reference point for all policy-makers everywhere.[12]

The OECD is a statistical powerhouse, but it is also a consensus organization, relying heavily on peer reviews. The *Starting Strong* report was also, to an extent, a consensus exercise. Similar statistical data were collected throughout the study, but each of the 20 countries who hosted the study asked for the OECD team to take particular issues into account, a view from the outside of how their policies appeared. (The review team that visited the UK highlighted the very early start to school as a major concern!)[13] The review teams which visited each country were made up of a researcher/rapporteur who drafted the report, a representative of the OECD, and two or three policy-makers from other countries participating in the study. For example, I was rapporteur of the team which visited Canada, along with a representative from the OECD, and senior ministry officials from Finland and Belgium.[14] Each OECD country study used information from multiple sources. The host country was required to produce a *background* country report highlighting policies and giving standard statistical data on children, on services, on women's employment, on poverty levels, and other demographic information. The teams, armed with the background report, met with leading officials and politicians, as well as various stakeholders including researchers, and accepted any material they chose to give. The team had to review the consistencies and inconsistencies between these accounts and the background report to provide a negotiated overview, the *country* report, paying particular attention to the issues raised by the host country. In the last resort the officials and politicians who commissioned the report had to recognize themselves. (In one country they didn't, and no country report was produced.) The *country* report then became the official OECD report on early education and care on that country.

The final report *Starting Strong* was a synthesis of the 20 country reports. In addition the OECD held a number of expert seminars, at which leading researchers were commissioned to present papers on key topics. These too were incorporated into the final report.

Even although countries differed considerably, there were important commonalities. Using examples from each country in the study, it suggested that the following factors were the key to a quality early education and care system.

- A systemic and integrated approach to ECEC policy – co-ordinated national policy frameworks, a lead ministry, co-ordination between central and decentralised levels,[15] a collaborative and participatory approach to reform, and links across services, professionals and parents at local level

- A strong and equal partnership with the education system – not only a unified and consistent approach to learning, but also a recognition of the particular requirements of young children
- A universal approach to access – ensuring equitable access for all children whatever their circumstances
- Substantial public investment in services and infrastructure – including controlling the cost to parents
- A participatory approach to quality improvement and assurance – including regulatory systems and curricular development
- Appropriate training and working conditions for early childhood education and care staff – qualified staff, decently paid
- Systematic attention to data collection and monitoring, including participatory approaches
- A stable framework and long-term agenda for research and evaluation.

However the OECD, like all other large organizations, has problems with the left hand not knowing what the right hand is doing. At the same time as the *Starting Strong* project, the Employment division of OECD brought out a series of reports *Babies and Bosses* with a different and somewhat contradictory emphasis.

Based on OECD-wide indicators, the *Babies and Bosses* synthesis examines tax/benefit policies, parental leave systems, child and out-of-school-hours care support, and workplace practices that help determine parental labour market outcomes and family formation across the OECD. The *Babies and Bosses* reviews of work and family reconciliation analysed policies and family outcomes in Australia, Denmark and the Netherlands;[16] Austria, Ireland and Japan;[17] New Zealand, Portugal and Switzerland;[18] and Canada, Finland, Sweden and the United Kingdom.[19,20]

As Rianne Mahon points out, these reports operate within substantially different frames of reference. *Starting Strong* is concerned with best outcomes for young children. *Babies and Bosses* on the other hand is about economic utility – how to promote a flexible and efficient labour market – a process in which both women and children are viewed instrumentally. *Babies and Bosses* 'promotes a shallow version of "gender equity" and does little for the rights of children.'[21] Moreover, whereas *Starting Strong* is written within the consensual OECD approach of contextualized learning for the countries who participate, *Babies and Bosses* is in the quick-fix policy transfer tradition – this is the policy which works best and here is how you can apply it.

These conflicting rationales, as we have seen, run through most contemporary policy-making in early childhood. Is it an education policy, concerned with children's well-being and progress, or is it an employment policy, concerned with a smoother running workforce in a more dynamic economy?

United Nations Educational, Scientific and Cultural Organization (Unesco)

Unesco was founded in 1945, as part of the United Nations and is also based in Paris. It is a global organization and currently has 193 member states. Because it had strong representation from the former Soviet Union and its satellite states, as well as a majority of poor countries, for a time it was regarded as too left-wing by the USA and UK governments, who withdrew their membership (the USA 1985–2003, and the UK 1986–1997). Most countries now have permanent delegations at Unesco. Unesco in turn maintains offices in many countries, especially in Africa, one of its priority areas. It is part of what is called 'the United Nations family' and shares its goals of world-wide efforts to achieve social justice and reduce poverty.

> The broad goals and concrete objectives of the international community – as set out in the internationally agreed development goals, including the Millennium Development Goals (MDGs) – underpin all UNESCO's strategies and activities. Thus UNESCO's unique competencies in education, the sciences, culture and communication and information contribute towards the realization of those goals.[22]

Unesco pursues six strategic goals, as part of its Education for All initiative, which were agreed at a world conference held in Dakar, Senegal, in 2000. Overall it recognizes that:

> Basic learning needs . . . comprise both essential learning tools . . . and the basic learning content . . . required by human beings to be able to survive, to develop their full capacities, to live and work in dignity, to participate fully in development, to improve the quality of their lives, to make informed decisions, and to continue learning.[23]

The goals set out in Dakar are global in nature, drawn from the outcomes of regional EFA conferences and the international development targets to which countries are already committed. The first goal is:

> Expanding and improving comprehensive early childhood care and education, especially for the most vulnerable and disadvantaged children.

Every year Unesco brings out an annual report exploring the degree to which these targets have been met. The 2007 Education for All report *Strong Foundations* dealt mainly with progress in achieving early childhood targets.[24] It emphasizes the importance of a rights based approach, and rehearses the rationales (again!) for developing early education. It discusses costing, financing and governance. In the 2009 EFA monitoring report, it stresses the adverse effects of inequality and the importance of good, transparent governance in meeting all the EFA goals.

Unesco covers both rich and poor countries together, and unlike the World Bank for example, it takes its early childhood examples from rich countries other than the USA. The difficulties of this kind of transnational knowledge generation are discussed in detail in Chapter 10. Ideas and concepts tend to get exported from rich countries into poor ones, often without enough care. However, Unesco does offer good background data, compiling international statistics, and in the case of early childhood, providing country profiles, policy briefs (52 so far) and occasional publications. The four interrelated themes of the policy briefs are access, quality, investment and governance. The latest publication on early childhood at the time of writing is *Caring and Learning Together*, a review of countries that have integrated early childhood services within education departments.[25]

Unesco then is a good source of information about early childhood. It provides examples from across the world about how things work, and suggestions about how they might work better, from the most abstract principles to the most down to earth practice. Within poor countries it takes the lead on educational reform, working alongside many other international non-governmental organizations and charitable foundations to develop ideas about early childhood.

The international consensus

The consensus, clearly, is that governments have a responsibility to promote early childhood policy, in order to achieve high quality services. Conversely although there may be a few exceptions because of the work of exceptional individuals in particular places, quality services are unlikely to be achieved at a local level without considerable intervention on the part of government. High quality means at the core, considered rationales embodied in a national plan that covers both education and care with agreed targets for the number of places. It means prioritizing the most vulnerable children at every level of the service. It means having a view on what is taught (the curriculum) and how it is taught (pedagogy). It means having regulatory measures in place which ensure the consistency and continuity of services. It means having information and data collection systems to make sure services are carefully monitored and updated and revised in the light of the evidence. It means funding services adequately and efficiently and ensuring they have the means to do the job which they are asked to do. It means ensuring there is an adequately trained and adequately rewarded workforce.

But as we have seen, for the key international organizations even this is not enough. For Unicef/IRC it means above all controlling child poverty. For Unicef/IRC, OECD and the EU it means working on maternity/paternity and parental leave arrangements to make sure that the youngest and most vulnerable children are fully protected, and that their families are not under undue stress because of the difficulties of reconciling work and family life. For the EU too, it means the rights of the workforce should be very seriously considered, and their entitlements carefully outlined. For Unesco, it means that we should include poor countries as well as rich countries within the remit to support and develop ECEC services.

Notes

1 Unicef/IRC (2008) 'Introduction.' In *The Child Care Transition: A League Table of Early Childhood Education and Care in Economically Advanced Countries. Report Card 8*. Florence: Unicef/IRC.
2 See http://europa.eu/about-eu/institutions-bodies/index_en.htm
3 Eurydice (2009) *Early Education and Care in Europe: Tackling Social and Cultural Inequalities*. Brussels: Education, Audiovisual and Culture Executive Agency.
4 European Commission/NESSE (2009) *Early Childhood Education and Care: Key Lessons from Research for Policy-Makers*. Brussels: European Commission, Education and Culture DG. See www.nesse.fr/nesse/nesse_top/tasks
5 European Childcare Network (1996) *Quality Targets in Services for Young Children*. Brussels: European Commission, p. 6.
6 European Childcare Network (1994) *Quality in Services for Young Children*. Brussels: European Commission. Both these European Childcare Network documents are now out of print.
7 See http://europa.eu/rapid/pressReleasesAction.do?reference=MEMO/08/592& format=HTML&aged=0&language=EN&guiLanguage=en
8 The Czech presidency held its first conference in 2009 on the issue of the Barcelona targets and whether they should be revised.
9 Plantenga, J. and Remery, C. (2009) *The Provision of Childcare Service: A Comparative Review of 30 European Countries*. EU Directorate for Employment, Social Affairs and Equal Opportunities/European Commission's Expert Group on Gender and Employment Issues (EGGE). Brussels: EU.
10 OECD (2005) *Economic Survey of the United Kingdom*. Paris: OECD, Chapter 5.
11 OECD's *Social and Family Database* gives updated detailed figures on childcare payments by household: see www.oecd.org/els/social/family/database
12 OECD (2006) *Starting Strong II: Early Childhood Education and Care*. Paris: OECD.

13 OECD (2001) *Country Note: UK*. Paris: OECD.

14 A full list of all the teams is given in OECD, *Starting Strong II*.

15 A particular issue encountered by some countries is federalism. Australia, Canada, USA and a number of European countries such as Germany and Spain are federal states; that is they have devolved much of their administration to a state level, and the different states have adopted different policies, rules and regulations concerning ECEC services. In the UK, administrative powers, including regulation of ECEC, have now been devolved to England, Scotland, Wales, and Northern Ireland. These countries present particular problems of co-ordination of levels.

16 OECD (2002) *Babies and Bosses: Australia, Denmark and the Netherlands*, vol. 1. Paris: OECD.

17 OECD (2003) *Babies and Bosses: Austria, Ireland and Japan*, vol. 2. Paris: OECD.

18 OECD (2004) *Babies and Bosses: New Zealand, Portugal and Switzerland*, vol. 3. Paris: OECD.

19 OECD (2005) *Babies and Bosses: Canada, Finland, Sweden and UK*, vol. 4. Paris: OECD.

20 See also OECD (2007) *Babies and Bosses: A Synthesis of Findings*, vol. 5. Paris: OECD.

21 Mahon, R. (2006) The OECD and the work/family reconciliation agenda. In J. Lewis (ed.) *Children, Changing Families and the Welfare State*. Cheltenham: Edward Elgar, pp. 173–191. The quotation is from p. 174.

22 See www.unesco.org

23 Unesco (2000) *World Declaration on Education for All*. Paris: Unesco, Article 1, Paragraph 1.

24 Unesco (2007) *Strong Foundations: Early Childhood Education and Care. EFA Global Monitoring Report 2007*. Paris. Unesco. Available at http://unesdoc.unesco.org/images/0014/001477/147794E.pdf

25 Bennett, J. and Moss, P. (eds) (2010) *Caring and Learning Together*. Paris: Unesco. Also available at http://unesdoc.unesco.org/images/0018/001878/187818E.pdf

5 Childcare markets

In Chapter 4 I explored the position of leading international organizations on ECEC services. I argued that in order to judge what works and what doesn't work, what is high quality and what is not, at a national level, you also need international comparisons and standards.

In the view of the OECD: 'A public supply-side investment model managed by public authorities brings more uniform quality and superior coverage of childhood populations than parent subsidy models'.[1]

Yet a number of countries, especially the USA, do not agree with this summary. One of the most contentious areas in delivery of services is how much provision should be left to the private market, and whether the private market does indeed deliver on quality. Can market-driven services deliver high quality? In neo-liberal English-speaking countries, especially in the USA where ECEC services are marketized and corporatized to an exceptional degree, for-profit care is more likely to be seen as not only acceptable but necessary. The ubiquitousness of for-profit provision in the USA has led many researchers, US-based international organizations such as the World Bank, and prestigious think tanks based in Washington such as the Brookings Foundation, to assume that for-profit provision is an inevitable and positive feature of the ECEC landscape.

In this chapter I explore several aspects of the private market, and the issues it raises when considering quality. Then I discuss regulation, which is about the attempts to set limits on the operations of the private market. I try to briefly summarize the evidence about quality in the for-profit sector, across a number of countries, using the UK as a particular example.

The importance of parental choice?

Gary Becker, the US Nobel prize-winning economist whose views on the family have been very influential, argues that economics should consider families as well as individuals as a unit of economic analysis. The economic approach to the family assumes that all decisions can be explained in terms of economic costs and benefits. Even intimate decisions like marriage, divorce, and family size are ultimately reached through weighing the financial advantages and disadvantages of alternative actions. The purchase of childcare is part of the economic activity of the family, and can only be decided within the family. It is one of many investments that the family makes. As an investment opportunity, it is much more efficient to have better off families buy childcare services in a private competitive market than to spend tax revenue on preschool government-run programmes for the children of these families. This is because families themselves must make the choice of investing or not investing in childcare, and the right to make this choice should not be taken away from them. For those children in poorly functioning families where intervention might be desirable a demand led system (giving parents tax credits or vouchers) is still better than supply-side system (direct subsidy to the provider of services). The subsidies for poor families take the form of vouchers which poor families can spend on any approved *private* daycare. In Becker's view the market will ensure a sufficient and adequate supply of provision for all types of demand.[2] He argues that *any* state intervention undermines family choices. This kind of economic reasoning has provided an influential intellectual justification for ignoring or downplaying social policy issues in the USA.

Gary Becker represents an extreme view, in which all family transactions are commodified (given a price) in a society which is itself highly competitive and market driven. But other USA economists who have specialized in childcare are also wedded to a market approach. One of the best known is David Blau, who has focused his work specifically on childcare markets.[3,4,5] He too argues that because childcare is a service that is bought and sold in markets, economics can provide a useful framework for thinking about its problems. As with any commodity, supply, demand, cost, price, and quality are key elements of market analysis. In many respects, he claims, the childcare market functions much better than is commonly believed. He believes that childcare workers have low wages because they are willing to work for low wages, not because they are exploited by centre owners or forced to subsidize consumers. But he does acknowledge the childcare market is not working as smoothly as it might. His analysis of the problem is that parents, as consumers do not have enough information about childcare, and make bad choices. Classic economic theory holds that in a competitive market, fully informed consumers will choose the best products. So demand for excellent childcare will not increase unless consumers have sound information about the quality of care as well as stronger incentives to purchase better care.[6]

However two comprehensive reviews of the economic literature on early childhood education and care, carried out for the Canadian government in 2009, suggest that giving parents information about quality is not straightforward, and is only a relatively minor factor in the purchase of childcare. Parental views about quality often differ from those of professionals. Generally the higher the fees, the less likely mothers are to use childcare, but this is tempered by geographical availability and family circumstances (such as numbers of children).[7,8]

Parents are consumers in the sense that they choose the provision on behalf of their children, but not in the sense that they experience it. Their information about the provision is usually partial and limited, and their children are not in a position to report back. Many parents have never purchased childcare before, and may never purchase childcare again. Working parents have little time to seek out and evaluate childcare, even if they know what they were looking for. Furthermore, the direct consumer of the care – the child – cannot easily communicate with the parent about what kind of care is being delivered. There is some evidence that parents may have difficulty assessing the quality of childcare. Parents substantially overestimate the quality of care received by their children relative to evaluations made by trained observers. While parents valued the same kinds of things that professionals valued, their rankings differed significantly: 90 per cent of parents rated their child's classroom as high quality, while trained observers rated the same classrooms poor to mediocre.[9]

The argument for giving parents 'choice' is that they are the best judges of their own and their children's needs, and can pick what suits them best. But quite apart from the nature of the information available to them, and the cost of the provision, their choices are likely to be limited. Parents cannot usually afford the time or the money to travel in search of provision; they are mostly confined to the local, where choice may be very limited. The regulatory requirements and cost structures mean that provision itself is not very variable, and the choice parents can exercise is mainly limited to time availability.[10] But convenient times for parents are not the same as convenient times for young children. If being with and learning alongside friends and peers is an important aspect of learning, even for the youngest children, it is very disorientating to children to be with a different set of children (and probably adults) each time they attend. It is as if going to a workplace, our friends and working colleagues are never the same two weeks running. It presumes a degree of individuality in learning which is quite unreal.

The Canadian reviews do claim that there are significant benefits *to the wider economy* in providing childcare. Childcare provision, in economic terms, acts as a *multiplier*. There is a general increase in economic activity if more women are in the workforce, and also if more women – and men – are employed as childcare workers. Those people additionally employed as a result of childcare provision spend money on other goods and services and contribute to taxes.

One of the key issues in relying on the market is its lack of equity. The market is not inherently an equitable place, since people buy what they can afford. A Ferrari motor car for example may be a very successful product, well made, well marketed and garnering a huge profit for its company in the marketplace; but in no sense does it promote equity, rather it is a marker of social stratification. Ferrari is a successful company, but it is directed at the top end of the market, and is uninterested in any other consumers. Companies find market niches, and promote their product accordingly.

It is a noticeable feature of US social policy that equity is not an issue, except in the very limited sense of the access of women's and minority groups to the labour market (for a fuller discussion of toleration of inequality in the USA and in other neo-liberal countries, see Chapter 10). But for most European countries, by contrast, social citizenship and social inclusion are important goals, and it is a fundamental principle of policy that all children should have equal access to provision. If equity is a legitimate goal for children's care and education, then the marketplace, which is by its nature stratified, is not the best way to provide it. The market needs tempering. If the provision of childcare is reliant on the fees that parents pay, only those that earn sufficient money can pay the fees; poor women and poor children lose out. Even where parents are subsidized, the inequalities remain (no parental subsidy scheme is foolproof). Parental choice is a highly problematic concept, an apparently simple (and politically popular) idea but it essentially implies that early education and care are goods to be bought and sold in the marketplace.

Knowledge sharing or competition?

Private for-profit care is so entrenched in the USA as to be beyond comment. Conversely, providers are unashamed of making a profit; childcare is a good and legitimate business activity and competition is natural. Childcare businesses need to do everything they can to secure the future of their own enterprise, and attract customers, irrespective of the cost to others or the need to co-operate. For example, the website for *Childcare Exchange*, a US-based networking early years practitioners, carries many items like this:

> Child Care Marketing Solutions is excited to announce the launch of their new Child Care Business Success System, a comprehensive toolkit for marketing and enrollment-building. The system features ten learning modules with ten accompanying audio CDs, designed specifically for early childhood business owners and administrators. By using these innovative, cuttingedge, and cost-effective strategies, centers and schools can easily increase their enrollment, improve customer satisfaction, and improve their return-on-investment on marketing and advertising budgets. Includes actual examples, templates, and worksheets. Discover the hidden wealth buried in your child care center![11]

Economic rationality governs the conduct of the all businesses, including early childhood businesses. The precepts of choice, competition, supply and demand explain the behaviour and responses of commercial organizations within the early education and childcare sector. Businesses analyse and predict what purchasers (parents) will pay for the commodity of childcare, how profitable financial investment in nursery businesses, especially corporate nursery businesses, is likely to be, and how government regulatory frameworks are likely to restrict or reshape their activities.

From a market perspective, knowledge and information are themselves market commodities. The market view of intellectual property is stated succinctly by this major UK childcare provider.

> Why give away techniques and confidential information which have taken time, energy and a great deal of expense to develop? In a competitive environment this intellectual property or pool of trade secrets represents one of the most important assets a company owns . . . this is exactly what the government is expecting the best nurseries to do in an effort to raise standards . . . Both the private and the maintained sector will be expecting to spend time sharing best practice with other nurseries even if they are competitors . . . this is neither fair nor reasonable[12]

The difficulty of access to information under business confidentiality clauses is a well-known phenomenon of privatization more generally. Business confidentiality in the field of private nurseries necessarily limits mutual co-operation and learning. So, on the one hand, while consumers ideally base their choices on good information about the product (childcare) they are purchasing, on the other hand, businesses have a vested interest in selling their product and marketing it to their best advantage, playing up the best features of their business, and downplaying the less satisfactory attributes. In this sense the interests of parents and providers are at odds. Parents want to know about not only the strengths but also the drawbacks of the service they use; providers have a vested interest in portraying themselves in the best light possible.

Market volatility

The market is also inherently unstable, as providers expand in anticipation of profit or contract in order to avoid loss, and as parents shop around to make their choice. Successful businesses expand and take over other less competitive businesses; unsuccessful businesses which cannot attract and enrol enough customers fall by the wayside. Many nurseries, originally 'mom and pop' or single trader operations, have consolidated into larger operations. A distinctive feature of the childcare market in the UK and USA is the growth of large chains of nurseries. Shareholder companies provided about 8 per cent of all UK childcare places in 2009, and a much higher percentage in the USA. So nursery businesses that do well expand their operations, and unsuccessful nurseries contract their business or close down altogether. The childcare market is volatile, and the market profile is likely to change from one year to another, although these figures are difficult to obtain. This market volatility is exacerbated in a recession, when it is more difficult to make a profit. In the UK for example, where there is centralized record keeping through Ofsted, it is possible to get some indication of turnover. In 2008/2009 every two childcare business start-ups were matched by three closures, and there was an overall fall in provision. In 2009 some 870 nurseries in the UK closed their doors, and some 11,000 childminders withdrew.[13]

At the other end of the scale, successful businesses expand. One of the most notable features of any childcare market is the consolidation of successful companies – they buy up other less successful companies and what may have been once a successful 'mom and pop' operation becomes a large company. The large companies that float on the stock exchange are bought up by equity firms and others keen to make a profit. About 8 per cent of the UK market is now in the hands of very large companies, some of them subsidiary enterprises of offshore companies, whose headquarters and operations are located outside of the countries where they operate. Knowledge Universe, for example, is a company based in Singapore. Its chief executive is a convicted fraudster, who has served time in a US prison for junk bond trading. He is now apparently a reformed character, and has been buying up chains in the UK (Busy Bees) and in the USA and is attempting to break into the Canadian market. Other offshore companies are located in regions of the world where regulation (and taxation) are lighter. From these tax havens they can restructure childcare businesses to maximize profits and minimize external costs. For these reasons, it is argued, regulatory controls need to be international as well as national.

The Australian corporate childcare giant ABC Learning is a salutary example of expansion. Once a 'mom and pop' operation, it grew very rapidly. ABC Learning ran over 1000 centres in Australia (30 per cent of the Australian childcare market) as well as having investments in a number of other countries including Singapore, New Zealand and the UK (it owned the UK chain Busy Bees, which was then sold on to Knowledge Universe). At the end of 2008 the company collapsed amidst accusations and counter-accusations of fraudulent accounting by its one-time chief executive Eddie Groves and others involved with the company (including his ex-wife and other relatives). The ABC share of the Australian market was so substantial that the government could not let the centres themselves go under – too many nurseries faced closure. It has taken the receivers over a year to sort through the business and to decide about the future of the nurseries. The government has spent well over 100 million dollars to keep the nurseries open while the mess was being unravelled. (Meanwhile an unashamed Eddie Groves was still claiming to the receivers that he was owed a 3.3 million dollar bonus under the terms of his contract.) The Australian Senate committee, set up in the wake of the ABC failure, commented on 'the deficiencies in childcare policy and regulation' that led to the collapse. It recommended that small-scale or individual independent operators and not-for-profit and community-based organizations should provide services, rather than childcare being left entirely to the market.[14]

Market failure is integral to a market approach. Successful businesses compete and expand; unsuccessful businesses fail and close. Unlike public services which are intended to provide a consistent service whatever the vagaries of the market or vulnerabilities of the clientele, the private market responds primarily to profit and loss. The balance sheet is the primary consideration rather than, for example, the well-being of poor or vulnerable children.

If for-profit nurseries fail, however, then what becomes of the assets they have accumulated? For many private owners the most substantial asset they may have is the property in which they operate. But if the government has paid out grants and subsidies to the nursery, who owns these assets? Can owners walk away with everything if they decide to close the nursery? The market answer is that the owners took the risks, so they should be entitled to any assets. Schools are public assets for example, and even if a school closes, the assets revert to the government or the community. Should similar controls be put on private nurseries? This is a fundamental aspect of the debate about public–private partnerships of any kind in the UK. Who benefits from the government funding and government contributions when the private sector also invests?

Alternatives to the market

But not all economists agree that a market approach is the best way to understand or predict the nature of dealings between people. Economic theory itself is undergoing revision, partly because of the severity of the current recession, but also because leading economists and political thinkers are beginning to ask radical questions about the application of economic theory. Michael Sandel, a leading political scientist, argues that the last 25 years have been characterized by 'market triumphalism'. Market precepts have expanded into spheres where they have not previously operated – such as education – thereby undermining traditional social norms and values such as citizenship, social justice and social inclusion, and treating as irrelevant personal values and attributes such as sharing, caring, loving, intellectual curiosity, honesty, moral obligation or duty etc. Because human skills, capacities and capabilities are undervalued or disregarded in standard economics, in this sense the market is inefficient rather than efficient, and biased rather than value-free.[15]

Sandel's critique is increasingly widely shared. A report from the New Economics Foundation uses some of the principles and valuation techniques of social return on investment analysis to quantify the social, environmental and economic value made by certain groups. Do people contribute to citizenship and social inclusion in their work? Unlike bankers or accountants, whose activities may detract from the social return on the economy, childcare workers create a social value of between £7 and £9.50 of value for every £1 of pay. That is, they can be said to contribute to social cohesion of society, and this contribution can be costed.[16]

Rejecting a market approach

In many European countries, the market has never taken hold in the field of early education and care. Making a profit out of children (or any vulnerable person) and discovering 'the hidden wealth' that can be extracted from them, would be anathema. The Swedish curriculum for example is heavily value based. It not only does *not* mention money or costs, but also stresses the value of mutual support and solidarity.

> An important task of the preschool is to establish and help children acquire the values on which our society is based. The inviolability of human life, individual freedom and integrity, the equal value of all people, equality between the genders as well as solidarity with the weak and vulnerable are all values that the school shall actively promote in its work with children.[17]

There is then a spectrum of approaches to the provision of private for-profit services for young children, and the relationship between auspices and quality. At one extreme is the USA. Countries like Australia, Ireland, the Netherlands, and the UK also support market-based childcare. Where the state puts money into childcare, it does so through parent subsidies or tax credits (demand led funding) rather than funding services directly (supply-side funding). From an economic point of view, such an approach is said to encourage business efficiency and provide a better balance between supply and demand, while extending consumer choice. At the other end of the scale, some countries consider that early childhood services are essentially a public good, and the arguments for equality, mutuality, and shared citizenship outweigh those of the market – a different view of economic efficiency.

Most European countries, including Eastern European countries, have little in the way of for-profit provision, less than 5 per cent of childcare provision (the UK has 70 per cent for-profit provision of childcare). In many countries, like Germany, there is a lot of provision in the voluntary or non-state sector. Norway is an interesting country from this point of view. Only 46 per cent of provision is directly provided by the state (via the municipality).

The other 56 per cent is provided by a range of organizations including for-profit entrepreneurs. In Norway any provider who meets the licensing conditions is *entitled* to a per capita grant given directly to the provider, rather than to the parent through tax credits

However, the licensing conditions for Norwegian nurseries include the following:

- A cap on the fees parents pay, related to household income. Poor parents or parents with several children pay least, but nurseries cannot charge anyone more than 15 per cent of household income.
- Standards which include staff qualifications (mostly tertiary qualifications), and staff ratios, and the requirement to provide an annual plan, updated each year, for the nursery, outlining the activities and curriculum. The plan must be *agreed with parents and other community stakeholders*, and revised in the light of their comments. The plans are then further discussed at a municipal level.
- Open access, for all children. Nurseries must accept anyone who applies, whatever their income, subject to the availability of places.
- Sustainability, guaranteeing the availability of the place as long as it is required.

The nursery place then is not a commodity to be bought and sold according to market diktats, but a well-financed and serious place of learning and democratic participation, run by trained and knowledgeable people, with clearly articulated goals. If this framework is in place, it does not matter who actually provides the service. Norwegian law allows for any kind of provider who meets these criteria to receive a grant, but it makes it very unlikely that for-profit providers would choose to operate in circumstances where profit margins are very low and assets are controlled. Other countries go still further in some respects and choose to legislate on pay and conditions; employees must be paid at rates negotiated with trades unions, and have conditions of service that match those of other employees in the state sector. Another Nordic country, Denmark, regards trades unions as important partners and stakeholders.

Regulation and enforcement

In many business circles regulation is synonymous with 'red tape', an unnecessary curb on competition. Yet it is also widely accepted, even by the most ardent pro-market economists that the market requires some degree of regulation and standardization in order to function and to control 'unfair competition'. International rules about competition and monopolies, about standards of accounting, safeguarding of copyright and rules for data protection are generally welcomed and observed. Companies in breach of these regulations face heavy fines or penalties by national and international bodies. But most other forms of regulation, in various degrees are seen to restrict competitiveness and to affect the profitability of individual businesses. (The world banking crisis has indicated how important regulation is; bad investments could have been controlled through regulation and enforcement. The countries that were least affected by the banking crisis were those, like Canada, that had fairly tight regulatory procedures for regulating the financial sector.)

The standard view in the US literature is that quality in early education and care is a reflection of structural and process variables. Structural variables are those that can be directly controlled: adult–child staff ratios, group size, teacher education levels, space and hygienic requirements. Process variables are those describing relationships and activities: how adults and children relate to each other, what they do and how they do it when they are together such as the richness of 'turn-taking-talk' and the amount of warmth and cuddling between caregivers and babies. These process variables are not so easily quantifiable and more difficult to regulate.[18]

The process variables that have received the most attention in research to date involve the caregiver, including the correlations between training and teacher–child interactions. In licensed childcare homes with moderate group sizes (averaging around six children), caregiver training or education was a better predictor of childcare quality than child-to-adult ratios. Caregivers with training were less detached with the children.[19] In this research, none of the structural characteristics predicted caregiver sensitivity.

A growing number of nursery businesses view quality accreditation as a kitemark which adds value to their business, as opposed to regulation over which they have no control. Accreditation can help a nursery distinguish itself from its competitors.[20] Accreditation is voluntary, and does not involve any kind of monitoring or enforcement procedures, and is perceived as less demanding and coercive than regulation. The accreditation agency is a knowledgeable body, for-profit or non-profit, and it sets up a list of criteria for businesses seeking accreditation. In the field of early education and care, checklists of structural and process variables have been extracted by various organizations concerned with accreditation. For example the Council on Accreditation in early childcare and development services in the USA (one of many accreditation boards in operation) identifies eight aspects of high-quality infant care, mixing both structural and process variables: (1) health and safety; (2) small groups of three or four infants per caregiver; (3) assigning each baby to a primary caregiver; (4) ensuring continuity of care with the same provider over time; (5) caregiver responsivity to infant signals; (6) meeting each infant's needs in group care with a focus on individual learning style and temperament; (7) cultural and linguistic sensitivity; and (8) provision of a physical environment with variety, stimulation, and planned activities.[21]

In the private market regulation is supposed to be a guarantee of quality, but it can have the very reverse effect: its sets a lowest common denominator below which standards must not fall. The regulatory framework is intended to prevent bad practice and then becomes the mark of 'quality'.

Regulation can be very expensive, although some of the costs can be recouped through fees from providers. In the field of childcare, monitoring very many small independent businesses, arranging visits (for Ofsted in the UK, 90,000 visits over three years – see below), appointing and paying inspectors, publishing their reports, negotiating the challenges to those reports, requires a costly bureaucracy. But like everything else regulatory costs are a market phenomenon, and in the EU, in particular, there are attempts to provide a tool-kit for regulatory efforts across a wide range of issues. Some regulatory interventions are more cost efficient than others. The costs of regulation have been broken down into information duties, payment duties, cooperative duties, supervisory duties, training duties as well as target fulfilment and other requirement fulfilment duties.[22] These are technicalities but the point of raising the topic here is that all markets are regulated to some degree, and for economists, how the market is regulated is a key condition of how well it functions.

Regulation in the UK

England provides a classic case of the regulation dilemma. Regulation in England has been a response to a very diverse market; a way of trying to achieve some semblance of fairness even though the provision on the ground is very diverse, and this diversity is encouraged by the government in the name of parent choice. The result of regulation (and low levels of funding) has been to dumb down provision and inhibit experiment. The *Statutory Framework for the Early Years Foundation Stage (EYFS)* in England is (comparatively speaking) obsessed with health and safety and permits little leeway or innovation to those wishing to build new nurseries, deploy staff imaginatively, or experiment with curricula activities, indoors or outside.[23] EYFS comes with packages of information and guidance, which have been widely disseminated by regional experts appointed by the Department for Education. But basically it is a regulatory document written by civil servants to forestall any exceptions. It is based on a distrust of professionals; that is an assumption that judgements about quality, except within relatively minor parameters, cannot be devolved to those working in or using the system at a local level or within institutions themselves. This distrust arises partly because the workforce is minimally trained (comparatively speaking again) and standards may slip without regulatory controls.

The government has now introduced training requirements into the regulatory package. But attempts to upgrade staff within a diverse and privatized system are crucially dependent on the willingness and ability of private organizations to invest in training and to pay the salaries that well-trained professionals might reasonably expect. As Kate Goddard and Emma Knights suggest, childcare in England is woefully underfunded for what it aims to do, and trained staff in the private sector are poorly paid and remunerated compared to the conditions that pertain in the maintained sector.[24] If the investment to pay staff is lacking, regulation is the next best option to try to secure standards. And in protecting standards, the regulatory framework necessarily focuses on what must be prevented.

England has a monitoring and inspection system for ECEC, but in a privatized system this is still insufficient to ensure quality across a large section of the private sector. Ofsted prides itself on its transparency and lists all inspection details on its website. I wrote to Ofsted under the UK Freedom of Information Act 2000 to ask how many nurseries it had actually closed because they failed to meet standards. In 2008, Ofsted closed seven nurseries. I also complained to Ofsted about a local shopfront nursery on a main road, which from my very short visit appeared to be infringing health and safety regulations. Ofsted did in fact pay a visit, six months later, to the nursery, but merely asked them to provide a plan to suggest how they might improve their provision. No further information about this failing nursery is listed on the Ofsted website, a year later. A further 18 months later, apparently unchanged, the Ofsted inspection rating was 'good'. This possibly suggests that monitoring is not vigilant, and enforcement is a last resort. This situation is likely to be made worse, because of the privatization of Ofsted itself.

Set the bar too high, and too many nurseries will fail to meet it; set the bar too low, and bad practice is condoned. This is the dilemma faced in a much more acute way in poor countries. There is a mushrooming childcare market in most cities and large townships in the developing world. Parents may be so poor, and can pay so little, that nurseries which are reliant on fees offer a very meagre service that does not meet any recognizable standards. Any attempt at regulation would drive those nurseries out of business. Many poor countries, working with advisers from international non-governmental organizations (NGOs) concerned about protecting children, have worked with governments to introduce regulatory standards that in fact are inoperable. The whole business of regulation then becomes a collusive farce. The real issue is not regulation but lack of funding for services.[25]

Quality of for-profit care

Katherine McCartney comments that 'the importance of child care quality is one of the most robust findings in developmental psychology'.[26] Poor quality care leads to poor outcomes in language, sociability and cognitive abilities for children. The amount of time spent in poor quality care also appears to affect outcomes; the longer children spend the worse it is.

So 'red tape' has a purpose. It aims to prevent bad practice and protect children in situations where exploitation and abuse might otherwise occur. Regulation in market economies – where there are many private childcare and education providers – is a balancing act between prevention and realistic acceptance of what the market will bear. But it is not aspirational. It will never lead to the cutting edge.

Where the links between for-profit provision and quality have been explored they provide a depressing picture, even in those countries like the UK where regulation is relatively wide ranging, and monitoring and enforcement are in place. Gordon Cleveland and his colleagues using a reanalysis of large-scale Canadian data sets estimate the difference in quality between for-profit and non-profit care to be 7.5 per cent to 22 per cent. Quality is significantly higher in the non-profit sector, although the trends are slightly modified in thick (lots of demand for places) and thin markets (little demand for places, e.g. in a rural area). There are fewer incentives for entrepreneurs in thin markets to improve quality. In a subsequent study Cleveland reviewed the impact of the Quebec '$5 (now $7) a day programme' of universal childcare and also concluded that for-profit care was of poorer quality than non-profit care.[27] A further study in Quebec by Christa Japel demonstrated that as the number of private providers increased, quality fell.[28]

Using the NICDH data (the largest cohort study in the USA) Laura Sosinsky and her colleagues examined the relationship between childcare quality, cost and type of provision, and concluded that for-profit care, especially corporate care, was likely to have more poorly trained staff, to pay them less, and to be rated lower for quality than non-profit provision. After corporate care the next poorest group was childcare provided by religious organizations.[29]

In 2005 the Netherlands Government switched from supply-side funding to demand-led funding, and removed most regulatory controls. Noailly and Visser suggest that the introduction of a free market in childcare in the Netherlands has led to a shift away from non-profit nursery provision in poorer areas to for-profit nursery provision in high-income urban areas.[30] The latest findings of the Dutch childcare quality research academic consortium suggest quality of provision is deteriorating.[31]

Because of the rapid expansion of the childcare market in England, there has been a tranche of work which identifies the scope and evaluates the impact of private for-profit early years provision. Penn traces the development of for-profit private – and increasingly corporate – care in England.[32] Mathers, Sylva and Joshi,[33] and Mathers and Sylva,[34] in each case using a different data set, conclude that while the quality of the private sector is very variable, the poorest provision is to be found in the private sector, and the most reliable in the state sector; and that poor quality provision impacts adversely on vulnerable children.

An Ofsted survey of 90,000 inspection visits to 84,000 providers (daycare, out-of-school clubs and childminders) over a three-year period suggested that only two-thirds of those inspected were good quality, falling to about half in deprived areas. 24,000 complaints were recorded.[35] The Ofsted report also found that the better provision was in the better areas; good nurseries were significantly more likely to be found in prosperous than in poor areas. A UK parliamentary answer relating to the data conceded that in poor areas, 10 per cent of provision does not even achieve minimal compliance.

Local regulation and initiatives

Regulation is problematic but it is often argued that creativity and innovation are more likely to arise where there is some kind of local autonomy, with little red tape. Some systems of early education and care are devolved by default (as in the case of Italy) or by intention (as in the Nordic countries) to a local authority or project level. Some of the most innovative practices have arisen as a result of local experimentation. Loris Malaguzzi, the renowned psychologist behind the famous Reggio Emilia nurseries writes of the *municipality* as being the unit of operation, the level at which practice gets shared, discussed and tested.[36]

The flip side of local autonomy is that bad practice may also flourish. While Reggio Emilia in the north of Italy is an outstanding example of good practice, other regions of Italy, especially in the south, in Calabria and Sicily, are much more problematic both in terms of quality and quantity. Governments nationally need to provide a regulatory framework which enable local authorities and do more than consider them as just enforcers – as in the UK. To do this requires investment, a commitment to the professionalism of those working in and delivering the service – as in the Nordic countries.

When I interviewed private providers when they were first starting up in the UK (after the Child Care Act 1989 permitted the care of children under 3 years outside of domestic settings, which until that time had been heavily frowned upon) many of the new private providers were escapees from the public sector. Nursery nurses and teachers who felt they had been hamstrung by the restrictions of working in local authority day nurseries and nursery schools, revelled in the opportunity to try to give the care and education they thought was better and more imaginative.[37] Some of their ideas were innovative. But on the other hand some of the provision was very poor. At that stage there were relatively few checks and balances. But in any case the need for financial viability became a more important consideration than altruism. Some few nurseries expanded into childcare chains, and others fell by the wayside; they were taken over or their owners gave up. Competition, consolidation and expansion are standard features of any market. So the financial underpinning of any innovation is a crucial issue; without it providers are forced to cut corners. One interesting study in Canada found that without regulatory checks, for-profit providers cut back significantly on the number of trained staff they employed, and on the wages they paid.[38]

Childcare markets or not?

The overriding argument for using private providers is that they are more flexible, they can reflect market demand more quickly, and they do not get bogged down in red tape when opening new facilities. This is true to an extent, but it does not recognize the many difficulties involved in regulating the market and ensuring its equity and sustainability. As Sandel comments,[39] any marketization of human services devalues our humanity. Children are treated as objects and loving, caring and educational relationships with children are assessed as financial transactions.

In my view childcare markets do not work, for the kinds of reasons I have explored here. Unless they are heavily subsidized, directly or indirectly, they are very costly to parents which in turn leads to social stratification and social exclusion. If they are heavily subsidized, then regulatory controls and contractual obligations become very important, if public money is not to be misused, and if vulnerable workers are not to be exploited. The drive to make profits most often distorts, or is in conflict with, the need to provide the highest possible quality of provision for young children, a particularly vulnerable group. There are many areas where the government accepts that it needs to intervene in order to provide good and equitable services for all its citizens, and to make sure that whatever circumstances occur, those entitlements remain. Health care is one area. Education is another. Early education and care should be a third.

Notes

1 OECD (2006) *Starting Strong II: Early Childhood Education and Care.* Paris: OECD, p. 114.
2 Becker, G.S. (1991) *A Treatise on the Family.* Cambridge, MA: Harvard University Press.
3 Blau, D.M. (1999) 'The effects of childcare characteristics on child development.' *Journal of Human Resources* 34: 786–822.
4 Blau, D.M. (2000) 'The production of quality in child-care centers: Another look.' *Applied Developmental Science* 4(3): 136–148.
5 Blau, D.M. and Mocan, H.N. (2002) 'The supply of quality in childcare centres.' *Review of Economics and Statistics* 84(3): 483–496.
6 Blau, D.M. (2001) 'Rethinking US childcare policy.' *Issues in Science and Technology* 18(2): 66–72. Available at www.issues.org/18.2/index.html

7 Child Care Human Resources Sector Council (CCHRSC) (2009) *Literature Review of Socioeconomic Effects and Net Benefits: Understanding and Addressing Workforce Shortages in Early Education and Care (ECEC) Project*. Ottawa: CCHRSC.

8 Child Care Human Resources Sector Council (CCHRSC) (2009) *Literature Review of ECEC Labour Market: Understanding and Addressing Workforce Shortages in Early Education and Care (ECEC) Project*. Ottawa: CCHRSC.

9 Cryer, D., Tietze, W. and Wessels, H. (2002) 'Parents' perceptions of their children's childcare: A cross-national comparison.' *Early Childhood Research Quarterly* 17(2): 259–277.

10 The English government now awards nursery education hours on a pick and mix basis; parents may choose the hours which best suit their needs.

11 See http://ccie.com/favoritethings_exchange.php

12 Bentley, A. (2008) 'To the point.' *Nursery World* June, p. 12.

13 Ofsted (2010) *Registered Childcare Providers and Places in England at 31st Dec 2009*. London: Ofsted.

14 The website www.childcarecanada.org provides extensive coverage of the fiasco of ABC Learning and includes many contemporary newspaper reports as well as the findings of the Australian Senate Committee which investigated it.

15 Sandel, M. (2009) *Justice: What's the Right Thing to Do?* London: Penguin.

16 Lawler, E., Kersley, H. and Steed, S. (2009) *A Bit Rich*. London: New Economics Foundation.

17 Swedish Ministry of Education and Science (1998) *Curriculum for the Preschool*. Stockholm: Fritzes.

18 Clarke-Stewart, K.A., Vandell, D.L., Burchinal, M., O'Brien, M. and McCartney, K. (2002) 'Do regulable features of child-care homes affect children's development?' *Early Childhood Research Quarterly* 17(1): 52–86.

19 Clarke-Stewart et al., 'Do regulable features of child-care homes affect children's development?'

20 Laing & Buisson (2009) *Children's Nurseries: UK Market Report 2009. Eighth Edition*. London: Laing & Buisson.

21 Council of Accreditation for Early Child Care and Education (2006) http://coastandards.org/downloads/ECCD/ECCD%20Reference%20List.pdf

22 Schatz, M., Schiebold, M., Kiefer, S. and Riedel, K. (2009) *The Handbook for Measuring Regulatory Costs*. Berlin: KPMG/Bertelsmann Stiftung, p. 52.

23 See www.teachernet.gov.uk/teachingandlearning/eyfs/

24 Goddard, K. and Knights, E. (2009) *Quality Costs: Paying for Early Childhood Education and Care*. London: Daycare Trust.

25 Penn, H. (2008) 'Working on the impossible: Early childhood policies in Namibia.' *Childhood* 15(3): 378–398.

26 McCartney, K. (2004) 'Current research on childcare effects.' In R.E. Tremblay, R.G. Barr and R.DeV. Peters (eds) *Encyclopedia on Early Childhood Development*. Montreal: Centre of Excellence for Early Childhood Development. Available at www.child-encyclopedia.com/documents/McCartneyANGxp.pdf

27 Cleveland, G., Forer, B., Hyatt, D., Japel, C. and Krashinsky, M. (2007) *An Economic Perspective on the Current and Future Role of Nonprofit Provision of Early Learning and Childcare Services in Canada*. Toronto: Toronto University and Human Resources and Skills Department, Canada.

    Cleveland, G., Forer, B., Hyatt, D., Japel, C. and Krashinsky, M (2008) 'New evidence about childcare in Canada: Use patterns, affordability and quality.' *Institute for Research in Public Policy: Choices* 14(12), www.irpp.org/choices/archive/vol14no12.pdf

28 Japel, C. (2011) 'The Quebec childcare system: Research results and lessons to be learned.' In N. Howe and L. Prochner (eds) *New Directions in Research in Childcare in Canada*. Toronto: University of Toronto Press.

29 Sosinsky, L., Lord, H. and Zigler, E. (2007) 'For-profit/non-profit differences in center-based childcare quality: Results from the National Institute of Child Health and Human Development Study of Early Child Care and Youth Development.' *Journal of Applied Developmental Psychology* 28(5): 390–410.

30 Noailly, J. and Visser, S. (2009) 'The impact of market forces on the provision of childcare: Insights from the 2005 Childcare Act in the Netherlands.' *Journal of Social Policy* 38(3): 477–498.

31 de Kruif, R., Riksen-Walraven, J., Gevers Deynoot-Schaub, M., Helmerhorst, K., Tavecchio, L. and Fukkink, R. (2009) *Pedagogische Kwaliteit van de Nederlandse Kinderopvang in 2008*. Amsterdam: Nederlands Consortium Kinderopvang Onderzoek.

32 Penn, H. (2007) 'Childcare market management: How the UK government has reshaped its role in developing early education and care.' *Contemporary Issues in Early Childhood* 8(3): 192–207.

33 Mathers, S., Sylva, K. and Joshi, H. (2007) *Quality of Childcare Settings in the Millennium Cohort Study*. SSU/2007/FR/022. London: DCSF.

34 Mathers, S. and Sylva, K. (2007) *National Evaluation of the Neighbourhood Nurseries Initiative: The Relationship between Quality and Children's Behavioural Development*. SSU/2007/FR/022. London: DCSF.

35 Ofsted (2008) *Early Years: Leading to Excellence. A Review of Childcare and Education Provision 2005–2008*. London: Ofsted.

36 Hoyuelos, A. (2004) *La etica en el pensamiento y obra pedagogica de Loris Malaguzzi*. Barcelona: Rosa Sensat. This book offers a very comprehensive and well-evidenced account of the work and philosophy of Loris Malaguzzi. Unfortunately it is not available in English.

37 I was commissioned by BBC Television's *Panorama* programme to undertake a review of private nurseries in 1992.

38 Cleveland, G. (2008) *If It Don't Make Dollars, Does that Mean It Don't Make Sense: Commercial, Non-Profit and Municipal Child Care in the City of Toronto*. A report to the Children's Services Division, City of Toronto.

39 Sandel, M. (2009) *Justice: What's the Right Thing to Do?* London: Penguin.

6 Curriculum and training

Governments set the frame, by intention and by default, for early childhood services. The transnational knowledge generation organizations like the OECD, the EU, Unesco and Unicef, whose job it is to provide international comparisons, have made general recommendations about the structure and financing necessary to produce and support quality in early childhood services. A broad and internationally accepted view of quality in services for young children is that they ensure equality of access for all children, provide especial care for the most vulnerable, and pay attention to both the present well-being of children as well as their future as learners in school. In the actual delivery of quality services, there are two factors strongly linked to quality; the curriculum and activities provided for children, and the level of training of the staff that provide them. These aspects are discussed again in other chapters – in Chapters 7, 8, 9 and 10 – which explore how practitioners go about their daily work in a wide range of situations. But here I focus on the content or curriculum of the daily life that occurs in a nursery, and the staff who deliver it.

The pedagogical or curricular framework may vary considerably between countries, but it is usually intended to identify the key goals of services in that country and guarantee some consistency of approach. In some cases they are the result of widespread, participative consultation and trialling among a range of stakeholders. The recent (*and first*) Australian curriculum, Belonging, Being and Becoming, was introduced in this way in 2009. The development of the curriculum was tendered out to a group of academics, who held many meetings with interested groups of practitioners, parents, policy-makers and academics, and produced many drafts for discussion. They achieved a remarkable consensus, although there were some hitches in the tight timescale imposed by the government, and in securing political acceptance on all the diversity issues.[1] There is also an implementation group, who are reporting on the ways in which the curriculum is now being developed across Australia.

The OECD in 2004 held a cross-national research seminar on curricula, with country representatives and leading researchers in the field.[2] Five curriculum outlines were discussed at the meeting, demonstrating the range of options different countries had adopted. The curricula discussed were:

- Experiential education (Flanders, Belgium)
- High Scope – USA
- Reggio Emilia
- Te Whariki
- The Swedish curriculum.

These curricula were developed in response to rather different situations. In Flanders, all nursery education, from 2½ years onwards, is provided in nursery classes attached to schools, and an important issue has been to differentiate nursery education from mainstream primary schooling – to loosen it up and take a less didactic approach, to 'deschoolify' it.[3] The 'plan-do-review' High Scope curriculum was developed as a simple (simplistic) solution to the marginalization of highly impoverished communities, in the absence of any coherent government system.[4] High Scope is run by a non-profit company. It operates within a private market and has no particular roots; its curriculum is a free-floating product which has to compete with other similar products. It has been very successful in its self-promotion, thanks to the highly effective marketing techniques of the company, which emphasizes the 'scientific' evidence on which it is based. Unsurprisingly, it argues that 'children are all the same everywhere' and its curriculum can be adopted (bought) anywhere in the world.[5] Reggio Emilia is the outcome of 25 or more years of consistent investment by a small socialist municipality that has safeguarded the freedom to experiment and develop its nurseries, and offered them substantial resources in doing so. It has invested in pedagogic theory and practice as no other system has done.[6] Te Whariki is a response to a bicultural society. One in every four or five children in New Zealand comes from a Maori background, from a strong and well-articulated cultural tradition. Unlike other countries with indigenous populations, New Zealand chose to adopt an inclusive bicultural curriculum to reach out to its various population groups. 'Te Whakiri' means a woven mat, and it is the linking metaphor of the curriculum. The Swedish curriculum reflects the very high commitment to equality and gender issues within that society. As well as insisting on equality of access, children have to learn how to live and act together, to be part of a community rather than isolated, competitive individuals.[7]

Other countries have responded to other situations. The Soviet curriculum emphasized the importance of comradeship, citizenship and the priority of the group over any individual preferences. It also emphasized *bodily* well-being, especially nutrition, and exercise designed by physiotherapists to support muscular development and suppleness (swimming, dancing, callisthenics). These exercise routines were designed to improve children's physical skill and co-ordination as well as their circulation (rather more than the 30 minutes of vigorous exercise three times a week that is recommended in the UK, and rarely achieved in nurseries, especially if they lack outside space!). This physical well-being is an aspect all but missing from most Western European curricula.[8] Post transition, countries have reacted against all-encompassing and expensive state provision, and have turned to promoting individual creativity and democracy, even entrepreneurship.[9] Far Eastern curricula reflect other values, including spiritual values, and may hold very different expectations of children's learning activities and behaviour.[10]

The OECD report *Starting Strong* distinguishes between school-based curricular traditions and social pedagogic traditions. In the former, the emphasis is on a gradual introduction to school-based learning, especially emergent literacy and numeracy, and the acquisition of key skills. In the latter, there is more emphasis on a broad or 'holistic' approach, which is mainly project and play based. Table 6.1 summarizes the differences between these approaches. Table 6.2 compares some examples of curricula across the OECD.

Table 6.1 Distinctions between school-based and social pedagogic traditions

	Readiness for school	*Social pedagogic tradition*
Understanding of child and childhood	Child as an investment, as a mind to be shaped in predetermined sequences and by prescribed pedagogic routes; a productive citizen to be formed by appropriate instruction; mind more important than body; learning an indoor phenomenon	Child as subject of rights, autonomy and well-being. Child sets pace, chooses learning strategies, with adult support. Child as a participative member of a caring community of peers and adults. Learning takes place inside and outside
The early childhood centre	A service based on individual demand and parent choice, a place of learning and instruction appropriately equipped. Competitive targets	A life space, where adults and children learn 'to be, to know, to do and to live together'. Provides experience of democratic living, little pressure on children
Curriculum development	A prescribed ministerial curriculum, detailing goals and outcomes. Assumption that curriculum can be delivered by individual teacher in a standardized way, whatever the group or setting, measured by children's achievement in reaching prescribed goals and subsequent performance at school	A broad national guideline, devolving detail and implementation to municipality or centres themselves. Responsibility for implementation on staff as a group, in a setting of collegiality, measured by staff's own evaluation of their progress within their community

Focus of programme	A focus on learning and skills needed for schooling, mainly teacher directed and controlled	A focus on 'whole child' and her family/community; nature of the interactions between children and adults; quality of life in the institution important
Pedagogical strategies	A balanced mix of instruction, child-initiated activities and thematic work, managed by teacher, who delivers. National curriculum. An emphasis on individual autonomy and self-regulation by child	National curriculum guides choice of themes and projects, but interpretation local. Confidence in child's own learning strategies and learning through play with others
Language and literacy development	A focus on competence in national language. Oral competence and phonological awareness (even in a non-phonetic language like English!) and letter recognition. Standards may be set for pre-literacy and pre-numeracy knowledge	A growing focus on competence in the national language as a means of communicating with others. Children encouraged to find many ways of expressing themselves, '100 languages of children' including art, dance and rhythm
Targets and goals for children	Prescribed targets, set at a national level, to be reached in all centres	Broad orientation, rather than prescribed outcomes
Indoor and outdoor spaces for young children	Indoors is the primary learning space. Outdoors an additional amenity, if it is provided	Indoors and outdoors have equal pedagogic importance. Children may spend 3–4 hours daily outside, in summer and winter. The environment and its protection is an important theme
Assessment	Graded individual assessments by teacher required for each child as prelude to school entry	Formal assessment is not required; multiple assessment procedures – involving parents – are favoured
Quality control	Standardized inspection regimes, achievement of specified learning outcomes	Undertaken at municipal level by pedagogic advisors. Emphasis on centre rather than on children

Source: Adapted from Table 6.2 in OECD (2006) *Starting Strong II*

Table 6.2 ECEC curriculum in selected OECD countries

	Age group covered by curriculum	Page length of CR	Level of govt responsible	Assessment related to CR	% staff with tertiary training	Child:staff ratio	Place delivered
Belgium: Flemish/ Belgian	2.5–6 years 2.5–6 years	30 pages 498 pages	Regional Regional	None None	100% 100% (excluding assistants)	No national regulation; on average 20:1 plus assistant	Usually nursery class attached to state school. A few free-standing schools. All publicly provided
Denmark	0–6 years	2 pages	National and local centres	None	65%	No national regulation; average 3.3:1 (under 3) 7.2:1 (3–6)	Free-standing public kindergartens
France	2.5–6 years	150 pages	National	Yes	100% excluding assistants	No national regulation; average 25:1 (excluding assistants)	Free-standing écoles maternelles, publicly provided
Germany	Mostly 3–6 years	18–320 pages	Regional	Mostly none	2%	No national regulation; ratios vary approx 12:1	Mostly free-standing kindergartens, variety of providers
Italy	3–6 years	24 pages	National, regional and local	None	None, but new legislation underway	25:1 or 12:1 if open 8 hours, variable	Mostly free-standing kindergartens, but variety of arrangements including church provision
Korea	3–6 years	39 pages	National	None	100% teachers	20:1	Mixture of providers and settings; 51% publicly provided

	Age	Curriculum	Level	Assessment	Staff training	Staff:child ratio	Settings
Mexico	3–6 years	142 pages	National	Informal assessment	70%	No national regulation; approximately 20:1 sometimes higher in urban areas	Mixture of providers and settings but only 10% in private sector
Norway	1–6 years	29 pages	National and local	None	32% trained pedagogues, rest assistants with vocational training	No national regulations 3–6 yrs average 15:1; 1–3 yrs average 8:1, excluding assistants	Free-standing public kindergartens
Sweden	1–6 years	22 pages	National and local	None	50%	No national regulations; average 5:1 including assistants	Free-standing public kindergartens
UK (England)		Early Years Foundation Stage has 142 pages	National	Yes	100% teachers in schools; assistants basic vocational	1:13 in schools including assistant	Nursery classes or reception classes attached to schools; very few free-standing nursery schools. Approx. 50% 3 year olds in private for-profit nurseries

Source: Adapted from Table 6.3 in OECD (2006) *Starting Strong II*

If curricula are so very different, are there any general lessons to be learnt about their development? The Swedish researcher Ingrid Pramling and her colleagues from Göteborg University argue that even though content and context may differ considerably, there are some common principles for a quality curriculum.[11] They outline these, although they are necessarily very general principles.

- Values and norms: the curriculum needs to articulate what kind of goals it wants to see, what kind of child it is trying to create.
- The largest freedom possible within the overall goals: the curriculum should set the aims, and make suggestions about how they might be realized, but should allow practitioners a maximum amount of discretion in implementing them. Practitioners need freedom to develop their own ideas and adjust their interactions and responses for individual children or especial or unusual circumstances.
- A combination of pedagogic methods: children need to learn to think logically, and systematically (logical analytic thinking), but they also need to be creative and responsive (narrative or associative thinking).
- Consistency of learning goals but at different levels of complexity: children return to the same themes again and again in their learning, but as they gain more experience, their questions and answers become more complex. (The example the Swedish authors give is that young children should be introduced to collective living based on democratic principles, but only much later are they able to discuss how to vote!)
- A continuity of perspectives through schooling and beyond, lifelong learning: learning literally never stops, and the same general themes and concerns, including societal concerns, should be evident throughout formal school, and beyond. Early childhood curricula should be regarded as a foundation for subsequent schooling.
- Creating meaning: young children are above all 'meaning-makers' and are developing models in their head of how the world works, physically, emotionally, artistically. Creative staff need to focus on the creativity of children and understand how they are constructing meaning, rather than imposing adult meanings upon them.
- Looking to the future: it is a truism that the world is rapidly changing; curricula need to anticipate future directions. Obvious examples are the destructiveness of war, and the sustainability of the environment and global warming.[12]
- Resolve the issue of play: play is sometimes thought of as activities allowed to children outside of the curriculum or learning agenda. Is play an activity by and for itself, or is it a means to learning? In what way is it different from learning? These are questions which need to be addressed within a curriculum framework.

- Quality of staff: all of the above principles imply thoughtful, skilled staff, staff who have been well trained and who can competently take decisions for themselves.
- Strong evaluative processes built in, long term and short term: services to young children, like any other services need to be accountable – how is the appropriateness of the curriculum or the efficacy of the pedagogies going to be judged without some kind of evaluative record? Relying solely on school-based methods such as learning outcomes is problematic, especially since early childhood services lay claim to resolving a variety of societal issues (see Chapter 3). Much more needs to be done on devising appropriate evaluative methods.
- Democracy and gender: 'Democracy needs to be embedded in the curriculum both as an object of learning and as an act of praxis'.[13] A key aspect of the curricula is redistributive justice, in the sense that, whatever their social class or background, children come together in a nursery or school setting as equals, learning from each other and learning to be together.
- Care and education: the routines of care, especially for younger children, are often viewed as a 'natural' activity, which can be carried out by women (and much less frequently by men) who have basic qualifications or none at all. But a truly integrative curriculum would incorporate both equally.

This is a useful summary of curricula issues although it omits some questions which might be regarded as very important elsewhere – in particular questions of bodily prowess (discussed again in Chapter 7), language and diversity (discussed again in Chapter 10), art and music (regretfully not discussed). But it is a summary that arises out of the social pedagogue tradition (see Table 3.2) and it is relatively unsympathetic to knowledge and skills acquisition and outcome measures that characterize provision in the UK, and even more in the USA.[14] This latter view, that the role of education is to bring poor children who are falling behind up to scratch on basic numeracy and literacy as efficiently and cheaply as possible, has a long history in England,[15] and has been given renewed emphasis in the Early Years Foundation Stage framework.

But even if one favours a more functional view of education – children must learn the basic skills – as Pramling-Samuellson points out,[16] the question of play needs to be addressed within the curriculum. What is the role and importance of imaginative drama and make-believe in young children's learning? Is play a kind of practice for living and learning, for children who do not yet have a fixed sense of reality, an experimenting with possible options? Is play jokey or serious or both? Is it part of learning or apart from learning? As the American historian Paula Fass has pointed out, ideas about what constitutes play and relationships between play and useful learning, and between learning and work, have changed enormously over time and in different places.[17] In rich societies play is now almost inextricably associated with consumerism. It is easily assumed that play needs a great range of props and children's playthings have also, unfortunately, become a matter of fashion and marketing.[18] Somewhere, in the ideal curriculum, the phenomenon of play and playthings needs to be explored, defined and found some kind of place.

Training and qualifications

It is part of the litany on quality that children have better outcomes if staff are professionally trained to tertiary level. Tertiary training has certainly been accepted as a necessary condition for quality by the transnational knowledge generation bodies – OECD, EU, Unesco and Unicef. But as we have seen, over and over again, countries differ considerably in their rationales for early childhood services and in the spectrum of services they provide. The curricula are set by governments or states or local authorities – depending on the country – and they vary between 2 pages long and 498 pages long (and in China, at one point, the curriculum ran to 18 volumes, because every lesson was prescribed). Depending on the curriculum, the nurseries and who attends them and for how long, the requirements for training are likely to differ. Quality, as ever, is contingent on values and context.

Gendering

Before discussing the range of training options that have been adopted by different countries, I want to raise one issue that bedevils discussion on working with young children, namely gender. Working with young children is one of the most heavily gendered of all occupations. Why is it the case and what are the implications for training? Feminists claim that caring and emotional labour is a special type of work which is almost always undertaken by women.

> Woman's work is of a particular kind. Whether menial or requiring the sophisticated skills involved in childcare, it almost always involves personal service . . . emotionally demanding labour requires that the carer gives something of themselves to the person being cared for, so that even while childcare is capable of immense variation within societies, across societies and across time, it remains the case that nurturance – a matter of feeding, touching, comforting and cleaning bodies – is culturally the preserve of women[19]

In the UK there is certainly a prevalent view about the naturalism of childcare, and therefore its suitability as an occupation for women who otherwise have little in the way of qualifications or expertise. With a colleague, Susan McQuail, I carried out research for the then Department for Education and Employment (now Department for Education),[20] on childcare as a gendered occupation – as part of a wider OECD project on gendered occupations.[21] We used focus groups to interview young women training as nursery nurses at colleges of further education. We also spoke to their tutors and looked at curriculum documents. The women we interviewed felt that they all brought 'natural' talent to the job of childcare, and that this talent was at least as important, if not more important, than any training. These were typical comments:

> 'The caring bit attracted me. I feel comfortable around children and they feel comfortable around me.'

> 'It's intrinsic to being a woman.'

> 'All the courses in the world will never give you that feeling of knowing and working with children. That feeling comes from within, it's a good, good feeling.'

> 'You need to be a little bit mumsy to work with babies, it comes from within.'

> 'Whether trained or not, if you are not a natural, you can't hack it, you've got to get down to their level.'

For this reason, young women, who otherwise have low self-esteem and little confidence in their abilities, are steered towards childcare since it is one of the few things they know about and can do. This research was undertaken in 1996, a long time by research standards, but Carol Vincent's more recent research along the same lines suggests that little has changed, in England at least.[22] Mothers attending Sure Start Children's Centres in England who were expected to go on and seek employment were often (more often than not) steered in this direction of childcare.[23] Michel Vandenbroeck reports a similar phenomenon in Flanders, where refugee women or first generation migrant women are encouraged to go into childcare work, because it is something they can easily do.[24] Liane Mozère reports a similar situation for daycarers in France.[25] In many countries marginalized women are encouraged as a matter of self-emancipation to work in childcare, precisely because of their gender, irrespective of the low pay they are likely to earn – a limitation which they recognize and appear to accept. In Carol Vincent's research, women undergoing vocational training in childcare were asked to rate themselves in the job market. They likened themselves to hairdressers. In our research, they also placed themselves near the bottom of the manual worker scale.

Relying on women's gendered labour in this way has paradoxically led to a lowering of standards and an acceptance of the low place of childcare in the pecking order. But also if childcare is 'natural' it implies that the theory and knowledge of practice, and the ethics and standards associated with professionalism, are to an extent superfluous.

Vocational training in childcare is fairly basic in many countries, for two years post-16 level. Success on such vocational courses is defined by performance of a narrow range of predefined 'competencies'. Mostly the work available after such training is with infants or as assistants to teachers or pedagogues. But some countries have deliberately adopted a non-academic and vocational career route for childcare, even although internationally there has been a drive to professionalize the early childhood workforce in the name of quality. Eva Lloyd and Elaine Hallet have traced in detail how this promotion of non-academic vocational routes has happened in the UK through the operation of the Children's Work Force Development Council (CWFDC). The attempt to persuade women to undertake further training in order to qualify as 'lead professionals' or 'teachers' through further workplace based training has largely failed, partly because of the limited nature of the training, but also because, in a private childcare market, there is relatively little financial reward for having undertaken such training.[26]

So if women are recruited into childcare work because of their gendered 'natural' aptitude, what are the limitations of this vocational route? For the women we interviewed, tied in with this view of themselves as already caring and competent women, there was also a predominant view of young children as a more vulnerable group, uniquely susceptible to their influence.

> 'They are vulnerable, I want to protect them, they depend on you. When they are older, they don't.'

> 'I enjoy helping them, the first five or seven years are important to their life, it's important to help them on their way, by 9 or 10 they have learnt it all, the older children answer you back, they are harder to control.'

> 'They are more open to learning, older children are more stubborn.'

> 'We can control them more. You say "don't do it" and they understand. You say it to an older child and they get back at you.'

These vocational routes then are likely to come as part of a class and gender package; poorly educated working-class women feel that their instincts and accumulated experience as mothers and carers are the most important things they have to offer, although they also understand it is not worth much in any competitive job market. At the same time, this caring role is contingent on working with very young children who are perceived as vulnerable individuals in need of help and guidance. The women's status was enhanced, at least in their own minds, because they could exercise control over someone else. As one respondent put it, 'You get more self-esteem, it confirms what you already know. I am able to do it.'

Men in this situation are an anomaly. If childcare is a 'natural' occupation for women, then it follows that it is 'unnatural' for men. Michael Chabon's book *Manhood for Amateurs* wryly and wittily captures how odd it feels to be a man engaged in traditional women's pursuits of caring and childrearing – and the domestic tasks that go with it.[27] Most of the men and women in our student sample thought that men working with children was 'unnatural' and would be perceived as such by the outside world. This could be resolved only by arguing that men brought something special and different to childcare. Men were said to offer 'a male role model'. Men were perceived as being more physical, more able to engage in rough-and-tumble play, better at organizing children, but less able to deal with babies or very young children.

> 'For a man, he's a wally if he doesn't fit in.'

> 'The man is seen as a woman when he changes a nappy.'

> 'It's good to have male role models, it's essential but the skills of the men are different . . . it's an attitude to physical activity, an ability to team lead children.'

> 'They play with the children differently, they get the rough play.'

There is little concrete evidence that men either behave like this or serve as a role model if they do; the gender consciousness appears to be in the eyes of adults rather than children.[28] In the UK and other English-speaking countries, if not more widely, stereotypes of gender permeate basic childcare training, even if some exceptional individuals manage to overcome them. It is a real dilemma. On the one hand, it is right that women's deep culture of caring should be recognized. One of the criteria for good infant care is that carers should offer 'warm contingent care' to children, the archtypal picture of mothering.[29] On the other hand, where does it fit in with the push towards a highly trained, professionalized workforce? One argument is that however much it may involve hands-on caring, looking after other people's children in an institutional setting is not the same as looking after one's own children at home.

The biological bond described by the socio-biologist Sarah Hrdy is not there.[30] Infant care as well as care of older children requires additional, definable skills and knowledge (I discuss the differences between children's behaviour and language at home and at nursery further in Chapter 7).

Given the overwhelming dominance of women workers in early childhood, the underpinning stereotypes of gender and class need much more debate. Most of the work on men in childcare has focused on strategies for increasing the number of men working in the sector.[31] Instead, or as well, concepts of gender need unpicking.

Models of training

Pamela Oberheumer and her colleagues, in a series of papers, have investigated models of training across Europe.[32] Inevitably, these reflect the spectrum of services and curricula that exist. She distinguishes three main training routes for professionals (the crucial role of childcare assistants is discussed below):

- early childhood specialists
- teachers
- social pedagogues.

Early childhood specialists are specifically trained to work with children aged 0–5 (or 1–6, or whatever the age range in the country is). They are expected to study a range of issues arising from work with young children, including their care and education, and their upbringing with their families. Typically these specialists work in some kind of early childhood centre, where they will be with the same group of children for more than three years. Training varies, but in the countries that have adopted this route (including Austria, Czech Republic, Finland, Hungary, Italy and Sweden) it tends to be a three-year tertiary training.

Teachers are explicitly trained to promote children's learning, according to a curriculum, in a school-based setting. Teachers are among the best qualified of all early years professionals, typically with a three-year tertiary training, not necessarily in a related subject, and an additional postgraduate professional qualification. Teachers usually cover a wider age range than preschool and can teach in primary school as well. Their salaries and conditions of work (including hours and holidays) are similar to or just below those of primary school teachers. Australia, Canada, France and the UK, for example, train teachers to deliver the primary and preschool curriculum in this way in nursery schools and classes.

Social pedagogues have a wider remit than working with young children. They are 'social network experts with a clear educative function',[33] who may work across the range from the very young to the elderly. Their job is to promote positive living and lifelong learning, and their training tends to include artistic and practical skills – dancing, storytelling, artwork etc. – in order to engage in pleasurable communal activities. Countries which promote social pedagogy include Denmark, Germany and Norway.

There is also a view, especially in the UK, that looking after children and their families and promoting their learning is a very complex and challenging affair. This is related to the perception (or possibly vain hope) that early childhood services can cure poverty, or at least ameliorate it. This strong welfarist tradition in early childhood led to the Sure Start programme, discussed in Chapter 3. Because so many publicly funded programmes are aimed at 'dysfunctional' families (even if the programmes claim to be universalist) a range of professional skills are needed to deal with the problems that parents and children present. This extraordinary degree of surveillance is summed up in the phrase *The Team around the Child*.[34] Multi-agency working, deploying the skills of social workers, health visitors, psychologists as well as teachers and childcare workers, is seen as necessary to deliver early childhood services. The question then arises, who is in charge of directing the multi-agency work, and all the professional boundary issues it gives rise to? What kind of training do they need? This has led in turn to the ideas of 'lead professional'. As mentioned earlier, Eva Lloyd and Elaine Hallet have tracked the development of the notion of 'early years professional' introduced in the English Childcare Act 2006.[35] They argue because of the diverse or fragmented nature of UK provision and the particular vocational route such training has taken, problems of 'multi-agency working' remain unresolved, or as they kindly put it 'a work in progress'.

So although the level of training – tertiary – may be related to quality, the format of training is not. A well-qualified practitioner is qualified to deliver the curriculum in whatever country she or he is working, but as we have seen, there are considerable differences in how and what children are expected to learn, and in what kind of place they pass (or enjoy) their time.

Whichever route trainees take, initial training is only part of the story. In-service training also seems to be important. No job stays the same for a long time, at least in the competitive market economies and however much experience counts, experience is worth more when people can reflect and systematically examine and build on their practice, preferably with the help of others. The theory underpinning practice also changes; ideas current in one decade are superseded in the next. Theory is always provisional, rather than fixed, and keeping abreast of changes in theoretical perspectives and new developments in research, is arguably part of being a good professional. This access to in-service training may consist of access to professional development courses and conferences, self-study, or in-house training. This latter has been the principle of the famous early childhood programmes in Reggio Emilia and other Northern Italian cities. Each week time is built in to the timetable for a detailed discussion of the documentation gathered, led by the *pedagogista* or local adviser. A number of countries insist on in-service training time as a condition of employment, around 10 per cent of employed time. However it is usually the most highly qualified of staff who are eligible for in-service training, rather than the least well qualified.[36]

Care assistants

Many systems of early education and care make use of care assistants, staff whose job it is to assist the fully trained professional, mainly in terms of domestic duties like washing and toileting, or serving and clearing up meals. In some countries care staff are included in the ratios and in some they are supernumerary. According to the OECD report, the importance given to these staff and the training they receive is also part of quality provision. The report cites Sweden as an example of a country where care roles are taken very seriously.[37]

In the UK, within the school system, nursery nurses once fulfilled the role of care assistants. They undertook two years' post-16 vocational training, the NNEB (National Nursery Examination Board childcare qualification). This qualification is also offered as a workplace-based vocational qualification, the NVQ, with a similar content, but intended as a practice-based rather than college-based qualification. As indicated in the section on gender, many academically unsuccessful young girls and women are routed into this kind of training. As part of the UK government's attempt to systematize early childhood services, this basic vocational training then became the basis of professional training for early years professionals. The Children's Workforce Development Council (CWDC) specified the processes whereby this basic vocational training could somehow be transformed into the equivalent of tertiary academic training, without the university education. The Open University in particular has played an important role in offering workplace-based training to transform childcare workers into early years professionals.[38] While in some respects these options are laudable in offering a second chance qualification, in others they reinforce the divisions between those who have had the privilege of full-time university-based education, and those who have not, and who have to undertake tertiary education as an extra alongside their employment. The least able and most poorly qualified students experience the most gruelling and least well-resourced tertiary education conditions.[39] And if they work in the private sector, they are unlikely to gain the wide experience of practice in different settings that is supposed to be the advantage of vocationally based routes. Relying on the upgrading of a workforce with weak basic skills and limited practice opportunities to staff an expanding early years sector, and pursuing a training route that is part of the care sector and is entirely separate from teacher education, is not the best recipe for development of early childhood services.

Pay and conditions

Well-qualified professionals like teachers usually earn a reasonable salary with standard benefits and conditions. The level of staff wages is also a proxy for quality. As Sharon Kagan has pointed out:

> Research has indicated that teachers' wages are associated with quality of care provided. Professional quality is hard to find in a market place where ECE providers do not earn as much as funeral assistants or garbage collectors . . . not surprisingly given the low salaries, staff turnover is high in early childhood programmes outside of schools, around 36 per cent per annum.[40]

If the job is poorly paid and working conditions such as paid holiday leave and sick benefits are non-existent, then workers will have little loyalty to their job. It compounds the vicious circle of childcare being a woman's job therefore it comes naturally and does not require much training, and does not warrant decent pay. In Chapter 5 I discuss the work of US economists including David Blau, whose position is that childcare workers have low wages because they are willing to work for low wages.[41] To an extent it is true that women childcare workers have low expectations – women with poor academic qualifications are routed into childcare work because it is something they can do by virtue of being female and because they have low self-esteem and consider that many other avenues are shut to them, even though they know in advance they will not earn good money. These critiques are particularly pertinent to a private market. Chapter 5 has dealt with questions of quality in a private market in more detail.

In Chapter 8 I discuss questions of leadership, hierarchy and staff morale. Although leadership is an important topic related to quality, and raises further questions about appropriate training, the organization of work and the representation of the workforce are important issues too.

More generally, questions about the status and training of the workforce go back to the same starting point, what are services for, what are the rationales to justify them? If it is just warehousing childcare for the children of working mothers, training, pay and conditions may not matter too much. If staff are expected to work wonders in terms of realizing the education and social potential of young children it matters much more. As the OECD comments:

> All countries in the coming years will have to address the professional education, status, pay and working conditions of ECEC staff. If not, the sector will remain, at least in some countries, unproductive where quality and child outcomes are concerned, and non-competitive with other sectors for the recruitment and retention of staff.[42]

The content of the curricula

In this chapter I have discussed curricula and training very generally, focusing on the principles that underpin them. The content of the curricula is of course very important, although this book is not intended to be about suggestions for everyday practice. From the point of view of a child, the range of activities that is provided, the ingenuity and the intelligence and sympathy that has gone into planning it, matter enormously. Children can pace themselves of course, but they need grist to their mill. There are various 'atelier' schemes with artists in residence: dancers, singers and other musicians, storytellers, sculptors, chefs and gardeners. The notion that those very good at their trade, but not necessarily teachers, can share their expertise, with children as apprentices, is a very traditional view of learning, the way in which children used to learn before schooling was widespread. There are plenty of ideas about the materials that can be used with children, from 'treasure baskets' of natural materials such as stones, hessian, buttons and onions for the youngest children, to more sophisticated tools for art and design of all kinds, indoors and out, for preschool children.[43,44]

The more prescribed the curriculum, the more limited to plastic materials, the more risk-averse it is with regard to the adults who contribute and the activities that take place, the duller it is. There are many reference books, indeed many consultancies, to cull for ideas; the point is to use them.

Notes

1 Sumsion, J., Barnes, S., Cheeseman, S., Harrison, L., Kennedy, A.M. and Stonehouse, A. (2009) 'Insider perspectives on developing Belonging, Being and Becoming: The Early Years Learning Framework for Australia.' *Australasian Journal of Early Childhood* 34(4): 4–13.
2 OECD (2004) *Starting Strong: Curricula and Pedagogies in Early Childhood Education and Care. Five Curriculum Outlines*. Paris: OECD.
3 OECD (2001) *Country Note: Flanders*. Paris: OECD.
4 OECD (2001) *Country Note: USA*. Paris: OECD.
5 See www.highscope.org. The High Scope founder, David Weikart, gave many presentations about his work, for instance at an NAEYC international seminar in Toronto in 1998, where he made claims about the exportability of High Scope. The Canadian government then brought in High Scope as a special programme aimed at its aborigine population!
6 Rinaldi, C. (2005) *In Dialogue with Reggio Emilia: Listening, Researching and Learning*. London: Routledge.
7 Swedish Ministry of Education and Science (1998) *Curriculum for the Preschool*. Stockholm: Fritzes.

8 Bronfenbrenner, U. (1974) *Two Worlds of Childhood*. London: Penguin.

9 International Step by Step Association: www.issa.nl/philosophy.html

10 Tobin, J., Hsueh, Y. and Karasawa, M. (2009) *Preschool in Three Cultures Revisited: China, Japan, and the United States*. Chicago, IL: University of Chicago Press.

11 Pramling-Samuelsson, I., Sheridan, S. and Williams, P. (2006) 'Five preschool curricula in comparative perspective.' *International Journal of Early Childhood* 38(1): 11–30.

12 'Save our planet' is a regular theme of the *CBeebies* BBC television programme for young children. Readers of the 'Charlie and Lola' series by the author Lauren Child will also be familiar with the theme of sustainability!

13 OECD, *Starting Strong: Curricula and Pedagogies in Early Childhood Education and Care. Five Curriculum Outlines*, p. 30.

14 No Child Left Behind Act was passed by the US Senate in 2001. It is based on theories of standards-based education reform – that setting high standards and establishing measurable goals can improve individual outcomes in education. The Act requires states to develop assessments in basic skills, in order to receive federal funding for schools. If a school fails to meet the targets set two or more years running, the school must offer eligible children the chance to transfer to higher-performing local schools, receive free tutoring, or attend after-school programs.

15 Robin Alexander compares primary education in England, France, India, Russia and the USA. See Alexander, R. (2000) *Culture and Pedagogy*. Oxford: Blackwell. The UK has always had a parsimonious view of education as cramming the masses, rather than developing cultured or well-rounded individuals.

16 Pramling-Samuelsson et al., 'Five preschool curricula in comparative perspective.'

17 Fass, P. (2003) 'Children and globalization.' *Journal of Social History* 36(4): 963–977.

18 Brian Sutton Smith is a New Zealander who has written widely about toys as culture. See, for example, Sutton Smith, B. (1999) 'The rhetorics of adult and child play theories.' In S. Reifel (ed.) *Advances in Early Education and Daycare*. London: JAI Press.

19 Rose, H. (1994) *Love, Power and Knowledge: Towards a Feminist Transformation of the Sciences*. Cambridge: Polity Press. The quotation is from p. 22.

20 The department has changed its name at least four times since 1997, and between 2007 and 2010 was familiarly referred to as the Department of Curtains and Soft Furnishings (from its acronym DCSF).

21 Penn, H. and McQuail, S. (1997) *Childcare as a Gendered Occupation*. DfEE Research Report 23. London: DfEE.

22 Vincent, C. and Braun, A. (2010) 'And hairdressers are quite seedy . . . the moral worth of childcare training', *Contemporary Issues in Early Childhood* forthcoming

23 Clarke, K. (2006) 'Childhood, parenting and early intervention: A critical examination of the Sure Start National Programme.' *Critical Social Policy* 26(4): 699–721.

24 Vandenbroeck, M. (2003) 'From crèches to childcare: Constructions of motherhood and inclusion/exclusion in the history of Belgian infant care.' *Contemporary Issues in Early Childhood* 4(2): 137–148.

25 Mozère, L. (1999) *Travail au noir, informalité: Liberté ou sujetion?* Paris: L'Harmattan.

26 Lloyd, E. and Hallet, E. (2010) 'Professionalising the early childhood workforce in England: Work in progress or missed opportunity?' *Contemporary Issues in Early Childhood* 11(1): 75–88.

27 Chabon, M. (2009) *Manhood for Amateurs: The Pleasures and Regrets of a Husband, Father, and Son.* London: Fourth Estate.

28 My colleague Richard Harty undertook a review of the literature on men in childcare, which he presented at the New Zealand Early Childhood Conference in 2007. Although many of the papers he reviewed mentioned male role models, there was no inquiry which set out to explore if and how young children were in fact influenced by men who worked with them into thinking about gender roles or acting them out.

29 Belsky, J. (2009) 'Quality, quantity and type of childcare: Effects on child development in the U.S.' In G. Bentley and R. Mace (eds) *Substitute Parents: Biological and Social Perspectives on Alloparenting.* Oxford: Berghahn, pp. 304–324.

30 Hrdy, S.B. (1999) *Mother Nature: Maternal Instincts and How They Shape the Human Species.* New York: Ballantine, p. 506.

31 Childcare Exchange, the US-based advocacy forum, organizes an annual World Forum, a conference for childcare practitioners. It has a number of special interest groups, one of which is 'Men in Childcare'.

32 Oberheumer, P. and Ulich, M. (1997) *Working with Young Children in Europe: Provision and Staff Training.* London: Paul Chapman.
Oberheumer, P. (2005) 'Conceptualizing the early childhood pedagogue: Policy approaches and issues of professionalism.' *European Early Childhood Research Journal* 13(1): 5–16.

33 Oberheumer and Ulrich, *Working with Young Children in Europe.* The quotation is from p. 23.

34 Blachford, I., Clarke, K. and Needham, M. (2007) *The Team Around the Child.* Stoke-on-Trent: Trentham.

35 Lloyd and Hallet, 'Professionalising the early childhood workforce in England.'

36 OECD (2006) *Starting Strong II: Early Childhood Education and Care.* Paris: OECD.

37 OECD, *Starting Strong II*, p. 164.

38 The Open University seeks employer-based sponsorship for courses ranging from certificate courses to a degree in early years and early years professional status. It is currently working with the Asquith Day Nurseries chain of nurseries to offer qualifications on this basis.

39 As someone working in a modern university which offers an early years professional training, I am acutely aware of the less than ideal conditions of

learning for early childhood students (a generally undemanding academic content, very large classes, often in the evening after work, little time for study, limited tutorial support, and little or no opportunity to remedy the literacy and numeracy weaknesses that led the students to take vocational routes in the first place).

40 Kagan, S. and Rigby, E. (2003) *Policy Matters: Setting and Measuring Benchmarks for State Policies*. Discussion Paper. Washington, DC: Centre for the Study of Social Policy. Cited in OECD, *Starting Strong II*, p. 169.

41 Blau, D.M. (2001) 'Rethinking US childcare policy.' *Issues in Science and Technology*. 18(2): 66–72. Available at www.issues.org/18.2/index.html

42 OECD, *Starting Strong II*, p. 170.

43 Duckett, R. and Drummond, M-J. (2010) *Adventuring in Early Childhood Education*. Newcastle: Sightlines.

44 For example, the practitioners' magazine *Nursery World* carries regular features about such initiatives.

7 Working spaces

In this chapter I focus on working spaces, for children and for adults. Here there are major differences in understandings of quality.

The physical characteristics of the building and the space in which it is located matter to those who work inside them. In the Far East there is even a name for the influence a building wields – Feng Shui. Children in nurseries are in an important sense at work. Arguably buildings and spaces matter even more for the young children who must spend part or all of their day in them, perhaps for more hours than do staff. Features such as the degree of natural light, the ventilation, sympathetic acoustics, no echoes, usable, cleanable and attractive surfaces, texture and colour, adequate storage, doors that can be held open – there is a long list. Even the absence of smell is a bonus (children's lavatories are usually smelly places and having them in a central position, not separated from the work space, can be very unpleasant). Nowadays environmental friendliness is also a major consideration. But over and above the hardware, there is the question of fitness for purpose. Understandings of childhood, learning and schooling, mothering, family and work, and poverty all feed into what we consider to be appropriate environments for children.

Embodiment and physicality

The neurologist Oliver Sacks has written famously about his cases, adults who have suffered neurological damage. One of these cases is entitled 'The disembodied lady'. One of his clients, called Christina, had suffered rare neurological damage and most of her neurological receptors carrying information from her muscles appeared to be blocked. She had no bodily sensations. She felt as if her body were dead, as she put it: 'I feel my body is blind and deaf to itself . . . it has no sense of itself'. Sacks comments that Christina 'is condemned to live in an indescribable unimaginable realm – though "non-realm", "nothingness" might be a better word for it.'[1]

This example illustrates the absolute importance of 'embodiment' the fact that consciously or not, everything that happens to us happens through our bodies. In a rather curious way, in dealing with young children, current theories of learning and development give enormous priority to cognitive attributes. Instead of treating the body as a total organism, we have an extraordinary inflated view of the importance of the brain as the central organ – despite the fact that for example there are more neurotransmitters like serotonin in the gut than in the brain. The notion of embodiment has a long philosophical history.[2] It is worth making the argument very strongly that children's mobility and physicality is essential to their sense of themselves, their very identity, not merely to their learning. So much more is involved in physical expression than gross motor skills or hand–eye co-ordination.

There are recognized concerns today about children's immobility and obesity. Obesity is recognized as being partly caused by eating too much, and eating too much of the wrong things, in particular processed food. But it is also to do with children being couch potatoes. Most small children are naturally very active; they run and bob about, they squirm and fidget, they stagger, they touch, they want to walk on the tops of walls and jump off into puddles. Look at any place where young children gather, in a playground, in a school yard, in the street with their parents, and it is hardly an exaggeration to say that small children are as frisky as young lambs. The French sociologist Michel Foucault came up with the insight that in order to control minds we have first to control bodies. In the case of children, regulating bodily activity and motion is a way of disciplining their minds and shaping them into compliant adults. Trisha Maynard presents an interesting case study of young children attending a Forest school, and the ambivalence of their teachers in seeing children have the bodily freedom to explore and run around in their new environment.[3] Children who are made immobile or whose mobility is limited are easier to control.

In the early days of nurseries in the UK, indeed of the nursery school movement in general, the outside space, the freedom to move and the fresh air were regarded as an essential aspect of education for young children.[4] Most nurseries in the 1940s and 1950s were built with verandas, a covered space to bridge the gap between inside and outside, especially in poor weather. Nurseries were designed to recompense children who lived in cramped quarters or in flats. Before health and safety became such an overwhelming preoccupation, nursery and primary school design in the UK had rather a good reputation. David Medd and Mary Crawley, the inspirational architectural partnership (in Hertfordshire, and then at the Department for Education), were responsible for many landmark designs.[5] They worked with school inspectors, teachers and children in the 1950s and 1960s throughout the UK and beyond to reflect pedagogical ideas about child-directed creative learning. For 30 years they were 'the world's most enlightened creators of primary schools'.[6]

This need of children for exercise and movement, spontaneous or otherwise, was also recognized as a necessary part of the day in former Soviet systems. Even in crowded city centres in China, in kindergartens with restricted space, there would be regular 20 minute intervals of exercise or callisthenics, even for the youngest children. Each child would have a marked spot on the playground or roof terrace, where they would perform carefully thought out exercise routines, designed to improve their circulation and stretch their muscles. By contrast in industrialized countries, adults can go to the gym or to aerobics classes, or partake in some other indoor sport, but young children can be cooped up all day without a second thought.

As an example of rather different expectations of children's prowess and stamina, Children in Scotland has translated the booklet *Adventures in Nature* (*Avventure in natura*), an account of young children's experiences of abseiling, potholing and white river rafting. These activities are built into the curriculum in some northern Italian nurseries. The booklet's illustrations show competent young children engaged in sophisticated activities to test their strength and agility.[7] These activities would be almost impossible to arrange, unless there was a facilitative local authority with a lot of money, and the scenery to match! But they do indicate the degree of underestimation of children's physical ability in most circumstances.

The natural world

An earlier view of nursery provision was that 'nature' was restorative, especially for children living in restricted environments. This was a central tenet for Margaret McMillan, the Scottish pioneer of nursery schools. The garden in her nursery in Deptford, London, rapidly became a legend, with its herbs, flowers and vegetable plots and outside sleeping places. The garden was more than just a space but a metaphor for education itself, a place where children's inborn capacities could also flower.[8] This philosophy of the importance of nature and natural objects is still held by the Steiner school movement. Many Steiner schools have environmentally friendly buildings that look as if they nestle into their surrounding landscape; inside colours are always muted, and natural objects prevail.[9]

Again, this view of the importance of nature and the natural environment is widely recognized. The Finnish preschool curriculum is not on the whole a prescriptive one, but it requires that children spend a *minimum* of two hours everyday outside whatever the weather – and Finland is snowbound for much of the winter. In Denmark, Sweden and Norway, curricula guidance lays great emphasis on imaginative use of space, and on coming to terms with and understanding the natural environment. The Forest kindergarten movement, where children are taken out by bus into surrounding wild places in forests or by lakes, is a familiar feature of Danish childcare. It has also been taken up in the 'Waldkindergartens' of Germany.

Richard Louv's evocatively titled book *Last Child in the Woods: Saving our Children from Nature Deficit Disorder* is a sentimental but moving account of childhoods spent in rural and wild environments. He claims such environments have a particular meaningfulness to children; indeed their daily life is impoverished without such roving experiences.[10] Having the freedom to potter around in the earth, fingering worms, woodlice, spiders, beetles and caterpillars and foraging for herbs and berries, is, in his view, infinitely more enriching than playing with manufactured plastic toys. There are now many websites and environmental centres devoted to environmental education,[11] although Louv had more self-directed experiences in mind.

From seeing nature as restorative, it is now being seen as a *right* for children, an endorsement of their legitimate and heartfelt preferences and interests. Brazilian-Italian writer and pedagogue Gianfranco Zavalloni has also been pioneering young children's re-engagement with nature. In his book 'The pedagogy of the snail' he describes what he calls 'slow pedagogy', the idea that children can pace themselves outdoors, and find many natural things to occupy themselves, at their own learning speed, and with minimal intervention from adults.[12] He has outlined 10 'natural' rights for children: the right to leisure, to get dirty, to appreciate smells, to make things for themselves, to experience night and day and changes in the light, the right to experience wilderness etc.[13]

It is now fashionable at least to have small gardens and grow vegetables as part of the nursery curriculum – if there is space to do so. Beans, potatoes, radishes and carrots are all relatively easy to grow, even in tubs (pumpkins seem to be super fertile seeds!). The yield may not be high, but the experience of cultivation is a complex learning experience – about time, growth, weather and soil, as well as about taste and nutrition. Growing food is a fundamental part of Steiner education.[14] But children also need to prepare and cook the food they grow otherwise growing it is merely decorative. The Steiner nurseries also have accessible cooking facilities for children. Health and safety rules may forbid children any access to kitchen facilities, restricting them yet again to their minaturized play worlds.

Making the environment look good

I have written elsewhere about nursery building, in particular about the Frankfurt Nursery Building programme.[15] The Director of Architecture in the German city of Frankfurt celebrated the 1200th anniversary of the founding of the city of Frankfurt by commissioning a series of new kindergartens, through international tendering. These buildings, all of which were environmentally innovative, promoted a celebratory view of early childhood and its status in society. The buildings were mostly in poor areas, and in some cases on very difficult sites. For example, one prize-winning nursery (the Kiefernstrasse kindergarten designed by Peter Wilson) was built on a long narrow site sandwiched between a motorway and a railway line, among social housing serving a poor immigrant community. It was a heart-stoppingly original work of art. I thought it was one of the most beautiful and playful buildings of any kind I had ever visited, because it experimented with light, levels and widths. It was a vivid visual demonstration of how, in a fair society, poverty need not be restrictive; the best can – and should – be available to everyone. (I've come across the opposite view too; that the poor can't be expected to move too far out of their comfort zone, and a grand building in a poor neighbourhood is an invitation to vandals.)

The Frankfurt kindergartens offered childcare and education for children aged 3 up to school starting age of 6 years and after-school care for older children. Part of the design specification for the programme was to respect child autonomy. Each kindergarten had to have child-only spaces where adults could not enter; children had free movement within the buildings. The specification also included a child-friendly kitchen, where fresh meals were prepared and served. A real workshop area had to be provided for out-of-school children. The Frankfurt nursery programme was a deliberate attempt by architects to meditate on the nature of space for children and how it might be used – length, width, height, proportion, light, colour, contour and surface.[16] It was however an architectural project; their control of the design predominated, sometimes over the heads of their more cautious and less inspired welfare colleagues.

In 2006 the organization Children in Scotland, which has led the way on promoting such issues in the field, held an international competition for nursery design. The results were published as a booklet and DVD called *Making Space: Award-Winning Designs for Young Children*.[17] Regulations for physical space for young children have been increasingly parsimonious in a number of countries, not just the UK. So this competition was held to demonstrate what is still possible, even where money is short and space is tight. The prizes were awarded to buildings and spaces that

> appealed to the senses, that acknowledged the natural world, that encouraged participation in the designing process, that included the children's wider community into the building or space, that paid close attention to the details that matter to children, for example coats storage and toilets, and that allowed for an integrative approach to children's services.[18]

The first prize was awarded to a Japanese centre 'Bubbletecture', a wave-like structure made of wood. The runner-up was a nursery from the hot and poor

Island of Réunion in the Indian Ocean. It used a bioclimatic air-conditioning system: it was built on a slope in such a way as to allow the breezes to flow through, so that even in the hottest weather, the building was cool. The architects said of their design: 'This nursery makes reference to the Creole way of living, in particular its intimate outside/inside relationship . . . the façade of the building is like a very porous skin.'[19] Another runner-up was Italian, 'a multi-sensorial environment' with a beautiful use of colour. The third runner-up was in London, the Forward Children's Centre (also listed for the prestigious Stirling Prize for architecture). Here (unsurprisingly), security was a major concern, and the colours were bright verging on garish. The architect had to reconcile different demands. 'Parents communicated their concerns over safety, and residents wanted to retain their pride in the centre as a community resource. The children mainly wanted trees and a lot of sand.'[20] This illustrates the difficulty for architects in relying on consultation and consensus with children, adults and staff. Where public expectations of what might be achieved are very low, architects have to lead the way.

In Italy, design has a much higher priority in considerations of quality. Loris Malaguzzi, for example, argues that it is a principle of quality that nurseries should always be a habitable *aesthetic* space.[21] I once attended a seminar in the Italian Renaissance city of Florence on how to site children's lavatories sensitively in a medieval building that was being converted into a nursery. The detail of the discussion, and its presumed interest to the audience of local people, was mind-blowing, at least to me. Renaissance cities in Italy are one place where architects do not have to lead the way: history has already done it.

Is an architect's vision a measurable mark of quality? Mark Dudek has written about kindergarten architecture across the world, and highlighted some of the best designs in his book *Kindergarten Architecture*.[22,23] Good buildings relate to the space around them, and incorporate not only a vision of childhood but also children's own vision of their childhood (see below). Pedagogically, as well as aesthetically, this has pay-offs. In a well-designed environment children can explore the limits of their bodily prowess and control, climbing, jumping, running, twirling, and dancing in an explosion of movement, and enjoy the self-confidence that comes from bodily mastery. As one barefooted 3-year-old girl, in a particularly spacious and imaginatively well-equipped nursery garden (rope ladders in the trees, a tree-house, a walk-in aviary, a huge sandpit, and a bicycle track) confided to us, 'Everywhere we can play. We can play outside and in the classrooms and on the monkey bars.'[24]

Working spaces for children

I have focused mainly on external space, because this is often the most neglected area. Internal space matters too. Here the debates are about children's autonomy and the extent to which they can be trusted to work in, utilize or even design the spaces for themselves. Alison Clark has worked with young children over a period of time listening and recording what they say about the spaces they use within early childhood education and care settings. She has set out ways of working with children to enable them to articulate their views, and enabling others – including architects – to act upon them: what she calls 'the mosaic approach'. Children have useful and insightful contributions to make, even the youngest.[25]

Typically, at least in those countries where there is a substantial private market, the inside space is frequently modelled on what Joseph Tobin has called 'the excesses of the shopping mall' – cheap bright standardized toys crowding the space offering children too many choices between not very well-differentiated goods.[26] In addition children are under constant surveillance, to make sure they do not abuse or harm the materials, and are not harmed by them – there are always watchmen on duty! Going outside is especially danger-ous, and access to the outside spaces are closely guarded. This lack of trust in children, the hyper-risk culture, bodily and mentally restricts children and is the antithesis of approaches which emphasize children's rights.

Many premises in use for young children now are rented or hastily con-verted, but not originally intended for children at all. They are leftover build-ings from some other activity. They were originally shop fronts or industrial units or church halls or sports halls or rooms in private houses or disused school buildings or, in very poor places, in shacks, sheds and garages. This cur-rent lack of concern about space is an extraordinary omission, given the intense physicality of young children.[27] There is very little solid evidence about the impact such restriction may have on learning or on physical development; it is a lacunae in the research as well as in the conception of provision. In the UK the preoccupation is with keeping children safe and secure, even when doing so results in an environment rather like a prison. In England the requirements are minimal – 'a safe and appropriate physical space'. Current regulations do not even require outside space![28] I've seen many places like this in England – the book cover features one of them – but never in the Nordic countries or former communist countries (at least until recently) and infrequently in other European countries.[29]

Working spaces for adults

How the space is organized also affects how workers can actually do their jobs, and whether they can do them efficiently. A very simple example is storage space. Unless the storage is well organized, handling lots of small objects and keeping track of children's work is much more difficult. I once had the misfor-tune to move into an office which had a filing cabinet without any drawers (a long story). The chaos this caused was terrible – every time we looked for a file we had to sort through piles of folders and rebalance the stack! The efficacy of the material environment is part of doing the job well.

If the environment and spaces are good for children, they will be good for adults too – like the spirit-lifting Kiefernstrasse Kindergarten mentioned above. But there is an additional question about whether staff *need* separate resources for themselves. Many institutions see the staff as doing a professional job with clients, a job which specifies the kinds of relationships they might have and the temporal, spatial and emotional limitations of their work. The radical French psychiatrist Félix Guattari, whose work is discussed in Chapter 9, attempted to break down all these barriers, and create a very fluid environment in his clinic. So if there is a view of co-construction in learning, of mutuality and sharing, what are the boundaries of this approach? Should the working space be designed for both adults and children to do all their necessary work, or should the staff have separate working/recreational areas where they can take a breather from the children? Most schools have such facilities. The roles and boundaries of the women (and few men) who work with young children were discussed in Chapter 6.

I use all these examples to suggest that, in the English-speaking literature at least, the visual and the physical are neglected as aspects of quality. 'A safe and appropriate physical space' is so unambitious an aim for a quality environment for children or adults as to verge on insult, especially when there are marvellous examples to learn from.

Notes

1   Sacks, O. (1998) 'The disembodied lady.' In D. Robinson (ed.) *The Mind*. Oxford: Oxford University Press, p. 331.

2   Clark, A. (1997) *Being There: Putting Brain, Body and World Together Again*. Cambridge, MA: The MIT Press.

3   Maynard, T. (2007) 'Encounters with Forest School and Foucault: A risky business?' *Education 3–13* 35(4): 379–391.

4   Penn, H. (2004) 'Round and round the mulberry bush.' In R. Aldrich (ed.) *Public or Private Education: Lessons from History*. London: Woburn Place.

5   The papers of David and Mary Medd, Photographic Archive at Institute of Education, London University, GB/366/DC/MG.

6   Burke, C. (2009) 'Inside out: A collaborative approach to designing schools in England 1945–1972.' *Paedagogica Historica* 45(3): 421–433.

7   Children in Scotland (2008) *Adventures in Nature: Building Better Childhoods*. International Perspectives Series. Edinburgh: Children in Scotland.

8   Steedman, C. (1990) *Childhood, Culture and Class in Britain: Margaret McMillan 1860–1931*. London: Virago, p. 82.

9 At the University of East London where I work, the on-site nursery is a Steiner kindergarten. The garden has running water, a thicket of trees, a vegetable garden, and a boat for children to play in. There is not a single plastic object in the nursery – everything is made of wood or natural materials, and where possible hand crafted.

10 Louv, R. (2005) *Last Child in the Woods: Saving Our Children from Nature Deficit Disorder*. Chapel Hill, NC: Algonquin Books.

11 See e.g. www.naturegrid.org.uk/children.html

12 Zavalloni, G. (2008) *La Pedagogica della limaca: per una scuola lenta e nonviolente* [The Pedagogy of the Snail]. Bologna: EMI.

13 Zavalloni, G. (2009) 'Children's natural rights.' *Children in Europe* 17/2009. Edinburgh: Children in Scotland, pp. 28–29.

14 The nursery at the University of East London is run along Steiner principles, and the productive garden is regarded as an essential aspect of children's activities.

15 Penn, H. (2000) 'Where should children learn: Space and segregation.' In H. Penn (ed.) *Early Childhood Services: Theory, Policy, Practice*. Maidenhead: Open University Press, pp. 83–89.

16 Burgard, R. (2000) 'The Frankfurt kindergartens.' In H. Penn (ed.) *Early Childhood Services: Theory, Policy, Practice*. Maidenhead: Open University Press.

17 Children in Scotland (2006) *Making Space: Award-Winning Designs for Young Children*. Edinburgh: Children in Scotland.

18 Children in Scotland, *Making Space*, p. 33.

19 Children in Scotland, *Making Space*, p. 37.

20 Children in Scotland, *Making Space*, p. 39.

21 Hoyuelos, A. (2004) *La etica en el pensamiento y obra pedagogica de Loris Malaguzzi*. Barcelona: Rosa Sensat.

22 Dudek, M. (2000) *Kindergarten Architecture*. London: Spon.

23 Dudek, M. (2007) *Schools and Kindergartens: A Design Manual*. Munich: Birkhauser.

24 Penn, H. and Maynard, T. (2010) *Siyabonana: We All See Each Other. Building Better Childhoods in South Africa*. Edinburgh: Children in Scotland, p. 18.

25 Clark, A. (2010) *Transforming Children's Spaces*. London: Routledge.

26 Tobin, J. (1995) 'Post-structural research in early childhood education.' In J.A. Hatch (ed.) *Qualitative Research in Early Childhood Settings*. Westport, CT: Praeger, pp. 223–243.

27 Even new buildings can be seriously at fault. The property manager of one well-known nursery chain in the UK hedged its property investments by making sure its new premises could all be converted into sports centres should the property market change or the nurseries not make sufficient profit.

28 I visited one brand new integrated showpiece children's centre in London: it had smart security doors which only authorized staff could open. One side of the two-storey building was for health personnel. The other side was for the children's centre, with rooms upstairs for adult activities. Downstairs the space

for children was lit by very bright neon lighting and was entirely open so all the children could be scrutinized at all times. It was badly ventilated and overheated, and it smelt. It had sealed windows which were also partly barred, and which gave onto an inner courtyard, a kind of well within the building. This had a rubberized ground surface which came partly up the wall. The children were let out into this rubberized well for a very short controlled exercise period when the weather was good.

29 When I showed these photos at a conference held in Paris for trade unionists from across Europe representing early childhood workers, there were astonished gasps!

8   Working practices

Management and leadership

Leadership is said to be a key indicator of quality in the early years. The early years market is becoming saturated with books on leadership and management, more or less empirical, which try to identify generic leadership and management skills and list the situations in which they can be applied.[1] In England there is now a national leadership course for early years, with Department for Education endorsement and obligatory CD-Rom.[2] In the USA too leadership has become institutionalized, and there is a scale to measure it.[3] The prescription for good leadership varies slightly, but this list is indicative.

- Identifying and articulating a collective vision
- Ensuring shared understandings, meanings and goals
- Effective communication
- Encouraging reflection
- Monitoring and assessing practice
- Commitment to ongoing professional development
- Building a learning community and team culture
- Encouraging and facilitating parent and community partnerships.[4]

In other contexts, this list might be rather puzzling. Why should it be necessary to ensure shared understandings of goals, or to build a learning community, unless of course these issues are problematic and these goals cannot be achieved without considerable effort. In the UK these goals *are* indeed problematic. As I discussed in Chapter 2, since 1997 there has been a unprecedented raft of new measures, changing the rules, although barely changing the rationales. These new measures have fragmented an already piecemeal system, one held together only by regulation. As the examples below show, there is no standard format for leadership that can easily be applied in the UK – or in other countries where there is a considerable diversity of provision.

In this chapter, I consider views of leadership which are common currency elsewhere, the first from the USA, and the second from Italy. Then I discuss some of the theories about leadership, management and workplace learning.

A business model

In a marketized economy, as in the USA, leadership requires very specific skills.

> Early childhood programs are essentially businesses, and successful administrators function much like the unit managers of their corporate counterparts. They are savvy financial managers who possess skill in budgeting and cash flow management. They are knowledgeable about book-keeping methods, accounting terminology and bank relations. They are well-informed about federal, state and local sources of revenue, and seek out grant raising and fundraising opportunities. Additionally effective administrators work with legal counsel to ensure compliance with the many regulations that govern early childhood programs. . . . They have a working familiarity of legislation relevant to contracts and negotiations, insurance liability and labor law . . . (they) are strategic marketers whose programs benefit from effective promotion, publicity and community outreach activities. . . . Their programs are promoted to the public on paper, through broadcast media and over the internet, through attractive brochures, websites, handbooks, newsletters, press releases and carefully placed advertising.[5]

In this analysis of leadership, having financial management and marketing skills are the prime considerations. The nursery is an independent business which must be kept afloat. The author doesn't go so far as to say the nursery must make money, but that is the implication. And if its aim is profitability, that frequently takes precedent over other aims. The books have to balance, preferably tilting towards the owners. This is of concern to those trying to regulate services, or tender services:

> However carefully you construct contracts, an organization primarily focused on profits can achieve greater profitability by providing a rather lesser service.[6]

In the USA, UK and other countries where there are corporate nursery chains,[7] company bosses are chosen for their business and financial expertise and acumen, and for their marketing skills, rather than for their knowledge about children or communities. The biggest children's charity in the UK, the National

Society for the Prevention of Cruelty to Children (NSPCC), is now run by someone recruited from the advertising and marketing industry.

A collective model

At the opposite end of the spectrum there are nurseries which are run as collectives and have no managers. In a number of countries there were shortlived attempts to run nurseries (and schools) as democratic and radical places where traditional views of childrearing were challenged, and staff attempted to relate to each other and to the children and parents and community in non-hierarchical ways. In doing so, they tried to challenge societal mores. These experiments happened in Russia in the 1920s,[8] in France in the 1970s,[9] even for a very brief period in the 1970s and 1980s in the community nursery movement in the UK. Chiara Saraceno discusses and compares some of these early experiments in Germany (in Stuttgart, Frankfurt and Berlin) as well as in Milan and the USA.[10] These community nurseries were intense places to work. The Stuttgart nursery, for example, was a place where the 10 men and women running it discussed and argued continuously, about politics, about pedagogical theory and about everyday practice, and how they related to one another. They agonized about being too middle-class and alienating working-class communities.

Most experimentation took place in Italy and Spain – the famous Reggio Emilia nurseries are still run along these lines. But in Spain and Italy the collective nurseries have older traditions to draw on. Agricultural co-operatives are a common form of organization across parts of Southern Europe. In Spain too there was a tradition of worker-schools, subversively operating under the Franco regime. These experiments might have been forgotten or ignored, had it not been for the influence of Loris Malaguzzi in Reggio Emilia. His ideas about social transformation through collective action in the nurseries are still being promoted.[11,12]

In England, for a time in the 1970s and 1980s, urban local authorities funded self-help community nurseries, a few of which were very radical. The Greater London Council funded over a hundred community nurseries before it was abolished by the Thatcher government. The Department of Health (DoH) also had a small community nursery programme funded under its voluntary grants programme. The advocacy childcare organization, the Daycare Trust, was asked by the DoH to pilot such a community programme. Because these programmes no longer exist, and many of the nurseries have closed, the records are scanty. They were outside the mainstream – neither flesh nor fowl, neither education nurseries nor social services day nurseries – and without pedagogical recognition or support they were regarded as making a marginal contribution to either education or welfare services.[13] Nowadays their aims would be more acceptable, but without grant subsidies, these nurseries have found it very hard to survive. Current demand-led funding mechanisms have made it nearly impossible for them to continue, certainly not in their original ambitious form.

I was a parent in one of these community nurseries, in South London, and for me and my co-parents, it was a rewarding if not transforming experience. (Some 25 years later the nursery held a reunion to which almost the entire cohort of parents and children turned up, such was the regard in which the nursery was held!) Partly because of this experience of being a parent in a community nursery I was interested to find out in more detail about the Italian and Spanish collective nurseries operated.[14] I carried out a comparative study in Spain (Barcelona) and Italy (various municipalities in the provinces of Emilia Romagna and Tuscany, but not Reggio Emilia, which by then was beginning to be very oversubscribed).

In the Spanish nurseries I investigated, all teachers and carers were paid on the same grade. Domestic staff – cleaners and cooks – were paid slightly less. No one was in charge, and decision-making was collectively undertaken. Most staff had completed or were undertaking a degree in early childhood at the local university, on an in-service basis. Staff took it in turn to undertake administrative duties for the nursery. This system, as far as I could tell from my observations and interviews over a period of six weeks, worked well. Staff turnover, usually an indicator of dissatisfaction, was very low indeed. I used a short job satisfaction questionnaire for staff, which included the question, 'Do you see yourself working here in five years' time?' Most staff did. As I wrote at the time, one of the nurseries in Barcelona (probably rather exceptional!) seemed to have a perpetual air of partying:

> In this nursery the pleasure the staff take in one another's company and in the children, is palpable. There seems to be an implicit view among the staff that of all the places in which one could choose to spend one's time, this is it. There is a kind of *joie de vivre* which expresses itself not only in the staff spending much more time in the nursery than they are contracted to do, staying on to help on each other's shifts, but also with much physical affection and laughter. I watch a young member of staff and an older cleaner stroll up and down the courtyard, their arms round one another, deep in conversation.[15]

The organization was crucially dependent on weekly staff meetings, and bi-monthly meetings with parents, rather jolly affairs usually, with (really) good food. At these meetings views were aired, problems discussed, and policies considered. In the job satisfaction questionnaires, I also asked staff to comment on their experiences of working in a co-operative setting.

> I'm in agreement with the structure and organization of the centre although from a practical point of view, working and deciding as a team takes longer, and things get done more slowly. Even so, I would

not change it even if certain aspects of punctuality and organization are lacking.

We have differences but they are not sources of conflict. Perhaps the fact that we have enough autonomy and we have friendships within the group means we have very few conflicts.

I have the good luck to be in a team where I have observed few conflicts, where people talk about things, a kind of dialogue that makes conflict unnecessary. And we have a lot of freedom within the group rooms and within the framework set by the nursery.

Even if I didn't like the work I would still like my colleagues. Bad relationships with colleagues would spread to work with the children.[16]

The municipality, the local authority funded the co-ops, handled much of the technical administration concerning fees and admissions, supplies etc., and provided background pedagogic support through local advisers. They also organized in-service training for staff.

In many cities in Northern Italy – including Reggio Emilia – similar co-operatives existed. Although there was also a complete absence of hierarchy within the nurseries, the staff had slightly less autonomy than in the Barcelona nurseries. The staff were also less well qualified. Here again, the local authority was the key. All the important administrative decisions and professional decisions were taken by the co-ordinators appointed by the municipality. The co-ordinators were well qualified, with a degree or postgraduate degree as well as practical experience. Each co-ordinator was responsible for a group of between eight and ten nurseries. The co-ordinators were in effect the managers of the nurseries and had a key role in the support and development of the service; they advised on training, they led the discussions on pedagogical theory and policy. However, they were not based in the nurseries, and on a day-to-day basis the nurseries ran themselves. Again, the municipality was responsible for the technical administration, admissions, fee collection, supplies, building maintenance and payment of salaries, appointments and human resource issues generally.

These Northern Italian co-operatives undoubtedly worked. (Or most of them did – there was one exception where there was some excruciating practice. There were many temporary staff and no handovers between staff, so there were a number of occasions where the staff did not even know the children's names. This was possibly because of poor relationships with the municipality concerned. But this was the only instance of the system not working.) Staff liked working in these co-operative nurseries, they focused knowledgeably on what the children were doing, and children produced impressive work. The parents who I met at meetings seemed very happy with the results.

At the time of writing, there is some talk by the Conservative party in the UK of 'co-operative schools' in England. But in so far as the idea has been worked out at all, these are rather different co-operative organizations from those described above. In the Spanish and Italian nurseries, the key to their functioning was in the input of the local authority, or municipality. The co-operatives did not have to deal with routine day-to-day administration; they did not have to raise money; and they were pedagogically inspired by highly trained and articulate people. They had autonomy, but they also had practical support and imaginative guidance of a high order.

Solidarity

Several of the workers quoted above said that work friendships were very important to them. The municipal co-ordinators frequently used the word 'solidarity'. 'Solidarity' is not a familiar idea in English-speaking settings. In the UK and the USA, individualism is rated as more important. Individuals have their own wishes and desires, make their own choices, and have to be responsible for their own decisions. Some nurseries or centres follow the social work practice of 'supervision' sessions with their manager, a regular individual counselling session with someone who is more senior. So the job of management in a sense is to bring tetchy or unsure individuals together and keep them to task. Rather like regulation, the more diverse the individuals, the more variety in their backgrounds, the more need to have strong leadership and management to make sure they work together within accepted parameters. But within many European countries, and indeed within the European Union, the idea of solidarity is constantly reiterated.

Solidarity is the notion that people have common interests and feelings and benefit from engaging in mutual actions. To show solidarity with someone is to sympathize with them, to stand by them, to support them, especially if they are in difficulty. Solidarity is a goal for children as well as for adults. The Swedish curriculum for example states that 'the task of preschool is to establish and help children acquire the values on which our society is based . . . the equal value of all people, equality between the genders as well as solidarity with the weak and vulnerable'.[17] In a hierarchical setting, where managers are in charge, paid more than others, and in the last resort, if not right away, expect some kind of obedience or compliance, solidarity is more difficult to achieve.

In hierarchical workplaces, solidarity has traditionally been pursued within trades unions. Workers may be the victim of injustices from their employer – for example women may be paid less than men for similar kinds of work, or white staff may be hired instead of equally well-qualified black staff. Bosses may redeploy people arbitrarily, or misinterpret their conduct, or try to make them redundant. Unions can offer an alternative avenue for redress. If the employer won't listen, unions can take up the complaint. Unions can also provide an opportunity for groups of workers to articulate a viewpoint which management has refused to consider. Union membership is discouraged in many private nurseries. It is viewed as disruptive and an indication of unnecessary polarization between managers and their staff. In the UK now more professionals than unskilled people belong to unions. Deskilled and low-paid workers working in private companies tend to be more fatalistic about their situation whereas teachers, social workers, academics and civil servants are more likely to consider it worthwhile to pay their union dues. Union membership does offer some kind of safeguard and a security for individuals in the face of unreasonable or unfair management practices – and it would be naive to suppose all managers were competent or empathetic. Some managers do a good job, but some certainly do not.

The right to trades union membership and collective bargaining at a local level is enshrined in legislation in most countries. The International Labour Organization (ILO), the branch of the United Nations concerned with work and employment practices states that:

> The right of workers and employers to form and join organizations of their own choosing is an integral part of a free and open society. In many cases, these organizations have played a significant role in their countries' democratic transformation. From advising governments on labour legislation to providing education and training for trade unions and employer groups, the ILO is regularly engaged in promoting freedom of association. The ILO's Committee on Freedom of Association was set up in 1951 to examine violations of workers' and employers' organizing rights ... Through the Committee on Freedom of Association and other supervisory mechanisms, the ILO has frequently defended rights of trade unions and employers' organizations.[18]

Within the EU, it is regarded as good practice in all workplaces, that workers have clearly defined rights:

> The adoption of legislation setting minimum requirements has improved labour standards and strengthened workers' rights and is one of European Union's main achievements in the field of social policy.[19]

So far I have discussed a range of views about what constitutes good management, and what safeguards can be put in place in case management fails. A key issue has been worker's voice, the extent to which staff have an independent avenue to express their interests and concerns, especially if they disagree with their managers. Within some international organizations – the ILO and the EU especially – it is regarded as good or essential practice, a component of a good quality service. But it is rarely, if ever, included or considered in discussions about leadership and management in the books I have cited.

Management theory

Critical reviews of the literature on management point to a dearth of theory and empirical evidence.[20,21] Much of the work on leadership and management is intuitive, a view of personal attributes successful leaders appear to show, rather than a critical account of the tasks undertaken. One management theorist who has attracted a great deal of attention in academic circles for his originality and his striking metaphors is the Finnish activity theorist Yrjö Engeström.[22] He has built on earlier work by Russian theorists, such as Leontev and Vygotsky, to suggest that leadership is situational. He argues that leadership itself is a misnomer. Getting things done is a social interaction in relation to specific tasks or activities undertaken in specific social contexts. Depending on the context, some approaches and some solutions work better than others; it is only possible to find this out empirically.

Engeström has worked in various workplace settings including a hospital clinic and a care home for elderly people. He argues that change and conflict are intrinsic to the workplace. Workers, whether professional and highly skilled, or unskilled, are always being presented with new and difficult problems, or recurring problems that don't seem to go away. This is especially the case in organizations where different groups of professionals come together, each with a different take on the problem, and a different set of responsibilities in relation to it. The problem tends to get bandied about between them without being resolved. For example, there might be a very difficult client presenting multiple problems which no one person can deal with. What often happens is that the client gets cast aside and ignored as being too difficult to deal with – in Engeström's word, becomes 'rubbish'. He argues that it only through dealing with intractable problems that the organization moves on and reassesses its activities and processes. He calls this process 'de-knotting'.[23]

Engeström is not an easy read, and his books and papers are peppered with complicated diagrams elaborating the stages of his theoretical approach. His work, although not dealing directly with education, has been fairly widely taken up by academic educationalists. But there are two empirical early childhood studies that suggest activity theory may provide a useful interpretative framework for service delivery.

Angela Anning carried out a study of two 'Centres of Excellence' (one of the many short-lived initiatives in England attempting to develop new interprofessional ways of working in the early years). She tried to explore how staff

changed their minds or developed their thinking in relation to 'critical incidents'. Staff were presented with vignettes representing conflicts and complexities in the delivery of services and asked how they would deal with them.
These included child sexual behaviour, grandparent gender (stereotyping),
and curriculum changes. She found that

> early years practitioners [are being asked] to operate at a highly sophis-
> ticated level in juggling the demands of their traditional, professional
> values/beliefs with each other, and at the same time with those of
> their host communities.[24]

The critical incidents revealed how difficult staff found it to change or adapt
their long-held beliefs, especially when there were also governmental expectations about what they should be doing. At the very least their attempts needed
to be documented so that there was some kind of real evidence and meaningful
theoretical framework to understand how they were coping in response to the
difficult situations that they encountered.[25]

Carol Aubrey and her team explored a group of 12 nurseries which were
recommended by local inspectors as providing a good quality service. But the
nurseries themselves were very different and so were the tasks carried out in
them.[26] Three were private nurseries, two were family centres provided by voluntary agencies, four were nursery and reception classes catering for 3–4 year
olds, and three were integrated children's centres. The leaders were asked to
keep video diaries of a 'typical' day, and all other staff were invited to contribute to a questionnaire (a 68 per cent response rate). Policies were often unach-
ievable in the context in which the leaders were working. The scale of the
organization – numbers of children, parent support, the qualifications and
experience of the staff who were recruited, the agencies involved, and the overall staffing levels – influenced the degree of specialization, delegation and distribution of leadership. In the three private nurseries in the study, for instance,
the managers were preoccupied with administrative tasks such as collection of
fees, arranging staffing rotas and so on. In the nursery and reception classes,
the leaders were almost entirely involved in high intensity interactions with
children. Leaders were variously guides, motivators, strategists and entrepre-
neurial. As with Anning's study, the leaders were committed to taking on
board the latest government policies, but were unclear what these policies
might mean in their practice, or how their practice might need to change as a
result.

This study too fitted the notion of 'distributed leadership'. In situations, as
in the UK, where there are very many different kinds of provision (and this is
certainly *not* the case in most European countries, where there are standard
and easily understood models of provision) it makes sense to think of leadership as the emergent property of a group or network of interacting individuals.

Capabilities and expertise are distributed across many in the organization (although this is not necessarily reflected in pay and hierarchical position within the organization). The study concludes that

> everything points to the need for continuing professional and inter-professional education and development as an effective means to create leaders and learning communities that are responsive to the needs of co-workers.[27]

Neither of these studies however considered pay and conditions – a key reason why people apply for jobs in the first place. The notion of 'fairness' in the distribution of tasks in the workplace, or conversely, exploitation, in asking staff to undertake jobs and work hours for which they are not sufficiently well recognized or renumerated, is not raised. Yet this is what trades unions deal with all the time.

Karen Evans and her colleagues have undertaken a series of studies on workplace learning, showing how workplace learning can be improved if close attention is paid to the relationship between organizational context, individual worker biographies, and regulatory frameworks.[28] She too argues that situated learning theories downplay the power structures in the workplace, and the regulatory conditions which shape working practices, by regarding them as benign or neutral, rather than a framing issue.

Where does inspired leadership fit in?

The discussion in this chapter has focused on management models of practice. As ever, context shapes what is done. Very occasionally an individual nursery with a visionary and articulate leader makes an exceptional impact. In Scotland in 1818 at New Lanark, Robert Owen made such a mark with his nursery that visitors flocked from many countries to visit it. Margaret McMillan achieved a similar iconic status with her nursery in Deptford in London in the 1920s. In the 1950s visitors came to Evelina Lowe school in Southwark, also in London, to see David Medd's revolutionary new building and the Piagetian ideas which it incorporated. In England now Pen Green Centre in Corby is a small Mecca for early childhood practitioners. But however inspiring these examples may be, they are contingent on the efforts of one or two people, and not embedded in the system. The question is how initiatives which break new ground can be recognized, encouraged, supported, monitored and extended. As this book has been at pains to point out, quality provision is not timeless or contextless and imperfectly reflected in government standards. Ideally ideas about quality are changed, refined and documented within a community of practice. This means that ideas are *consistently* shared and extended over time (a good deal of time) within a group of practitioners and pedagogues, in response to the wider context in which they operate.

In small countries, like Iceland or New Zealand, it is reasonable for this recognition of good practice to be a government task. But in large countries with large populations, it is more or less impossible for centralized governments to hone in on local initiatives, to understand, develop and promote them, to *embed* them. This needs to be done at a local level. As we have seen, it has been the municipality or the city authority in the famous nurseries in Reggio Emilia, San Miniato,[29] and so on, that have been able to provide this support for local practice, and enabled what was once an innovative idea to grow and develop over many years into a well-thought-out comprehensive, and internationally admired system of early education and care. Northern Italy is an exceptional example (and not a national one) but in Nordic countries, for example, responsibility for shaping services is devolved to local authorities, within a secure framework of government policy and funding. With this balance of national and local, the work of brilliant individual initiatives is less likely to peter out and can be incorporated into local practice by supportive local authorities. Devolution can be a risk, but if there is also a national framework and funding for ECEC, maverick local authorities, who do little to promote such services, still have to toe the line and provide a minimum.

Ideas of leadership too need a rethink. Where there are many diverse kinds of situations where children are educated and cared for, generic leadership skills may not be appropriate. Depending on the type of organization, the job is simply different. It has different priorities, and different requirements.

Notes

1 Briggs, M. and Briggs, I. (2009) *Developing Your Leadership in the Early Years*. London: Continuum.

Jones, C. and Pound, L. (2008) *Leadership and Management in the Early Years*. Maidenhead: Open University Press.

Moyles, J. (2006) *Effective Leadership and Management in the Early Years*. Maidenhead: Open University Press.

O'Sullivan, J. (2009) *Leadership Skills in the Early Years*. Stafford: Network Continuum Education.

Rodd, J. (2006) *Leadership in Early Childhood: The Pathway to Professionalism*. Maidenhead: Open University Press.

Whalley, M. (2008) *Leading Practice in Early Years Settings*. Exeter: Learning Matters.

2 Whalley, M., Whitaker, P., Fletcher, C., Thorpe, S., John, K. and Leisten, R. (2004) *Programme Leaders Guide: National Professional Qualification in Integrated Centre Leadership*. Nottingham: National College of School Leadership.

Department for Children, Schools and Families (DCSF) (2007) *Primary National Strategy: Developing Quality through Leadership: Action Research in Private, Voluntary and Independent Sector Early Years Settings*. London: DCSF.

3 Talan, T.N. and Bloom, P.J. (2004) *Program Administration Scale – Measuring Early Childhood Leadership and Management*. New York: Teachers College Press.

4 Siraj-Blatchford, I. and Manni, L. (2008) *Effective Leadership in the Early Years Sector*. London: Institute of Education, University of London, p. 28.

5 Bloom, P.J. and Clark, D. (2007) 'Administration of early care and education programs.' In R. New and M. Cochran (eds) *Early Childhood Education: An International Encyclopedia*. Westport, CT: Greenwood, vol. 2, pp. 307–313. The quotation is from p. 308.

6 Faulkner, K., chairman, Working Links (Welfare to Work Programme). *Society Guardian* 3 February 2010, p. 5.

7 In the USA the corporate market accounts for approximately 40 per cent of provision; in the UK about 8 per cent; in Australia, until recently, about 40 per cent.

8 Kirschenbaum, L. (2001) *Small Comrades: Revolutionizing Childhood in Soviet Russia, 1917–1932*. London: Routledge.

9 Mozère, L. (1992) *Le Printemps des crèches: Histoire et analyse d'un mouvement*. Paris: L'Harmattan.

10 Saraceno, C. (1977) *Experiencia y Teoria de las Comunas Infantiles*. Barcelona: Fontanella.

11 Hoyuelos, A. (2004) *La etica en el pensamiento y obra pedagogica de Loris Malaguzzi*. Barcelona: Rosa Sensat.

12 Dahlberg, G. and Moss, P. (2005) *Ethics and Politics in Early Childhood Education*. London: Routledge.

13 McCalla, D., Grover, C. and Penn, H. (2001) *Local Nurseries for Local Communities*. London: National Children's Bureau.

14 I described how these collective nurseries work in Italy and Spain in Penn, H. (1997) *Comparing Nurseries*. London: Paul Chapman. This book is now dated, especially the English nurseries which are described in it; the Spanish nurseries have also changed. But the book does give some idea of how these collective settings operated on a daily basis.

15 Penn, *Comparing Nurseries*, p. 82.

16 Penn, *Comparing Nurseries*, p. 38.

17 Swedish Ministry of Education and Science (1998a) *Curriculum for the Preschool*. Stockholm: Fritzes.

Swedish Ministry of Education and Science (1998b) *Curriculum for the Compulsory School System, the Preschool Class and the Leisure-time Centre* (Lpo94/98). Stockholm: Fritzes.

18 See www.ilo.org/global/Themes/Freedom_of_Association_and_the_Right_to_Collective_Bargaining/lang—en/index.htm

19 The EU Directorate of Employment, Social Affairs and Equal Opportunities devotes part of its website to explaining about European labour law. This

quotation is taken from the website: http://ec.europa.eu/social/main.jsp?langId=en&catId=82

20 Dunlop, A.W. (2008) *A Literature Review on Leadership in the Early Years*. Edinburgh: Scottish Government.

21 Aubrey, C. (2007) *Leading and Managing in the Early Years*. London: Sage.

22 Engeström, Y., Miettinen, R. and Punamäki-Gitai, R.L. (1999) *Perspectives on Activity Theory: Learning in Doing. Social, Cognitive and Computational Perspectives*. Cambridge: Cambridge University Press.

23 Engeström, Y. (2008) *Teams to Knots: Activity-Theoretical Studies of Collaboration and Learning at Work*. Cambridge: Cambridge University Press.

24 Anning, A. (2005) 'Investigating the impact of working in multi-agency service delivery settings in the UK on early years practitioners' beliefs and practices.' *Journal of Early Childhood Research* 3(1): 19–50.

25 Anning, 'Investigating the impact of working in multi-agency service delivery settings in the UK.'

26 Aubrey, C. (2007) *Leading and Managing in Early Years Settings*. London: Sage.

27 Aubrey, *Leading and Managing in Early Years Settings*, p. 139.

28 Evans, K., Hodkinson, P., Rainbird, H. and Unwin, L. (2006) *Improving Workplace Learning*. London: Routledge.

29 Bloomer, K. and Cohen, B. (2008) *Young Children in Charge*. Edinburgh: Children in Scotland.

9 In the (class) room

By the time we get down to considering the interactions between teachers and carers and the groups of children for whom they are responsible, the story of quality is more than half told. The nurseries are established within a policy and regulatory framework set by the government or local authority. Those who work in nurseries have mostly gone through some form of required training, which, however minimal and unsatisfactory, outlines the skills that are required of them. Their working spaces are shaped by others; unless they are unionized, their pay is non-negotiable (no bonus culture here!). In some countries, if not others, they will be working in a very hierarchical environment. There are rules, more or less specific and controlled, about what they can teach or how they can practise and what they are expected to achieve. The children who come to the nursery, their vulnerabilities, their circumstances, the length of their daily stay, how much or how little their parents must pay, these too are beyond the control of ordinary practitioners. The only thing which can be changed is how the person does her job on a daily basis, within those constraints. In some ways it makes sense for discussions of quality, as they most often do, to focus on the micro-issues of intent and behaviour of adults and children, separately and/or together. In this chapter I discuss some ideas about what good quality practice is in working directly with young children.

But before I engage in general discussion, I want to give an example – a personal one from outside of the classroom.

A breakfast conversation

My granddaughter Nobantu, who is 5 at the time of writing, stays with us one night a week. Brooding on how adults understand and communicate with children, and vice versa, I decided to record our ordinary breakfast time conversation – although I am reconstructing it from notes and it is not a verbatim tape-recording. She has spent the weekend with her Uncle Fritz, her

Aunt Sarah (known in the family as Lady Sarah) and her two young cousins. Nobantu refused the black pudding on offer for breakfast and opted for cornflakes.

N. You know I don't like black pudding.

H. It tastes like sausages. Uncle Fritz likes black pudding.

N. It's easy to get them muddled up. I call them Uncle Sarah and Lady Fritz.

H. Uncle Sarah! Lady Fritz! They don't look like each other.
There are noises upstairs where grandpa is rustling around in his room.

N. This is a noise-through house.

H. It's a different shape from your house. Your house is tall and thin, with the rooms on top of one another so you can't hear what goes on. This house is more open. Also grandpa is a very noisy person.

N. This house has got an attic. It's a tall house too. I heard grandpa snoring.

H. No, you were asleep.

N. He snores like this. Hrrumph . . .
Grandpa (appearing). It's Granny Helen who snores.

H. I'm coming to do your garden today.

N. I planted a toy and a toy tree came up. I planted an apple seed and an apple came up.

H. It takes a very long time for an apple seed to grow into a tree. You usually grow trees from cuttings. Like this cutting in the jar. Can you see its roots growing? (We look at the root system of the cutting in the jar) I'm going to plant this in your garden.

G. Would you like me to squeeze you some orange juice.

N. A blood orange.

G. Like a blood pudding. Black pudding is made of blood.

N. The orange juice isn't *real* blood. It's only the same colour as blood. Look at my muscles (rolling up her sleeve and flexing her arm). I've got muscles in my arm too, I can squeeze.

H. Terrific muscles.

N. Elsie (her cousin) said I'm so strong I can lift bricks. I'm going to be an entomologist *and* a builder when I grow up.

H. Did you see any bugs when you went to the park? (a school trip last week to the nature reserve in the local park)

N. I saw the chips on the path.

H. The wood chips?

N. The wood chips from the chopped up Christmas trees. I saw a stag beetle.

H. A stag beetle with horns? (I get the beetle book down and find a picture of a stag beetle)

G. We found a stag beetle in the garden once.

N. I saw three big stag beetles and three little ones.

H. Did your teacher see them too? Shall I ask her about them?

N. Just tricked you. I didn't really see any.

This gives a flavour of the conversation, which also went on to include a discussion about 'g' language, that is how to say words with a g in the middle so no one else could understand them, and another discussion about chocolate on toast. It is a meandering conversation, with many contextual references, drawing on memories of past events and understandings. We take apparent jumps from one topic to another, jumps which can be understood only because of the shared context. It is playful – we all tease one another. It's an attempt to conceptualize certain problems – how sound travels, the nature of physical strength. Going over the conversation, I see I am over intentioned, and anxious to capitalize on the knowledge-bearing aspects of the conversation (stag beetles – the entomology is an old joke – and rooted cuttings) but my granddaughter affectionately manoeuvres her way past my didacticism. Discourse analysis, the detailed examination of speech and the conceptual analysis of the use of words, inflections and pauses would probably reveal still more.[1] Anyhow, it's a real conversation, it lasts half an hour over breakfast, and like any good conversation, it is relaxed, stimulating, witty, reciprocal and enjoyable.

The point of reproducing this conversation here is to illustrate its complexity, embeddedness and mutuality, its playfulness with words. It may be an inescapably middle-class – and television-free – conversation, but it is also in many ways typical. Barbara Tizard in the 1980s compared children's conversations at home and at nursery school; whatever the social class of the child, the conversations at home were invariably richer, because of the importance of context and reciprocity.[2] It would be impossible for my granddaughter to have a long conversation like this in a classroom, within a group of busy children vying for attention with a teacher or practitioner. For all the claims about reciprocal relationships with families, a teacher or carer could not possibly have the knowledge of context that makes such a conversation possible. It is also unlikely that a postmodern approach based on 'the 100 languages of children' would have elicited a similar conversation. It would be very exceptional indeed for teachers and children to have long and reciprocal conversations. My granddaughter could probably have conversations a little like this with her friends, but even then, the conversations would be less rich, and have fewer memories to draw upon. Teachers and carers do a lot, but they also need to be modest about the reach of their involvement with the children with whom they work.

How do practitioners understand child development?

Learning relationships are mainly the domain of psychologists. How and what young children learn, how this varies with age, what stimulates learning and what inhibits it, how language shapes learning, how learning is assessed and measured: this is the stuff of child development. There are disagreements about the scope and content of child development, and there are some very senior renegades,[3] but it is an industry. Globally, the *most* influential, popular and most often cited application of child development to learning is the National Association for the Education of Young Children (NAEYC) manual *Developmentally Appropriate Practice [DAP] in Early Childhood Programs*, now in its third edition.[4] This is a series of practical guidelines for practitioners distilled from and relatively uncritical of psychological research, about how to care for and educate young children. It is an easily understandable guide, drawing from published research to substantiate its claims for particular types of practice. It is used as the basis for many accreditation programmes, including that provided by NAEYC. As well as being a standard reference in the USA, it is also used, for example, by many international non-governmental organizations (INGOs) to inform their work in the Global South.[5]

But DAP originated in the USA, and was designed to serve the mainly for-profit market in that country. It is meant to improve practice which it assumes (an assumption based on good evidence!) will be delivered by poorly trained workers and will be mediocre if not bad. It suggests straightforwardly what ordinary activities are most suitable for each age group of children, and what practitioners should be doing to promote these activities, since they may not know about these basics already. The third edition even includes a brief discussion of the USA policy context, although it does not refer to any non-USA contexts, and it does not comment at all on the venial nature of the for-profit market. DAP is summarized on the NAEYC website in this way:

Knowledge must inform decision-making: This knowledge is codified into 12 developmental principles.

1   All the domains of development and learning – physical, social and emotional, and cognitive – are important, and they are closely inter-related. Children's development and learning in one domain influence and are influenced by what takes place in other domains.
2   Many aspects of children's learning and development follow well-documented sequences, with later abilities, skills, and knowledge building on those already acquired.
3   Development and learning proceed at varying rates from child to child, as well as at uneven rates across different areas of a child's individual functioning.
4   Development and learning result from a dynamic and continuous interaction of biological maturation and experience.
5   Early experiences have profound effects, both cumulative and delayed, on a child's development and learning; and optimal periods exist for certain types of development and learning to occur.

6   Development proceeds toward greater complexity, self-regulation, and symbolic or representational capacities.

7   Children develop best when they have secure, consistent relationships with responsive adults and opportunities for positive relationships with peers.

8   Development and learning occur in and are influenced by multiple social and cultural contexts.

9   Always mentally active in seeking to understand the world around them, children learn in a variety of ways; a wide range of teaching strategies and interactions are effective in supporting all these kinds of learning.

10   Play is an important vehicle for developing self-regulation as well as for promoting language, cognition, and social competence.

11   Development and learning advance when children are challenged to achieve at a level just beyond their current mastery, and also when they have many opportunities to practise newly acquired skills.

12   Children's experiences shape their motivation and approaches to learning, such as persistence, initiative, and flexibility; in turn, these dispositions and behaviors affect their learning and development.

Goals must be challenging and achievable, and good teaching must be intentional: good teachers translate the developmentally appropriate practice framework into high-quality experiences for children through the decisions they make. They do this by:

1   Creating a caring community of learners
2   Teaching to enhance development and learning
3   Planning curriculum to achieve important goals
4   Assessing children's development and learning
5   Establishing reciprocal relationships with families.

DAP, like other practice guides, draws on a number of widely shared developmental assumptions about learning. First, children's needs, preferences and abilities crucially vary with age; a 6-month-old child will only be able to play with some objects and not others; an 18-month-old child can manage a different range of objects, and understand a different range of instructions; and a 36-month-old child will have different capabilities and understanding again. Age-related learning is a fundamental principle in providing for children. 'Quality' provision recognizes the importance of age-based learning.

Second, children may be in the same room together but they learn essentially as solitary individuals. Designing learning opportunities around individuality is a second fundamental principle of developmentally appropriate practice. Not only is individuality important, but also it is essentially expressed in the ownership, usage and consumption of physical objects. If a child wants something and is determined to get it, competitive pushy behaviour is not necessarily inappropriate (as it might appear in other cultures) but an essential aspect of individuality. Individuality is expressed by making choices between things, and since there are often not enough things to go round, children have to adopt strategies for getting what they want. 'Me first' is regarded as legitimate, if sometimes unpleasant, behaviour. Acquisitiveness and aggression are regarded as in some way natural, and indeed are praised as attributes in the competitive business world. Given this view of individuality, co-operative activities and sharing are regarded as unnatural, rather than as fundamentally human, and have to be worked at because 'learning how to share' is so difficult. The anthropologist Robert LeVine puts it powerfully like this:

> The American infant, unlike his African counterpart, has numerous possessions earmarked as belonging to him alone; their number and variety increase as he grows older, permitting him to experience the boundaries of his self represented in his physical environment . . . from infancy onwards, the child is encouraged to characterize himself in terms of his favourite toys and foods and those he dislikes; his tastes, aversions and consumer preferences are viewed not only as legitimate but essential aspects of his growing individuality – a prized quality of an independent person.[6]

Because individuality is so much tied up with having things, and making choices between them, children's learning is best enhanced in a resource-rich environment – having lots of toys to play with (even if they are predominantly garish manufactured toys made of plastic). The right to ownership is sacrosanct. So nurseries are in one sense battlefields, where children and those caring for them and teaching them must both acknowledge and reconcile 'natural' and 'individual' desires to compete, succeed and grab, with communal goals to share and learn together.

A third fundamental principle of DAP is the crucial role of the adult in children's learning and behaviour. Adults have a particular role to play as empathetic and attentive carers. Children's learning is governed and paced by appropriate adult interventions, by their praise, affirmation and verbalization of particular kinds of actions by the children. Practitioners must be 'intentional'; they must have a clear idea of what they are trying to achieve. They are in charge of the learning process. Conversely the implicit notion of the child at the heart of the process is that children need to be both stimulated and protected by adults to *become* fully functioning human beings. The young child is an incompetent half creature at the beginning of a long process of being moulded and shaped by adults.[7]

Not surprisingly there have been many critiques of DAP. It was designed to raise practice from the abysmal to the tolerable. It represents a professional consensus about working with young children and was designed as a practical talking point. But however well intentioned it may be, and however discursive the latest edition, it is also said to be simplistic, and culturally insensitive. It offers formulaic solutions.[8] More damningly, since it is supposed to be predicated on 'scientific' psychology, the application of DAP also appears to have no direct impact on later child outcomes. Research by Sharon Ramey (of Abecedarian fame) and M. Lee Van Horn followed up children coming from Head Start nurseries and projects that had adopted DAP, and found no difference between them and their school contemporaries at ages 6–8.[9]

DAP is the best established and well known of these guides to good practice. But it is an American tale not a European one, although there are recognizable overlaps. Good practice frameworks and guidelines in many countries may draw on a different context and content, but promote similar kinds of expert ideas about the right way to proceed in looking after young children – and in achieving the elusive balance between individuality and co-operation. For example, Ferre Laevers, working in Flanders, Belgium, has devised the 'Leuven Involvement Scale', which is also used quite widely in the UK, as part of the Effective Early Learning Project.[10] This is based on the concept of 'deep-level learning' and is a five-point rating scale to measure children's emotional well-being and involvement. This claims to be a process orientated scale – perhaps because in Flanders all provision for children aged 3 years and over is provided in the state education system in schools, and structural issues are dealt with at a national level. Laevers proposes 'Ten Action Points' for teachers, highlighting the initiatives that favour well-being and involvement. These are:

- Rearrange the classroom in appealing corners or areas
- Check the content of the corners and replace unattractive materials by more appealing ones
- Introduce new and unconventional materials and activities
- Observe children, discover their interests and find activities that meet these orientations
- Support ongoing activities through stimulating impulses and enriching interventions
- Widen the possibilities for free initiative and support them with sound rules and agreements
- Explore the relation with each of the children and between children and try to improve it
- Introduce activities that help children to explore the world of behaviour, feelings and values
- Identify children with emotional problems and work out sustaining interventions

- Identify children with developmental needs and work out the interventions that engender involvement within the problem area.[11]

This is practical if over-simple advice; you would probably do more good by
following it than not following it. It says more about the rigidity of the system
for which it was originally intended, than offering new insights into classroom
relationships. It implies a view of teachers and teaching in which the teacher
holds all the tricks. But essentially it too draws on the assumption that there is
a magic formula to teaching and learning.

There are many such magic formulae, and the best-sellers, like High Scope
for example, claim that their programme advice has been distilled from
detached and objective application of universal criteria. DAP offers the strong-
est statement that there is a body of undisputed scientific research findings
about the development of young children which will hold good whatever
the children's circumstances and wherever in the world the children are. To
apply those findings systematically is a guarantee of quality. Practitioners need
only to plug into 'ages and stages' and other scientific advice, to do their
job well.

Context and culture

The 'science' of child development is of course an illusion. There may be some
kind of current consensus on very general points of knowledge in child development – although this differs from country to country – but this does not
amount to a systematic and coherent body of knowledge, which leads to pre-
dictable outcomes. People might wish child development had more in common with physics, but it doesn't! One of the most serious omissions of most
guides to good practice is that context and culture are consistently under-
explored and underestimated in the child development literature.[12] I discuss
this in more detail in Chapter 10.

One of the people cited in Chapter 10 is an African educationalist who
took a very firm view about the extent to which she thought that Anglo-
European ideas about childhood were self-indulgent. She was informed by the
African notion of *ubuntu*, or mutual reciprocity, the idea of a common humanity with a common obligation to live together. She felt that children, even very
young children, had obligations to their elders, much as we might have obligations to them. When my colleague Trisha Maynard and I interviewed her, she
raised the question for us about whether we expect too little of children, and
indulge their selfishness and self-regard at the expense of others?[13] There are
fundamental differences in children's behaviour and actions in relation to the
groups and societies to which they belong, and there is little evidence in the
literature that these deep differences have been recognized or acknowledged.

Culture and context, fragmentary and changeable as they may appear, present profound challenges.

Alternative views of childhood have been given additional impetus by the UN Convention on the Rights of the Child (UNCRC). This international definition of the rights of children has prompted a considerable body of sociological, historical and legal work, which challenges a future orientated view of childhood, and downplays age as the key variable in understanding children. The present is more important than the future; children live in the present not in some far off future they can barely comprehend, and it is their present comfort and woes that need addressing. From this perspective it is young children's *capacities* which are acknowledged, their active and ingenious construction of the world around them. The intensity of children's feelings and the depth of their relationships matter to them as they would to any adult. From a UNCRC perspective, children should have as much a direct voice as possible. The considerable scholarship, in many disciplines, which has followed on from UNCRC, in academic journals, books, in research methodologies, and so on, is not reflected, or even mentioned in the NAEYC documentation.

Postmodern perspectives

The most sustained critique that has been mounted against these ideas about universality and quality has come from postmodernism. Postmodern critics working in the field of early education and care object to the 'grand narratives' of universalism and positivism, the idea that science can sort everything out, very soon, if not now. Research on the components of quality is not nearly as clear cut as it appears. From a postmodern point of view, professional 'experts' draw simplistically on research, to advise practitioners about how to interact with children. Experts derive their credibility from 'discourses of power' or 'dominant paradigms' or 'regimes of truth', ideas which appear to be so powerful and obvious that it is hard to disagree with them. But strongly normative advice takes away the possibility of critical and thought and analysis from practitioners, who in turn demoralize the children they work with who have to fit into the puppet outline expected of them. The only role open to practitioners is as 'technicians' whose job it is to carry out the practices defined by experts; the children are the manipulated bit performers.

Postmodernists point to the failure of experts (although usually without naming them or their work) in acknowledging complexity, diversity, ambiguity and uncertainty. The postmodern world is an uneasy place, and postmodernists take profound unease as their starting point. Apparently simple ideas and issues need to be 'problematized' to show how they implicitly draw on discourses of power. The theorists that postmodernists most often refer to are the French philosopher Michel Foucault (who coined the phrase 'regimes of truth'), Gilles

Deleuze (another French philosopher) and Félix Guattari (a French psychoanalyst). Deleuze and Guattari view all encounters between people as incredibly fluid and never the same twice. Recognition of this extreme fluidity or 'singularity' has to be the starting point for any work on relationships.

Postmodernists working in early childhood highlight the importance of privileging children's viewpoints. The postmodern perspective in early childhood emphasizes the 'construction of meaning' by children, the 'rich possibilities' that arise when children can initiate their own activities and follow them through, without oppressive interference from teachers intentioned on imposing their own meanings and shaping children in their own image. The 'pedagogical philosophy' of the municipal nurseries in Reggio Emilia, the '100 languages of children', is usually taken as the outstanding example of a postmodern approach, even though the nurseries operate in very stable conditions and within traditions that are centuries old. Giving children autonomy in turn becomes a model and a metaphor for the role of the nursery itself; it too can lead the way for a new kind of citizenship, a 'democratic space' where new 'democratic practices' can be forged (an uphill job you might say in Berlusconi's Italy!).[14]

But this emphasis on children's own meaning making and autonomy paradoxically downplays the context in which children find themselves. I have been arguing throughout this book that the policy rationales for and the structures of early childhood services make a great deal of difference to what happens on a daily basis when children are looked after by others. For postmodernists, indeed for many people who work with young children, this is an irrelevance. Practice itself is transformational; this is where progress happens and where attention must be focused. The 'ethics of the encounter' is a postmodern phrase, derived from yet another French philosopher, Emmanuel Levinas,[15] and is used to describe the responsibility of the adult to behave with great consideration in each encounter with another person or 'the other'.

As is probably obvious, I am sympathetic to some of the claims of postmodernism in early childhood. There is much that is troubling about the ways in which we understand and interpret young children's needs and capacities. But whatever the kernel of truth it contains postmodernism has in turn become a jargon ridden cult, or as Noam Chomsky described it 'pretentious rhetoric.' He writes 'my eyes glaze over when I read polysyllabic discourse on the themes of poststructuralism and postmodernism'.[16] He is not alone in his exasperation! Here is an especially dense extract from a published account of a postmodern analysis of an attempt to introduce outcome measures for a new early childhood programme in Canada.

> ECE (Early childhood education) subjects are, to borrow concepts from Deleuze & Guattari (1987), becoming more *rhizomatic* than *arborescent*. I equate arborescence to disciplinary societies and rhizomatics to control societies. Following Deleuze & Guattari's botanical

analogy, arborescence functions like a tree where all branches extend from a central root. The disciplinary subject operates this way where all movement (the branches) refers back to the subject itself (the root). We see this in the ab/normalization of subjects that are individualized through spaces and tasks: everything that they do refers back to them, whether it is their test scores or their ability to read and write by a certain age. Rhizomes function like grass, where the blades grow in infinite directions with no reference to a central root. . . . Power is territorialized in arborescence, where it is centrally located in formal hierarchies such as federal governments and ministries of education that prescribe the actions of ECE subjects. It is deterritorialized in rhizomatics, where subjects are controlled through the flows of knowledge and information.[17]

The baby has been thrown out with the bathwater, the baby being science – the method of systematic inquiry, description and comparison (and one might add clarity of language).[18] Science may not have a 'monopoly on truth' but some positions are much more tenable than others. Rational discussion – teasing out the inconsistencies in a position through critical scrutiny and by avoiding unnecessary jargon – is the only way to compare, reconcile or rank competing concerns, even if the decision to adopt one course or another is only provisional. Decisions about priorities have to be made all the time so how are those decisions made if not on the basis of critical reasoning and empirical results? As the philosopher Amartya Sen puts it, we need to be able to 'communicate, respond and altercate'.[19] Postmodernism, as it is used in the field of early childhood, is simply too fuzzy in its claims to a special kind of understanding, and in the language it uses to describe those claims. I return to this point in Chapter 11, when I discuss methods of evaluation of quality and questions about 'what works'.

Quality practice

What then should teachers and practitioners of young children be doing if the guides to practice aren't very good guides, and if the idea of a guide itself is suspect?

In the section on training in Chapter 6 I pointed out that the research, for all its limitations and caveats, does indicate that the highest quality provision for young children occurs when the staff are highly trained. For children over 3 years at least, the results appear to be better if the staff are trained as teachers, that is people whose job it is to promote children's learning. Intellectual training equips people to deal with abstract ideas and problems; vocational training is usually more basic and more didactic, a question of following rules. My breakfast conversation is a lesson that children are nothing if not enquiring, expanding their conceptual ideas at a great rate and playing around with them. They need grist for their mill. The writer Lilian Katz expresses this in her book *Intellectual Emergencies*, where she argues for an ability to recognize the challenges children continuously throw up, and the wit to deal with them.[20]

Another view of teaching or pedagogy is that young children should also have the chance to encounter interesting people who have independent skills and interests in their own right – as a dancer, a painter, a singer, a photographer, a poet, a carpenter, an embroiderer, a gardener, as a person who has a skilled repertoire of her or his own. Children need to encounter real people, not ciphers, to come across real skills and to live and work together with adults. As outlined in previous chapters, this is the idea behind the Danish pedagogical training,[21] the 'atelierista' of the Reggio Emilia nurseries,[22] or some of the artist in residence schemes described in the Children in Scotland booklet *Picture This*.[23]

When knowledge is regarded as something to transmit – or where circumstances are difficult – teaching is valued as performance. Some of the best teaching I have ever seen – in the sense of capturing audience attention – has been in a kindergarten in Nanjing in China. The teacher was working to a highly prepared curriculum,[24] in which the outcomes of the learning – the children's ability to repeat the messages of the lesson – was already prescribed. The teacher was like a brilliant actress, performing a story, with lines scripted for her. The film star quality of the teacher is partly what we mean by the idea of a role model; someone whose behaviour is so special that we want to imitate it. This Chinese teacher was not unique – I came across many teachers like her, presumably a reflection of the training they had received. But if knowledge is regarded as participative and co-constructed, additional or different skills are required. Being ingenious and inspiring in finding topics and projects and resources in working with children and vividly explaining them is only half the story. The other half of course is to be able to relate to the children themselves, to be able to listen, to enable them to voice their situations and enlarge their understanding.

Working together

Everyone has to move on with the times, to draw on contemporary resources and to keep abreast of contemporary culture from programmes like *CBeebies* or *Sesame Street*, or follow computer games. Even young children are not immune to pop idols or sports heroes. My granddaughter tucks her pink pop idol magazines alongside her the reading scheme book in her school bag. Despite the Pinkstinks campaign,[25] her teacher would be unfeeling to ignore her favourite icons. So how much freedom to innovate and experiment and relate to children's immediate interests is there, especially when one might feel disapproving of their passions? As well as being performers, empathizers, comforters and reciprocal thinkers

– already a tall order, especially for poorly paid and low-skilled staff – teachers and carers are also guides, giving some kind of moral compass to children. The difficulty in doing this is that, like my granddaughter, children are inextricably tied into their particular domestic contexts, and for many children this is a world away from their institutional life. Deliberately or not nurseries and schools offer very different sets of experiences to children, and the jury is still out on how and if these different worlds can be reconciled. It is an aim of most kinds of services to work with parents and families, but, to borrow a postmodern phrase, the aim has not been problematized, despite the very good work being done,[26] a point I return to briefly in Chapter 12.

Notes

1 Wetherell, M., Taylor, S. and Yates, S. (eds) (2001) *Discourse as Data: A Guide to Analysis*. London: Sage.
2 Tizard, B. (1984) *Young Children Learning: Talking and Thinking at Home and at School*. London: Fontana.
3 Jerome Kagan at Harvard University has always been highly sceptical of many of the traditional claims of developmental psychology. Two of his books debunk ideas about brain development, early nurturance and the objectivity of psychological investigations:
  Kagan, J. (1984) *The Nature of the Child*. New York: Basic Books.
  Kagan, J. (1998) *Three Seductive Ideas*. Cambridge, MA: Harvard University Press.
4 Bredekamp, S. and Copple, C. (eds) (1997) *Developmentally Appropriate Practice in Early Childhood Programs*. Washington, DC: National Association for the Education of Young Children. This influential document was republished in 2009 in its third edition, and comes with an accompanying position statement from NAEYC.
5 For instance, *Developmentally Appropriate Practice in Early Childhood Programs* is a linchpin for World Bank projects in early child development.
6 LeVine, R. (2003) *Childhood Socialization: Comparative Studies of Parenting, Learning and Educational Change*. Hong Kong: Comparative Education Research Centre, University of Hong Kong, p. 95.
7 Practitioners working with young children are often drawn from a pool of women who have not done well at school, for whom childcare is 'natural'; but such practitioners, who perceive themselves as powerless, get an especial satisfaction from being able to influence young children and exercise power over them. See Vincent, C. and Braun, A. (2010) 'And hairdressers are quite seedy . . . the moral worth of childcare training.' *Contemporary Issues in Early Childhood* forthcoming.
8 Hatch, A., Bowman, B., Jor'dan, J., Morgan, C., Diaz Solo, L., Lubeck, S. and Hyson, M. (2002) 'Developmentally appropriate practice: Continuing the dialogue.' *Contemporary Issues in Early Childhood* 3(3): 439–457.

9 Van Horn, M.L. and Ramey, S.R. (2003) 'The effects of developmentally appropriate practices on academic outcomes among former Head Start students and classmates grades 1–3.' *American Educational Research Journal* 40(4): 961–990.

10 Pascal, E. and Bertram, T. (1995) 'Involvement and the Effective Early Learning Project: A collaborative venture.' In F. Laevers (ed.) *An Exploration of the Concept of 'Involvement' as an Indicator of the Quality of Early Childhood Education.* CIDREE Report vol. 10. Dundee: Consortium of Institutions for Development and Research in Education in Europe (CIDREE), pp. 25–28.

11 OECD (2004) *Starting Strong: Curricula and Pedagogies in Early Childhood Education and Care. Five Curriculum Outlines.* Workshop Report. Paris: OECD, p. 6.

12 See www.aaacig.org/

13 Penn, H. and Maynard, T. (2010) *Siyabonana: We All See Each Other. Building Better Childhoods in South Africa.* Edinburgh: Children in Scotland.

14 Dahlberg, G., Moss, P. and Pence, A. (1999) *Beyond Quality in Early Childhood Education and Care.* London: Routledge. This book and others in the Routledge *Contesting Early Childhood* series give a good indication of the range of work and thinking on postmodernism in early childhood.

15 Hutchens, B. (2004) *Levinas: A Guide for the Perplexed.* London: Continuum.

16 Chomsky, N. (1995) 'Rationality/science.' *Z Papers Special Issue.* See www.chomsky.info/articles/1995——02.htm. He writes, 'Quite regularly, "my eyes glaze over" when I read polysyllabic discourse on the themes of poststructuralism and postmodernism'.

17 Ruffalo, D. (2009) 'Queering child/hood policies: Canadian examples and perspectives.' *Contemporary Issues in Early Childhood* 10(3): 291–300.

18 It is also botanically inaccurate!

19 Sen, A. (2009) *The Idea of Justice.* London: Allen Lane, p. 415.

20 Katz, L. and Katz, S. (2009) *Intellectual Emergencies: Some Reflections on Mothering and Teaching.* Lewisville, NC: Kaplan Early Learning Company.

21 Petrie, P., Boddy, J., Cameron, C., Heptinstall, E., McQuail S., Simon, A. and Wigfall, V. (2009) *Pedagogy: A Holistic, Personal Approach to Work with Children and Young People across Services.* London: TCRU Briefing Paper.

22 Vecchi, V. (2010) *Art and Creativity in Reggio Emilia: Exploring the Role and Potential of Ateliers in Early Childhood Education.* London: Routledge.

23 Children in Scotland (2010) *Picture This: Celebrating Children and the Arts.* Edinburgh: Children in Scotland.

24 At that time in the early 1990s the Chinese early years curriculum ran to 18 volumes!

25 See www.pinkstinks.co.uk

26 The Family and Parenting Institute, for example, contains some very useful material and research summaries on how practitioners can work with parents: see www.earlyhomelearning.org.uk/practitioners

10 Exporting quality

We live in a globalizing world. That means all of us, consciously or not, depend on each other. Whatever we do or refrain from doing affects the lives of people who live in places we'll never visit. And whatever those distant people do or desist from doing has its impact on the conditions in which we, each one of us separately and together, conduct our lives. Living in a globalizing world means being aware of the pain, misery and suffering of countless people who we will never meet in person . . . there is an abysmal gap between the suffering we see and our ability to help the sufferers.[1]

This chapter deals with the idea of knowledge transfer. How do ideas and practices about quality in early childhood get transported from one part of the world to another, and what direction does the traffic go in? This question has cropped up already in other chapters in the book – in the discussion of culture and context in Chapter 9, for instance – and it is an inescapable question. I am especially interested in it because I have worked in a few very poor countries; the distance Zygmunt Bauman speaks about is a distance I have crossed. What constitutes quality when resources of all kinds are extremely meagre, as they are for *most* children in the world? What constitutes quality when ideas about childhood bear little resemblance to childhood in rich countries?

The Unesco 2007 Global Monitoring Report provided an excellent overview of the issues concerning early childhood education and care in poor countries.[2] It should be recommended reading for anyone who cares about the lives of young children worldwide. The report provides data on a variety of topics, including policies adopted, uptake, data collection and so on.[3] Providing information of this calibre, updated every year, requires international resources at a level that only an organization like Unesco can provide, with its offices in many countries. I have reproduced some of the information here. But essentially this chapter suggests, Unesco notwithstanding, there are distortions in the way quality in early childhood education and care in poor countries is commonly viewed.

Exporting inequality

In many rich or developed countries – the UK and USA being two prime examples – the inequality between rich and poor means that in practice, whatever the government rhetoric about equality of opportunity, the life chances of children are radically different. But this pales into insignificance besides the differences in life chances experienced by children living in poor countries – such as Africa, and large parts of South Asia for example – and those living in Europe and North America. The debate about the rights of the child, in particular necessarily implies thinking through equity issues at a macro-level; the rights of the child are about the rights of *all* children or they mean very little.[4]

Many writers, philosophers, ethicists, demographers – and even economists – have warned about the dangers of inequality. It is not just that there is a moral obligation to help others less fortunate than ourselves. It is a practical question, since the damage done to the poor is likely to rebound on the rich. Books and reports suggest that unequal societies which favour the rich are fundamentally uneconomic in the sense that they waste resources, especially human resources. The demographers Richard Wilkinson and Kate Pickett, in their book *The Spirit Level: Why More Equal Societies Almost Always do Better*,[5] argue that in unequal societies, the poor suffer worse physical and mental health, which means in the long run greater expense for a country's budget. The poor are more liable to be unhappy and resentful, which means there is more public disorder – more crime, more drunkenness, more drugs – resulting in higher policing and prison costs. The poor also tend to be badly educated, and fail to learn even the most basic literacy and numeracy skills. By contrast the most economically successful societies – as opposed to individuals – are the most egalitarian. Their crime costs are lower, their health is better, and their education systems produce better results – without the need for endless quality assurance mechanisms and measures of outcomes to determine who is failing. The OECD report *Growing Unequal: Income Distribution and Poverty in OECD Countries* takes a similar if more soberly stated position about inequality in the world's richest countries.[6] The Unesco EFA Monitoring Report *Overcoming Inequality: Why Governance Matters* considers inequality globally, and its impact on education performance and concludes inequality is still more destructive in poor countries.[7]

As discussed in Chapter 3, there is a powerful contra-argument put forward by neo-liberal economists that individual success powers national and world economies, and society's job is mainly to nourish those who are successful. In this economic purview, the poor have mainly themselves to blame for not succeeding and the rich are entitled to keep their wealth, however generated. Generally speaking it is accepted that English-speaking countries in the developed world, especially the USA, the UK, Australia and Canada, are those most tolerant of inequality. They are most likely to hold to the view that individual success, entrepreneurship and competitiveness are paramount goals for society, and those at the bottom must either engage in superhuman struggle to improve themselves or suffer the consequences of their laziness, poverty and lack of aspirations.[8] So dealing with inequality is not a high priority; it is unfortunate rather than unjust.

Danny Dorling, a human geographer, who has charted the physical distribution of inequality in rich countries, is extremely dismissive of this neoliberal approach towards entrepreneurship and competitiveness. He identifies five sets of beliefs: elitism is efficient; exclusion is necessary; prejudice is natural; greed is good; and despair is inevitable. For injustice to flourish, inequality must appear as natural, normal, innate, and inevitable, and these sets of beliefs do just that: they uphold an unjust system that perpetuates extreme inequality.[9]

Unfortunately ECEC is sometimes put forward as a panacea for inequality. Economists tell us that investing in early childhood brings sure fire returns. Children who have had high-quality early childhood experiences will be become more profitable individuals; they will be less likely to commit crimes or be a burden on the state. As I've already suggested it is a bizarre argument for a number of reasons, although superficially it may appear as a good selling point for early childhood services.[10] However, the main reason for ignoring these arguments about human capital investment in early childhood is that the economists who argue for the long-term profitability of early interventions do not address inequality or injustice or the very difficult lives some children lead; rather, as a sop to conscience, they presume that in an unequal and competitive society, giving some children an early childhood experience will enable them to compete better. The World Bank has even provided a tailored economic calculator, so that countries can estimate what kind of returns on their investment they can expect as a result of investing in early childhood.[11]

If inequality is a problem in the developed world, it is far more so in the rest of the world. It is overwhelmingly the differences between rich countries, mainly peopled by white Europeans and their descendants, and poor countries, mainly peopled by non-whites, that the greatest inequalities occur. Some of the world's poorest countries also have the greatest degree of inequality, a super-rich echelon at the top, and the most abject poverty at the bottom. This great degree of inequality is true of South Africa and many other Southern African countries, and for most of South America. It is partly a legacy of colonialism, when white colonialists appropriated the most productive land and grabbed the most valuable mineral resources – oil, gold, diamonds and precious metals.

Toleration of inequality in the pursuit of economic development is one of the ideas commonly exported to the Global South, and its repercussions are most severe for young children. Children do not determine what kinds of families and communities they are born into, but the situation of their families and communities profoundly affects how they might live or even whether they survive at all. There are various recent international initiatives to try to promote what is sometimes called social protection – making sure international aid policies of all kinds consider their impact on the poorest children and families.[12] There are also attempts to give greater prominence to the rights of the child, in order to focus on the more extreme vulnerabilities of young children and their carers.[13] But being pro-poor in policies and strategies is not enough; it is also *inequality* that is damaging. Excessive wealth also needs to be curbed, in the interests of equality, but this is relatively rarely discussed.

Young children are especially vulnerable to inequality and chronic poverty, and least able to withstand it through their own efforts. Many millions of children *every year* die before they are 5 years old. Put more dramatically, thousands of children die every day unnecessarily. A common estimate is that between 9 and 10 million children under 5 die each year – around 27,000 child deaths per day.[14] The difference between 9 and 10 million deaths a year, the difference of 1 million or so in the figures, is because births and deaths of children in some places are such an insignificant event that they go unrecorded. Even in India, which is touted as a superpower, there are 2 million child deaths per year. In addition to the high mortality rates, at present roughly 60 per cent of the world's children are denied basic rights to the facilities that are deemed necessary for ordinary everyday life in the Global North. They lack access to water, sanitation, food, health care, education, and basic shelter.[15]

Exporting early childhood services

If so many children lack basic facilities, what is the point of developing early childhood services? One reason (apart from the specious human capital argument) is that they can serve as a focus of social protection for the most vulnerable. The large Integrated Child Development Services (ICDS) programme in India, discussed below, was directed at the poor, as are many programmes in other countries. Another rationale for services is that early education can ready children for primary school – although primary schooling in many countries is also highly problematic. Unesco's main rationales for including early childhood provision in its list of goals Education for All (EFA) are for these two reasons – to help the poor and disadvantaged and to improve school readiness. The first goal of EFA calls upon countries to expand and improve comprehensive early childhood care and education, especially for the most disadvantaged. The EFA Global Monitoring Report, produced annually, dedicated the 2007 report to a discussion of early childhood education and care.[16] However, the report also points to the slow and confusing take-up of this goal.

There are large disparities within countries. With a few notable exceptions, children from poorer and rural households and those socially excluded (eg lacking birth certificates) have significantly less access to ECCE than those from richer and urban households.

The children most likely to benefit from ECCE programmes – those exposed to malnutrition and preventable diseases – are the least likely to be enrolled.

ECCE staff in developing countries typically have minimal education and preschool training and are often poorly remunerated.

Governments accord relatively low priority to pre-primary education in their spending. The broad mix of public and private providers and a lack of data make it difficult to calculate total national expenditure on ECCE . . .

ECCE is not a priority for most donor agencies. Almost all allocate to pre-primary 10% of what they give for primary education, and over half allocate less than 2%.[17]

There are however outstanding examples of good early childhood policies in two of the world's very poorest countries – Cuba and Mongolia. These countries rank near the bottom of the United Nations Development Index in terms of annual per capita income, but nevertheless have (or in the case of Mongolia had until the 1990s) literacy rates of over 98 per cent and low child mortality rates. Cuba outperforms by far every other South American country on *all* standard educational outcomes. Exceptionally poor and rural children are as likely to have as good educational and health outcomes as urban children.[18] Martin Carnoy carried out a comparative study on schooling in Brazil, Chile and Cuba. He points out that, unlike the other two countries, 'a child in Cuba from a low income household is assured a childhood free from hunger, lack of shelter or isolation'. Because families believe and trust in the importance of the state's ability to provide high-quality education for all, he argues, there is a kind of unspoken contract. Families back education, and children in turn demonstrate 'a very high level of self-discipline and co-operative behaviour at all ages.'[19]

Similarly Mongolia had a good track record, with a high investment in education, despite its poverty. Its performance was better than the other Asian countries with whom it is regionally grouped. It also provided well for rural children – an extraordinary feat in a remote pastoralist society.[20] Demberel describes how a remote nomadic population with a 1 per cent literacy rate in 1926 was transformed into a fully literate society by the 1960s. As in Cuba, the education system was part of a revolutionary endeavour which inspired and brought the whole population together.

Pastoralist people deeply respect Mongolian traditions and nationality and their cultural upbringing bred a strong sense of collective obligation. These two factors, respect for traditional ways of life, and a sense of communal obligation, were understood and incorporated by the state which considerably helped towards the successful adoption of the education system. Now people criticize this state centralism. I consider it to be a humanitarian policy done for the well-being of the country, right for people at that specific time, when we were so behind in culture and education. This education programme succeeded phenomenally in a short period of time, because it earned the support of the people.[21]

Both Mongolia and Cuba developed very good kindergarten systems, which included outreach work for the most rurally isolated communities. Their systems had clear policies, and were fully integrated into the education system. These systems met the curricula and training goals discussed in Chapter 5, but used (very) low-cost resources to achieve good educational outcomes for all citizens. So the Unesco goal for poor countries is achievable, even if it has only been achieved so far in rather exceptional circumstances.

There is another reason, perhaps downplayed by Unesco and other INGOs, for supporting early childhood policies. Almost every city in every country *already* has nurseries set up mostly by small entrepreneurs. At the top end these cater for aspiring middle classes, and lead on to an equally flourishing private school system. These are nurseries which approximate to standards of the Global North – with hygienic facilities, running water, fenced and equipped playspaces, and trained staff who follow a curriculum of sorts.

But there are also nurseries which have grown up in response to the needs of poor urban women. Since the late 1980s in almost every country there has been a massive rural exodus, a movement of peoples from the countryside to the cities, which swell the shanty towns. There are all kinds of reasons why this is happening, but it is migration on a phenomenal scale. In China for example there are an estimated 30 million migrants from the countryside to the city. In South Africa, the shanty towns around Johannesburg are much bigger than they were under apartheid, despite all the government's attempts to rehouse people, because of the levels of migration not only from the countryside but also from other parts of Southern Africa. As many studies have shown, many of these dispossessed migrants are women with young children, who seek jobs as domestic servants or as market traders or some other unskilled lowly work. They work long hours and they live hard lives.

Jody Heymann, from McGill University in Canada, has carried out many studies of working women in shanty towns. In one such study in Botswana, she showed that around 29 per cent of children in the township were left unattended while their mothers worked, and that they had much higher accident rates than other children – as you would expect.[22] But some of the nurseries that cater for young children are not much better than no care. They are mostly small private businesses, shack and garage nurseries, run to make money, with children crammed into small rooms with no facilities and untrained staff. These small business enterprises cannot be regulated because they would fall short of every regulation in the book.

For those parents who can afford very little, the nurseries have no water, no latrines, dirt yards or no outside space, and untrained staff who are paid a pittance. Such poor provision is rarely regulated since most services of this kind could not afford to meet basic regulatory requirements, and to impose them would make a mockery of the system. As well as being unregulated, they are also unrecorded – there are very few available data about them. And at the very bottom are those children who are left untended at home and whose parents are unable to arrange even the most basic safeguarding. The reality is that very poor women, especially migratory women in townships or shanty towns or favelas, work exceptionally hard and make use of backyard nurseries of very dubious quality, or else make very unsatisfactory arrangements for their children, in order to earn a living and avoid starvation.

Most provision in Africa,[23] and a considerable proportion of it elsewhere,[24] is provided by for-profit providers. The word quality is inextricably bound up with ideas about resourcing and material environments. Nurseries in poor countries can never aspire to this level of resourcing and it puts them in a bad light. So are there other ways of conceptualizing what nurseries provide? The model that is relied on in many poor countries is that of small entrepreneurs, where the poorest always get the worst provision. Much more work needs to be done on what kinds of governance models work best – how co-operatives work for example, what private for-profit means in the operation of nurseries in poor places.[25] Another possibility is the notion of what I call fair trade nurseries. Fair trade is a popular concept; that is the purchase of goods from small producers who get a decent rate for their labour and who are not exploited and whose products are local and sustainable. Fair trade also implies ethical consumers, people who are concerned about the conditions under which trading takes place. Fair trade nurseries are rather a fanciful idea, but possibly one worth pursuing in a situation where ECEC investment in poor countries is more often than not directed at stimulating the private for-profit small entrepreneur market, despite the evidence that some of this provision may be almost worse than none at all.

The adverse effects of inequality have been a theme of another Unesco report stressing the incompatibility of equity goals within a market-led private system.[26] In three studies, in Swaziland,[27] Namibia,[28] and in South Africa,[29] I explore how cost is related to quality. If nurseries are entirely reliant on parent fees, the higher the parent fees, the more money the nursery can spend on its staffing and resources. At the top end, some of the provision in these countries is similar to European provision. The lower the fees, the less money there is to spend; and in some of the places I describe in these studies, the nurseries exist in the poorest places, have the least well-resourced premises, crowded, unhygienic and lacking in equipment; the workers are untrained or under-trained, and earn a pittance or are unpaid; and the children who attend are often ill or malnourished. These nurseries are also outside of officialdom – they rarely keep records about who attends, and they are unlikely to be visited or their activities supported or scrutinized. In these circumstances, early childhood development (as it is frequently called in the Global South) is rarely anything but grimly custodial. In extremely poor communities early childhood services *cannot* flourish without external financial support, yet the need is very great. The most recent EFA Global Monitoring Report *Reaching the Marginalized* yet again stresses the uneven access to provision.

> Living in one of Zambia's poorest households cuts the chance of access to early childhood care by a factor of 12 compared with a child in the wealthiest households, rising to a factor of 25 in Uganda and 28 in Egypt. Physical distance from facilities and unaffordable school fees are some of the other barriers faced by disadvantaged households.[30]

There are other extreme examples of need, where the traditional communal and mutually reciprocal lifestyles that used to characterize daily life for many communities has broken down, and some kind of extra protection is needed for children. The most dramatic instances of traumatic circumstances for children are those displaced by war and conflict, and living in refugee camps, and those affected by HIV/AIDS. There is a considerable literature about such children and their circumstances.[31,32] Rural populations too in the twentieth century were displaced by commercial farming, not only by white families, but also by big conglomerates taking over the most productive land. The commercial farms in Zimbabwe, for example, that have been such a cause of contention – and which produced flowers and vegetables for the UK market – employed mainly rural migrants rather than dispossessed local people, and were also places of extreme dislocation. Save the Children Fund ran an early childhood programme for farm workers, in order to protect children from the noxious chemicals that were regularly used on the crops. This provided minimal facilities – safe playspace, shelter, food, and sanitation – for young children while their mothers worked on the farms.[33]

Provision of early education has been increasing since the Education for All goals were established in 2000. Some 140 million children were enrolled in preschool programmes worldwide in 2007, up from 113 million in 1999. The gross enrolment ratio (GER) climbed from 33 per cent to 41 per cent over the same period, with the most pronounced increases in sub-Saharan Africa, and South and West Asia, albeit from a low base. It is decreasing in the countries of the former Soviet Union and its allies. Provision in central Asia was once reasonable, but has mostly declined in quality and quantity since 1990.[34] Where nursery education is now provided in these countries it is as an extra year before school. Instead of the holistic kindergartens (which still exist for elites) there are poorly resourced nursery classes, which no longer meet the needs of working women. The Unicef/IRC monitoring reports on Central Asia no longer include kindergartens as a category, and now report only on such nursery classes.[35]

The Young Lives project, which is following up 12,000 children in Peru, Ethopia, Vietnam and Anwar Pradesh in India, through early childhood into adulthood, has provided very comprehensive data on attitudes to and take-up of early childhood education and care. It also shows very clearly that the poorest young children have least access to services, and experience the poorest quality of provision.[36] Even if government services are provided for the poor, they tend to offer a poor service, and are shunned by the rich. The maxim 'a service for the poor is a poor service' applies here as well as in rich countries. If teachers don't turn up, if classrooms are overcrowded, if the resources are non-existent, as is frequently the case, the learning which takes place is impoverished.

The Young Lives project contributed to the Unesco 2010 report, and endorses the report's conclusion that government intervention is necessary to ensure that in poor countries, there are pro-poor services to guarantee access and quality, and that private services are regulated.

> These are the equity and quality issues that threaten to undermine the potential of early childhood education, the divisiveness of encouraging unregulated private schools while failing to improve government education systems, and the importance of viewing governance within a comprehensive framework that accommodates all sectors and age groups.[37]

There is still a view that problems can be solved in a straightforward scientific manner. In 2007 the prestigious medical journal, *The Lancet*, ran a series of articles on early child development, whose recommendations have in turn been taken up by the World Bank and Unicef.[38,39] Influential and important as they are in drawing attention to the issue, these strategies are medical and epidemiological (surveying very large populations). They are uncompromisingly 'scientific', that is they assume providing early childhood services is no more than a matter of systematically applying known scientific facts. Their view is that nutrient supplements contribute to brain and bodily development, and by analogy, early childhood stimulation contributes to psychological development. Both the facts and the recommendations are presumed to be universal and straightforwardly applicable in every country.

- Implement early child development interventions in infancy through families and caregivers, and add group learning experiences from 3 to

6 years, particularly for disadvantaged children as a poverty reduction strategy.

- Ensure that development programmes combine health and nutrition services with early learning, rely on families as partners, and have adequate quality, intensity, and duration to affect children's development cost-effectively.
- Incorporate early child development into existing services and systems to increase programme coverage.
- Monitor the effectiveness of programmes with outcome measures of child development.
- Increase advocacy on the importance of early child development and the consequences of the loss of developmental potential to individuals and to society.
- Include programmes in policies and financial allocations at national, local, or international levels.
- Create co-ordinating mechanisms for ministries that share the responsibility for early childhood development.
- Ensure that all children are adequately nourished, including micronutrients, such as iodine and iron.
- Identify the characteristics of child development programmes that are effective and can be expanded and implemented through existing health, nutrition, education, and social protection services.
- Examine the role of early child development programmes in mitigating the effects of multiple disadvantages, including poverty.
- Research parenting interventions to identify the most effective and scaleable strategies.
- Define a core set of globally accepted measurements and indicators for child development that can be adapted across countries for monitoring, planning, and assessment.
- Improve and assess strategies to increase effectiveness of outreach to disadvantaged children, including orphans.
- Strengthen the evidence base for the effects of maternal depression, exposure to violence, parental loss, toxins, malaria and other infectious diseases on child development and identify effective interventions to reduce their risks and adverse consequences.
- Create and test a method for estimating the costs of different models of early child development programmes.

The early childhood stimulation is based on Developmentally Appropriate Practice, a simplified version of which is now available on the World Bank Early Childhood website for use in developing countries. Measurement of children is regarded as crucial to implementation, and similarly, there is now a list of available measurement techniques on the World Bank website. There is no acknowledgement that any cultural context may be relevant. There is no requirement to seek 'the support of the people' and no obvious role for users or recipients of services.

There are cryptic references to 'families as partners' and 'parenting inter-ventions'. Many low-cost initiatives rely heavily on home visitors, especially for children under 3, and on volunteers, and are cast as parental intervention, that is programmes for parents who need to (be made to) improve their child-care skills. The gendered arguments about childcare are implicit here too. It is simply assumed that the task of promoting child development is reward enough in itself and that women have little else to do, and they will work/comply with programmes that are introduced. Nutrient supplements, or what-ever psychological equivalents are presumed to exist, are not going to change these lives without other political and social interventions.

The well-known and long-running Integrated Child Development Services Anganwadi programme in India, aimed at the poor and offering crèche provi-sion and nutritional supplements, has relied on voluntary women's labour, and there are now many protests about the exploitation of the women involved.[40] Many Unicef programmes in Southern Africa rely on unpaid 'family motivators' to stimulate community action and care for children.[41] Conditionality programmes in Latin America, in which women receive very small cash or nutrition benefits in return for their contribution, are also a pop-ular form of intervention. For example the Nicaraguan Red de Proteccion Sociale (RPS) has relied on mothers' (in)voluntary labour to roll out health and nutrition programmes to more than 22,000 children. As Susan Bradshaw com-ments, whatever their advantages, such conditionality programmes reinforce and draw on the idea of 'traditional' family values, including women's assumed altruism towards their families.[42]

It is a very real question whether poor provision is worse than none. The very minimal provision, offered for example in the Zimbabwe farmworkers' programme, at least allowed children to play together outside in a safe place (which they did) and gave them food. It was without any pretence of input or instruction. This minimal safeguard may be better than herding children inside a small classroom where all they do is to sit still with a poorly educated carer. In South Africa, a country where there have been strenuous efforts to develop early childhood education, the indicators that have been developed to measure quality (see Chapter 11 for further details)[43] first of all include such basics as birth registration and access to child support grants. Within settings they include the proportion of workers trained to level 4 (approximately the equivalent to two years post-16); a local authority or municipal plan for the area; a monitoring system in place against stated local and national policies; basic registration of settings, agreed staff child ratios and an annual provincial budget allocation. These are basic indicators indeed. Set against this stark real-ity, the kind of 'quality' discussions in some of the literature in rich countries is an indulgence by comparison, and to argue that a notion of quality is irrelevant or misplaced is the greatest indulgence of all![44] But the important aspect of these indicators is that they are very much concerned with government action, at provincial and municipal as well as governmental levels, and see these as crucially determining the nature of the interactions that are taking place within the classrooms.

So what conclusion should we reach about the export of early childhood services? First, that inequality, within and between countries, undermines any education or care or health initiatives; conversely equality makes education more likely to succeed. Inequality cannot be ignored as a dimension of policy.

Second, early childhood services are not a luxury in poor countries, even if you discount the specious human capital arguments about investing in the future. It is the present that is the problem. In most poor countries inequality has led to migration and dislocation, and rapid change. The young children of the urban poor, and women and children living in adverse circumstances, need basic protection, let alone a 'high-quality' experience of early childhood. The early education and care that already exists in so many places exacerbates inequality: it has to be recorded, improved and supported, and it is difficult or impossible to see how this can be done while it is being provided on an entirely ad-hoc basis by small entrepreneurs.

Third, in rich and poor countries alike, the government has a major role to play: building a positive equity agenda; setting clear policy objectives that are co-ordinated across the education system, recognising the link between educational and wider social and economic reforms; raising quality standards, and training teachers. But to do this in turn requires a central rationale – what are services for, what goals should they have, and who supports them? And here the questions of culture and context become very important.

Exporting childhood

On the one hand, there is a push to develop early childhood education and care across the world, and there are some strong reasons to support it, even in its most rigid applications. On the other hand, there is a considerable body of knowledge about childhood, mostly from the fields of anthropology, ethnography and cultural theory, which suggests that children are 'central figures – and actors – in contemporary contests over definitions of culture, its boundaries and its significance'.[45] There are fundamental differences in children's behaviour and actions in relation to the groups and societies to which they belong, and there is scant evidence in the development literature about early childhood that these deep differences have been recognized or acknowledged.[46]

It is not only in early childhood that there are export problems. Educationalists generally of course are not unaware of these dilemmas about global borrowing. The 'new literacies' movement has also been involved in redefining boundaries between home and school, and putting forward suggestions about literacy and numeracy not as individual accomplishments, but as distributed learning and social action.[47] Despite the global imperatives, local understandings are remarkably persistent.

The iconic studies, carried out by Joseph Tobin and his collaborators, illustrate the differences between Chinese, Japanese and USA nurseries. He used videotapes of the daily practice in the nurseries which he compared and discussed in each of the countries with audiences of parents, practitioners and policy-makers.[48] Some 20 years later he went back, and did the same again, also using the earlier records. He shows how at the same time there are pressures to evolve and to stay the same. The continuity was greater than he had expected, even in China where the material changes were most marked.[49] As Tobin points out, the 'preschools' he investigated were places where 'childrearing meets education' and where practice was implicitly and deeply cultural. So much so that children in the Japanese nurseries were regarded as dysfunctional by the US group, and the Chinese regarded both the Japanese and the US children as very problematic. But these nurseries were part of established systems in powerful countries. The examples of conceptions of childhood from the Global South are still more startling.

Drawing on Robert LeVine and others, I have tried elsewhere to describe some of the domains where cultural differences might apply: individual versus collective; family versus community; independence versus dependency; spirit world versus empirical world; gender, patriarchy and gerontocracy and so on. All these differences are encoded in language, in the very forms of address people use in their mother tongues.[50,51] However, as Brian Street has commented,[52] culture is a verb, not a state of being, and trying to dissect it and itemize it is something of a doomed enterprise. Instead, it makes sense to use what the anthropologist Clifford Geertz has famously called 'thick description' (although that also begs the question of who is describing whom).[53]

But scruples about cultural identity apart, here is a quotation that I use often to illustrate the astounding differences in expectations of young children's behaviour and capability. Alma Gottleib is describing childhood in a small West African village, where children are actively encouraged, from birth, to regard all the people around them as friends.

> Chantal, a feisty two year old in our compound disappeared from sight many mornings, only to emerge at noon for lunch and then around 5pm for dinner preparations. Although she was too young to report on her day's travels, others would chronicle them for us; she regularly roved to the farthest ends of this very large village and even deep into the forest to join her older siblings and cousins working and playing in the fields. With such early independence even toddlers are

expected to be alert to dangerous wildlife such as snakes and scorpions and they should be able to deal with them effectively – including locating and wielding a large machete.[54]

What Chantal is doing is nearly inconceivable to childhood experts in rich countries, preoccupied as they are with physical risk and the need for protective environments. Despite her lack of language, at 2 years old Chantal is secure, autonomous, curious and very capable. She has a sense of direction and a sense of time. She can use tools effectively. She and her parents are confident that if there is any kind of hazard she is sufficiently competent to deal with it, by recognizing and avoiding it or by calling upon others to help her. No one would ever advocate this lack of supervision in a modern city, but even in a rural village where everyone knows one another, and everyone can be assumed to be friendly, experts would not think it developmentally possible, let alone appropriate, to give Chantal this freedom. But if it is possible, then it suggests that the criteria commonly used to assess children's capacities and dependencies might need revising – Gottleib herself uses her research as a basis for challenging attachment theory.

Here is another example, this time from South Africa. Trisha Maynard and I visited a nursery near Pretoria, in South Africa, in the company of a Motswana academic, Dr Nikidi Phatudi, who was explaining to us about her expectations of young children:

> Children should be taught to respect adults and other children, not to have unnecessary arguments or disagreements. She said that in her own childhood, children were expected at all times to sit and be quiet in the presence of adults, but she could see that this had sometimes been inhibiting and prevented children from 'venturing out' and exploring for themselves. However, she felt that even young children should be able to act with dignity, helpfulness, respect and politeness, and to fail to teach them self-restraint was to deny them their culture.[55]

The question about the hierarchical nature of adult–child relationships, and the importance of docility, is one which occurs in many societies. Robert LeVine and his colleagues theorize that such behaviour is an evolved response to particular ecological conditions – the pressures of agrarian life in which physical demands on women are very heavy and there is little time or energy for any negotiated behaviour with children. This in turn has led to particular 'cultural scripts', the expectation that children will obey instantly.[56]

Yet another example of cultural confrontation is the San or Bushman people, the once nomadic groups of Southern Africa, who have mostly been brutally treated and resettled. They are a very unusual people. Their marvellous art work and paintings have achieved international fame.[57]

Their survival and tracking skills in hostile desert environments are legendary. They have been an object of fascination to anthropologists and ethnographers for many years, and are probably the most over-researched group of any humans. Their family kinship patterns and their warm and laissez-faire childrearing have been intensively studied.[58] But they are still the object of international child development programmes which pay no attention to their extraordinary and well-documented history. When I was in Namibia, there was a food programme that was distributing surplus tins of sardines to San communities. At the same time the local Unicef office had issued a video about a home visiting and family motivator programme, where one of the home visitors is recorded as saying, 'We have to teach these people to eat proper food not bush food!' Instead of their particular, unique and very difficult heritage being understood and recognized, the San were being treated as obtuse and hard to reach parents, who needed to learn about developmentally appropriate practice. Like other dispossessed indigenous groups, many people have been very damaged by the treatment they have received, and alcoholism and other problems are rife; but their cultural history, innovativeness, even their language(s) are generally ignored.

Jessica Ball, working with aboriginal communities in Canada, has used the expression 'cultural safety' to describe ways of working with indigenous communities who have been very marginalized (see Figure 10.1). She argues that cultural respect, or at least the avoidance of harm, is essential if any programme is to be effective. Cultural safety implies acknowledging not only what is often a damaging past, but an uncertain and hybridizing future, in which traditions will be lost or eroded.[59]

Ailie Cleghorn and Larry Prochner compared classroom practice in three settings, in an Anganwadi nursery in Tamil Nadu, India; an early childhood development centre in a township in South Africa; and an Aborigine Head Start programme in Little Lake, Canada.[60] The authors set out to study how two contradictory trends intersected: local indigenous ways of knowing about and working with children; and globalizing ideas about practice, such as those ideas derived from Developmentally Appropriate Practice put forward on the World Bank website. They noted the use of time and space in the settings, the ways in which timetables were adhered to, and rooms were laid out and resourced. Timing of events was more relaxed, and the resources that are usually taken for granted as a sine qua non of early childhood settings in rich countries were, according to the setting, more or less disregarded. They also compared adult–child interactions, the expectations adults had of children, and the ways in which children responded. In all three settings, children tended to learn by watching and observing adults rather than by doing things for themselves. In the Anganwadi setting in particular, there was whole group teaching, through chanting, rhymes and repetition.

These practices reflected the nature of the communities from which the children had come. They were expressions of local ways of doing things

early CHILDHOOD DeveLopment
intercuLturaL partnersHIPs

Cultural Safety in Practice with Chil

Jessica Ball, M.P.H., Ph.D. School of Child and Youth Care, University of Victoria

Cultural safety is respectful engagement that supports and protects many paths to well-being.

What can we do t

How

"Finding our way to wellness among diverse communities of children and families requires many pathways. No one approach, no one program model, will reach or work for everyone." **Meadow Lake Tribal Council Administrator**

Once upon a time...	*And then...*	*So now...*
Pre-contact:	Colonialism:	Present:
Cultural heterogeneity/	Cultural homogenization/	Cultural reconstruction
Insular communities	Silencing and resistance	Persisting racism and essentialism

Indicators of cultural un-safety

- Low utilization of available services
- 'Denial' of suggestions that there is a problem
- 'Non-compliance' with referrals or prescribed interventions
- Reticence in interactions with practitioners
- Anger
- Low self-worth
- Protests about lack of 'cultural appropriateness' of tools and interventions transported from dominant culture to minority culture

Culture: forms and goals of interactions among members of a group, and how they understand and communicate with one another.

Cultural sensitivity: appreciating that there are differences among cultures.

Cultural competence: being skilled in understanding interactions among members of a culture on their own terms.

Cultural safety: the outcome of interactions where individuals experience their cultural identity and way of being as having been respected or, at least, not challenged or harmed.

Cultural safety is an **outcome**. It is determined by the recipient of a service, or the participant in a program or project.

- Respectful relationships create cultural safety.
- Equitable partnerships appreciate that all parties have the right to influence the terms of engagement.
- The quality of engagement contributes importantly to outcomes.

Cultural perspectives on:

1 Goals for development

2 How to support optimal development and quality of life

3 How to respond to development or life problems

4 Who is best positioned to help

- Tools, curricula, intervention strategies, and treatment approaches.
- Practitioners, educators, researchers.
- Program participants, clients, parents, service recipients.

All are er
cultural h
and agen

Wha
they
and
goir

To learn more:

'Cultural safety' and the analysis of health policy affecting Aboriginal people.
V. Smye and A. Browne, Nurse Researcher (2002), 9 (3): 42-56.

Cultural safety in nursing: the New experience.
E. Papps & I. Ramsden. International Journal for Quality in Health Care (1 8 (5): 491-497.

Figure 10.1   Cultural safety in practice with children, families and communities

Source: Early Childhood Development Intercultural Partnerships: www.ecdip.org/docs/pdf/Cultural Safety Poster.pdf

Families and Communities

...urally safe environments and encounters?

...e the sense of personal risk that some people experience when coming to a program, service, or project?

*...andparents taught me that to truly understand the importance of something you must
...ck seven generations and you must look forward seven generations."* **Debbie Jette, Cree Elder**

In future...
Transnationalism:
Hybrid cultures and identities
Braiding together: "It's about *us*!"

...r implications:

...ram, services, or intervention

...derstandings

...ram activities, service method,
...rategy

...opment and deployment (recruitment,
...assignments)

...particular
...texts,

**...? How are
...interactions
...t what is
...n?**

*...tional Discourses in Anti-Racist
...lanning.*
*...d V. St. Denis, Canadian Journal
...a (2005), 28 (3): 295-317.*

...mation and updates:
...p.org

Cultural Safety 5 **Principles**

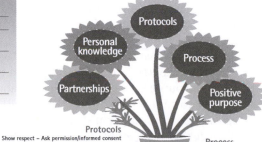

Protocols
Personal knowledge
Partnerships
Process
Positive purpose

Protocols
Show respect – Ask permission/informed consent
Seek cultural knowledge – Ask questions
Demonstrate reciprocity – Learning goes both ways
Engage community accompaniment –
Find allies, mentors in community of practice

Personal knowledge
Hone critical consciousness of social location/power
Who are you? Cultural affiliations, professional persona
Introduce yourself in terms of your cultural identities

Partnerships
Engage in relational practice founded on authentic encounters
Share knowledge vs. 'telling'
Collaborative problem solving vs. expert/authority
Strengthen mutual capacity vs. one-way 'delivery'
Co-construct ways to move supports into place

Process
Ensure equity and dignity for all parties
Negotiate goals and activities
Talk less, listen more

Positive purpose
Build on strengths
Avoid negative labelling
Ensure confidentiality
Be accountable
Do no harm
Make it matter: Ensure real benefits

C O N S C I O U S N E S S   E N G A G E M E N T

whatever the national requirements for the programme. The teachers were behaving, not as they had been trained – with play-based learning, constructivist teaching methods and so on – but according to what they felt was best for the children in their charge. But these early childhood settings had also to lead on to more formal schooling, which was more heavily influenced by international borrowing. For example in South Africa, the education system is organized around outcomes-based education and assessments, and particular literacy and numeracy requirements. This in turn was exerting pressure on the way early childhood development was being organized. The decision by the government, in the name of equality of opportunity, to offer 'grade R' education as a preschool year within schools, rather than as part of neighbourhood centres, exposed young children to international standards which are based on models of learning and resourcing in rich countries. The inevitable result is that failure rates are high, since children are not ready for schools which impose these standards. As the authors comment:

> It is understandable that a government should aim to develop its economy and to be competitive in today's world; however relying on the education system as the main vehicle for achieving these aims may be short sighted . . . National development does not occur among people who have lost their culture, language and identity.[61]

In terms of quality, it is evident that there are serious problems in developing criteria, if these are based on the standard indicators of rich countries and are fundamentally biased in favour of Euro-American beliefs about childrearing. Other quality criteria need to be created, however problematic a task it may be to reconcile local expectations and national standards. There have been various attempts to define quality on a local basis.[62] The difficulty is that such attempts may confirm rather than challenge existing inequalities, and in any case even local definitions of quality are contested.[63] The private for-profit nurseries that characterize much of African provision, for example, may reflect some local standards and understandings about entrepreneurship, but they also need external regulation and need to be matched against standards other than their own. In advocating the local, it is important not to ignore the national, or even the global.

Bringing it all back home

Rural–urban migration is a common phenomenon in most poor countries. But intercontinental migration is also increasingly common. Many rich countries have migrant or refugee populations, and public attitudes towards them are often hostile. Most European countries have right-wing anti-immigration political parties – for example the British National Party in the UK, the BZO in Austria, the Northern League in Italy or the National Front in France. So understanding and documenting cultural difference, and comprehending the limitations of monocultural approaches, is also important in rich countries. The sense of cultural complexity, of real diversity, of alternative views of parenting and childrearing, is not easy to accept, in any country which tries to present itself as monocultural. Immigrants are seen as outsiders who threaten a traditional way of life and traditional privileges. In some countries the very definition of immigrant is based on racial lines, so that even a third or fourth generation child is still regarded as unassimilated, and as coming from an immigrant community.[64]

There is a powerful diaspora literature in which migrants describe the view from their perspective, 'in a haze of history and pain' as one writer describes it.[65] Jhumpa Lahiri's book *The Namesake* is a description of motherhood in exile and the struggle for comprehension as the heroine tries to adapt to a very different kind of life from the one she grew up with, and how her children respond with equal incomprehension to her preoccupations.[66] Rawi Hage, an Iranian refugee, describes himself as a cockroach, despised and struggling to live on droppings.[67] Theirs are powerful and terrifying fictional accounts of what it is like to live as poor immigrants in rich cities. Knowledge about the depths of these experiences, and the resilience which young children show in coming to terms with this kind of heritage, should temper the way young immigrant children and their families are treated.

Nancy Scheper-Hughes, an anthropologist, has documented the struggles of marginalized families bringing up children. While mainly focusing on immigrant experiences in the USA, she also considers cultural conflicts over childrearing in a range of countries, in the present and historically. In her edited collection *Small Wars* she describes childhood as largely a story of resilience and survival against the odds.[68] These are the odds we should examine.

There is also a substantial early education and care literature about in-country diversity, which raises deep questions about practice. Celia Genishi and her colleagues argue that in the USA in dealing with diversity, 'any analysis must consider – and acknowledge – the three dominant paradigms that have defined social structures and interactions, as well as educational polices.' They list these as 'the inferiority paradigm, the deficit or culturally deprived paradigm, and the cultural difference paradigm.' They claim that these paradigms have shaped the design, delivery and curriculum of preschool programmes. Instead, they argue, there needs to be a collective responsibility for social justice and inclusionary policies. Recognizing diversity of all kinds is 'something to be enacted or expressed, something that is dynamic and agentic'.[69]

Paul Connolly, working in Belfast in Northern Ireland, which has been a bitterly conflictual society, has systematically investigated perceptions of difference by young children. His findings demonstrate how the development of young children's ethnic attitudes and identities, and their perceptions more generally, have to be understood within specific contexts.[70] Children unsurprisingly reflect who they grow up with and where they grow up, and in very divisive societies even more efforts are needed to promote equity and social justice. Connolly suggests the following strategies: a child-rights-based approach to the design, delivery and evaluation of early childhood programmes; rigorous and robust research to understand the effects of ethnic divisions on children, and to evaluate the programmes designed to address them; and the need to share good practice.

This research in Northern Ireland has led in turn to further funding from the Bernard van Leer Foundation for a network called the Joint Learning Initiative on Children and Ethnic Diversity (JLICED). Based in Northern Ireland, this research attempts to bring researchers, policy-makers and practitioners together in 'learning groups' from a number of countries where diversity is particularly fraught and problematic – the USA, Australia, Northern Ireland, Belgium, Canada, Colombia, Kenya, Mexico, Indonesia, Sri Lanka and South Africa – to compare and log projects that aim to reduce racial and ethnic divisions and conflicts and build socially inclusive and respectful communities through the promotion of effective early childhood programmes. It is still in its initial stages, but it is a challenging attempt to understand diversity from a global perspective, to track the connections, to compare and contrast contexts which spill over into each other.

Living in a globalized world, as Zygmunt Bauman suggests, is to be aware of the dilemmas and difficulties that exist in other places, especially poor places. In pursuing issues of child rights – and indeed ideas about quality – we have to engage with the experiences of childhood in poor countries. But to do that requires grappling with all kinds of issues previously outside of the traditional orbit of the early childhood community. Above all it means grappling with poverty and inequality on a vast scale. As well as professional responsibilities it raises personal responsibilities; we have to try to understand, at least in a rudimentary way, what causes poverty and inequality and whether there are particular actions we can take, in our lifestyles, in our consumption patterns, and in our work, to mitigate it.[71]

In offering remedies from rich countries for young children in poor countries, however virtuously it may be done, there are serious risks. As well as economic and social stereotyping, we do damage if we are not sensitive to diversity and context. The model of the family and of the individuality of the child that is current in the child development literature of rich countries is a simplified one, and does not do justice to the range of beliefs and experiences about childrearing which exist.

Ideas about quality then have both a global currency and a different edge in poor countries. But discussing quality in very different contexts presents an opportunity to enlarge meaning and understanding and to promote toleration.

Notes

1 Bauman, Z. (1995) *Life in Fragments: Essays on Postmodern Morality*. Oxford: Blackwell, p. 287.
2 Unesco (2007) *Strong Foundations: Early Childhood Education and Care. EFA Global Monitoring Report 2007*. Paris. Unesco. Available at http://unesdoc.unesco.org/images/0014/001477/147794E.pdf
3 Some of these data sets are based on ISCED data – that is they present a specific definition of early childhood education which excludes many kinds of provision. See Chapter 11 for a further discussion of data collection.
4 Overseas Development Institute (ODI) (2009) *Raising the Game: Mainstreaming Child Rights*. ODI Briefing Paper 56. London: ODI, November.
5 Wilkinson, R. and Pickett, K. (2009) *The Spirit Level: Why More Equal Societies Almost Always Do Better*. London: Allen Lane.
6 OECD (2008) *Growing Unequal? Income Distribution and Poverty in OECD Countries*. Paris. OECD.
7 Unesco (2009) *Overcoming Inequality: Why Governance Matters. EFA Global Monitoring Report*. Paris Unesco.
8 The USA, for example, has an extremely punitive justice system: it has a very high incarceration rate, and 2 per cent of all prisoners are held in total isolation, in what has been described as 'a rage to punish'. Craig Haney, Professor of Psychology at the University of California in his evidence to the Commission on Safety and Abuse in American Prisons, argues that the USA now celebrates and often demands, rather than lamenting or merely tolerating, official cruelty and the infliction of pain in its criminal justice system.
9 Dorling, D. (2010) *Injustice: Why Social Inequality Persists*. Bristol: Policy Press.
10 Penn, H. (2010) 'Shaping the future: How human capital arguments about investment in early childhood are being (mis)used in poor countries.' In N. Yelland (ed.) *Contemporary Perspectives on Early Childhood Education*. Maidenhead: Open University Press, pp. 49–65.
11 The World Bank website advertises the ECD calculator as a tool that provides a framework that will allow us to think about the economics of Early Child Development – to think about ECD programs as an investment. It will also help to put together the wealth of information on the effectiveness of ECD, to form coherent ECD policies. However, at the time of writing the ECD calculator is offline.
12 Department for International Development (DFID) and others (2009) *Advancing Child-Sensitive Social Protection*. Joint statement from the Department for International Development, HelpAge International, Hope & Homes for Children, Institute of Development Studies, International Labour Organization, Overseas Development Institute, Save the Children UK, United Nations Children's Fund (Unicef), United Nations Development Programme (UNDP) and the World Bank.

13 Overseas Development Institute, *Raising the Game*.

14 Save the Children UK (2009) *India Report, 2009*. London: Save the Children UK.

15 Gordon, D., Nandy, S., Pantazis, C., Pemberton, S. and Townsend, P. (2003) *Child Poverty in the Developing World*. Bristol: Policy Press.

16 Unesco, *Strong Foundations*.

17 Unesco, *Strong Foundations*, p. 4.

18 Gasperini, L. (2000) *The Cuban Education System: Lessons and Dilemmas*. Washington, DC: World Bank Country Studies: Education Reform and Management Publication Studies, vol. 1 (5).

19 Carnoy, M. (2007) *Cuba's Academic Advantage: Why Students in Cuba Do Better in Schools*. Stanford, CA: Stanford University Press, p. 156.

20 Steiner Khamsi, G. and Stolpe, I. (2006) *Educational Import: Local Encounters of Global Forces in Mongolia*. New York: Palgrave Macmillan.

21 Demberel and Penn, H. (2006) 'Education and pastoralism in Mongolia.' In C. Dyer (ed.) *The Education of Nomadic Peoples: Current Issues, Future Prospects*. Oxford: Berghahn, pp. 193–211. See pp. 97–199.

22 Heymann, S.J. (2006) *Forgotten Families: Ending the Growing Crisis Confronting Children and Working Parents in the Global Economy*. New York: Oxford University Press.

23 ADEA (2008) Working Group on ECD: see www.adeanet.org/workgroups/en_wgecd.html

24 Unesco, *Strong Foundations*, gives figures on the share of pre-primary enrolment in the private sector across countries, but it is likely to be highly inaccurate as many services are not registered, and the figure in any case excludes childcare.

25 Myers, R. (2000) 'Thoughts on the role of the "private sector" in early childhood development.' Paper prepared for presentation at the year 2000 Conference on 'Early Childhood Development, Investing in Our Children's Future: From Science to Public Policy', 10–11 April. Washington, DC: World Bank.

26 Unesco, *Overcoming Inequality: Why Governance Matters*.

27 Penn, H. (2005) *Unequal Childhoods: Young Children's Lives in Poor Countries*. London: Routledge.

28 Penn, H. (2008) 'Working on the impossible: Early childhood policies in Namibia.' *Childhood* 15(3): 378–398.

29 Penn, H. and Maynard, T. (2010) *Siyabonana: We All See Each Other. Building Better Childhoods in South Africa*. Edinburgh: Children in Scotland.

30 Unesco (2010) *Reaching the Marginalized: EFA Global Report 2010*. Paris: Unesco. The quotation is from p. 11.

31 Lloyd, E., Penn, H., Barreau, S., Burton, V., Davis, R., Potter, S. and Sayeed, Z. (2005) 'How effective are measures taken to mitigate the direct experience of armed conflict on the psychosocial and cognitive development of children aged 0–8?' In *Research Evidence in Education Library*. London: EPPI-Centre, Social Science Research Unit, Institute of Education, University of London. See http://

eppi.ioe.ac.uk/EPPIWen/home.aspx?page=/reel/review_groups/early_years/review_two.htm

32 Foster, G., Levine, C. and Williamson, J. (2007) *A Generation at Risk: The Global Impact of HIV/AIDS on Orphans and Vulnerable Children*, 2nd edn. Cambridge: Cambridge University Press.

33 Penn, H. (2001) 'Research in the Majority World.' In T. David (ed.) *Promoting Evidence Based Practice in Early Childhood Education: Research and its Implications*. Oxford: Elsevier, pp. 289–308.

34 IRC Transmonee 2008 database. Florence: Unicef/Innocenti Research Centre.

35 This is partly because Unicef/IRC has brought its data collection into line with OECD/Eurostat data collection, which focuses specifically on formal education systems.

36 Woodhead, M., Ames, P., Vennam, U., Abebe, W. and Strueli, N. (2009) *Equity and Quality?* Working Paper on ECD 55. The Hague: Bernard Van Leer Foundation.

37 Woodhead et al., *Equity and Quality?*, p. 80.

38 Grantham-McGregor, S., Cheung, Y.B., Cueto, S., Glewwe, P., Richter, L., Strupp, B. and the International Child Development Steering Group (2007) 'Child development in developing countries: Developmental potential in the first 5 years for children in developing countries.' *The Lancet* 369: 60–70.

39 Engle, P.L., Black, M.M., Behrman, J.R., Cabral de Mello, M., Gertler, P.J., Kapiriri, L., Martorell, R., Young, M.E. and International Child Development Steering Group (2007) 'Strategies to avoid the loss of developmental potential in more than 200 million children in the developing world.' *The Lancet* 369: 238–239.

40 Woodhead et al., *Equity and Quality?*

41 Penn, 'Working on the impossible'.

42 Bradshaw, S and Quirós Víquez, A. (2010) 'Even if conditionalities work, do women pay the price? *EIDIS Bulletin*: www.eldis.org/index.cfm?objectid= 786DBC92-BDA4-07FC-9592DE36FB92F88F

43 Dawes, A., Bray, R. and van der Merwe, A. (2007) *Monitoring Child Well-Being: A South African Rights Based Approach*. Stockholm: Save the Children Sweden and Cape Town: Human Sciences Research Council (HSRC) Press.

44 Dahlberg, G., Moss, P. and Pence, A. (1999) *Beyond Quality in Early Childhood Education and Care*. London: Routledge.

45 Stephens, S. (ed.) (1995) *Children and the Politics of Culture*. Princeton, NJ: Princeton University Press, p. vii.

46 Penn, H. (2010) 'Travelling policies and global buzzwords: How INGOs and charities spread the word about early childhood.' *Childhood* forthcoming.

47 Street, B. (ed.) (2005) *Literacies across Educational Contexts: Mediating Learning and Teaching*. Philadelphia, PA: Caslon.

48 Tobin, J., Wu, D. and Davidson, D. (1989) *Preschool in Three Cultures: Japan, China and the United States*. New Haven, CT: Yale University Press.

49 Tobin, J., Hsueh, Y. and Karasawa, M. (2009) *Preschool in Three Cultures Revisited: Japan, China and the United States*. Chicago, IL: University of Chicago Press.

50 Penn, H. (2009) 'International perspectives on participatory learning: Young children's perspectives across rich and poor countries.' In D. Berthelson, J. Brownless and E. Johansson (eds) *Participatory Learning in the Early Years: Research and Pedagogy*. London: Routledge, pp. 12–25.

51 Penn, H. (2009) 'The parenting and substitute parenting of young children.' In G. Bentley and R. Mace (eds) *Substitute Parents: Biological and Social Perspectives on Alloparenting*. Oxford: Berghahn, pp. 179–193.

52 Brice-Heath, S. and Street, B. (2008) *Ethnography: Approaches to Language and Literacy Research*. New York: Teachers College Press, p. 7.

53 Geertz, C. (1973) *The Interpretation of Cultures*. London: Fontana.

54 Gottleib, A. (2004) *The Afterlife is Where We Come from: The Culture of Infancy in West Africa*. Chicago, IL: University of Chicago Press, p. 32.

55 Penn and Maynard, *Siyabonana*.

56 LeVine, R., Dixon, S., LeVine, R., Richman, A., Keefer, C., Liederman, P. and Brazelton, T. (1994) 'The comparative study of parenting.' In R. LeVine and R. New (eds) *Anthropology and Child Development: A Cross-cultural Reader*. Oxford: Blackwell, pp. 55–65.

57 The Kuru Art project began in 1990, with a group of San artists in Botswana. The pictures they produced became famous, and at one stage one was used by British Airways for its tail-fin design. I have visited the printmakers working with the San artists and collected several of these prints, which I treasure.

58 Hitchcock, R., Biesele, M. and Babchuk, W. (2009) 'Environmental anthropology in the Kalahari: Development, resettlement, and ecological change among the San of Southern Africa.' *Explorations in Anthropology* 9(2): 170–188.

59 Early Child Development Intercultural Partnerships: see www.ecdip.org

60 Cleghorn, A. and Prochner, L. (2010) *Shades of Globalization in Three Early Childhood Settings*. Rotterdam: Sense.

61 Cleghorn and Prochner, *Shades of Globalization*, p. 134.

62 Woodhead, M. (1996) *In Search of the Rainbow: Pathways to Duality in Large Scale Programmes for Young Disadvantaged Children: Early Child Development. Practice and Reflections no. 10*. The Hague: Bernard van Leer Foundation.

63 Penn and Maynard, *Siyabonana*.

64 Heckman, F./NESSE (2008) *Education and Migration: Strategies for Integrating Migrant Children in European Schools and Societies. A Synthesis of Research Findings for Policy-makers*. Brussels: EU Directorate of Education and culture. Available at www.nesse.fr/nesse/activities/reports/activities/reports/education-and-migration-pdf

65 Hemon, A. (2009) *The Lazarus Project*. London: Picador, p. 1.

66 Lahiri, J. (2004) *The Namesake*. London: HarperCollins.

67 Hage, R. (2008) *Cockroach*. London: HarperCollins.

68 Scheper-Hughes, N. and Sargent, C. (eds) (1998) *Small Wars: The Cultural Politics of Childhood*. Berkeley, CA: University of California Press.

69 Genishi, C. and Godwin, A.L. (2008) *Diversities in Early Childhood Education*. London: Routledge, pp. 3–4.

70 Connolly, P. (2009) *Developing Programmes to Promote Ethnic Diversity in Early Childhood: Lessons from Northern Ireland*. Working Paper 52. The Hague: Bernard van Leer Foundation.

71 I develop these arguments further in Penn, *Unequal Childhoods*.

11 The measurement of quality

Scientific knowledge is most likely to display conspicuously the trappings of science in fields with insecure borders, communities with persistent boundary problems.[1]

This chapter reviews ideas about measuring quality in early childhood services. Quality is a problematic concept, for all the reasons discussed in this book. Quality in early childhood is difficult to define and measure, and as a result, as Porter suggests in the quotation above, claims of scientific rigour are often overemphasized and loudly asserted. I am not denying the need to try to provide measurable criteria, but this chapter suggests that the claims that are made for scientific knowledge and scientific findings need to be taken with a good pinch of salt.

There are many ways of organizing services, deciding who uses them, on what basis and for how long, and who pays. The content of what takes place, where it happens and what material resources are deployed varies enormously. The women (and few men) who are working in the service may have had a training of four weeks or four years. Quality might be measured by what happens at the time, or by what happens when children get to school, or even what happens when they are adult. Any notion of quality has to be based on the context in which the service is offered.

But I hope I have made it clear throughout the book that doing without a notion of quality is equally problematic. 'Evidence-based' policy is necessary (although not in everyone's view; it is sometimes described pejoratively, to indicate an overreliance on what is quantifiable over what is possible).[2] But almost all governments plan and pay for childcare and early education at some level, willingly or unwillingly, directly and indirectly, and they need some measure of value for money. At a local level and at a national level some kind of monitoring and data collection enables governments and others to understand how services are being used and if they are reaching the groups of children and parents for whom they are intended. Parents themselves want feedback on how their children are doing and what they are learning. Teachers want to know if they are effective.

In this chapter I discuss the kind of basic data that might be needed in order to monitor the take-up and distribution of early childhood services. At the most general level it is possible to devise a checklist about what governments themselves do in order to promote quality. In a sense that has been the main theme of this book. The OECD made recommendations about necessary government action to ensure quality. I presented these in Chapters 4 and 5, and each chapter in the book refers to them in one way or another.

Quality provision depends crucially on context. Children who come hungry to school or children who are from traumatized refugee families, or children from ghettos or sink housing estates, or equally children from leafy suburbs and well-cushioned backgrounds, bring their strengths and weaknesses with them. Given that early childhood services reflect the contexts in which they occur, I explore some of the measures of community well-being for children that are currently used.

I also explore measures that are used to judge quality in situ. On the one hand there are tests and scales that provide 'objective' or 'standardized' judgements of a situation, of which the best known is the Early Childhood Environmental Rating Scale (ECERS); on the other there are the kinds of self-reflection, documentation, and judgements that professionals (and others) make for themselves.

I also discuss – very briefly – the range of measures that are used to assess children's progress, many of which are retrospective, because of the difficulties of testing very young children. But increasingly there is a recognition that it is possible to ask children what they think and feel, and even though their answers may not be scientifically quantifiable, they certainly add to the picture of what services are like for children.

Measuring the context

In all these attempts to quantify and compare data about how children are being cared for and educated, there are prior decisions to be made about the domains of measurement. What is included, and what is omitted?

Andy Dawes discusses these dilemmas in his book *Monitoring Child Well-Being*. He and his colleagues are writing about South Africa, where there are particular problems of assessment – extreme poverty and devastating illness, and dislocation on a grand scale.[3] The book adopts a child-rights-based approach – the position that *all* children have entitlements or they are meaningless. In the light of these South African circumstances, the authors argue for the following approach:

- Incorporate the child's present while using a developmental perspective, that is, a positive quality of life is a legitimate goal, as well as any future outcomes.
- Assess both positive and negative outcomes – often measures focus on risk and negative outcomes.
- Generate child-centred statistics – the unit of analysis is the child, rather than the household or the institution; be able to disaggregate data in meaningful ways (e.g. gender, disability, education).
- Document the relationship between the quality of children's environmental conditions and child outcomes.
- Consider the timing of data collection – to try to dovetail with other surveys, or educational timetables.

At this point it may be useful to compare the South African approach with another major effort (although neither cross-reference the other) to introduce monitoring, that of the Canadian Early Learning Project, which is essentially an epidemiological monitoring programme conceived by public health and paediatric specialists.[4] This has been developed without the thoughtful background discussion about child rights that typifies the South African instruments. The Canadian project was developed principally by Clyde Hertzman and his associates at the University of British Columbia. It takes the view that it is possible to measure children's level of development in kindergarten (first year of school at age 5) by a kind of checklist (known as the Early Development Instrument or EDI, and similar to the Foundation Stage Profile in England) and map this onto other community indicators, in order to obtain a profile of particular communities and judge whether or not they are a good environment for children. The EDI is a checklist that kindergarten teachers complete online (on a voluntary basis) for each child in their class. It is a holistic measure of children's development across five areas:

- physical health and well-being
- social competence
- emotional maturity
- language and cognitive development
- communication skills.

Teachers complete the EDI in February, after they have had several months of interaction with their kindergarten class. Kindergarten teachers complete the EDI on individual children; however, the results are not used at the individual level. They are used to compile maps of where the most vulnerable children (those who do least well on the EDI) reside. There are three levels: high risk, moderate risk and low risk. Maps are produced to demonstrate patterns in vulnerability at the population level. The maps can be used flexibly (with sophisticated mapping technology) and may be produced at neighbourhood, school district, health area, and provincial levels.

Leaving aside the subjective nature of the assessment by kindergarten teachers (although they are offered training and guidance in completing them) what happens once the maps are made?

> we need an outcome measure that will inform communities about how the programs, policies and social environments that we provide for young children combine to support their development.[5]

Policy-makers are alerted but communities (which may be geographical, social or administrative or whatever) themselves are supposed to do something about the profiles of vulnerability which the maps reveal. Ideally there is a network of community activists, politicians, practitioners, well-meaning citizens with money and so on, who will act together to make changes. In practice they need coaxing, and they need to do their sums. The Canadian Early Learning project makes the following recommendations:

Get to Know your Community Assets

- Begin to think about community assets. Consider doing a survey of some parents with young children. What do they think of as assets for their children and how often do they access them?
  There are many possible ways to collect community asset data. Here are a few suggestions to get you started.
- Use driving and walking tours of the region, telephone books, community directories, maps of the region, municipal planning documents.
- Use personal knowledge, social contacts, and informal networks to identify community members with special talents, abilities, and capacities.
- Classify assets (for instance, individuals, organizations, natural resources, cultural assets).
- Think about relationships: how are assets interconnected and how do those relationships create yet another asset?
- Look out the window. You will be surprised at what you see when you consider how your surroundings might affect the development of a child.
- Can you be a barrier buster? What keeps families with young children from accessing services? Are there solutions that can be found locally or do the solutions lie in working with your funders and policy-makers.[6]

The impressive high-tech computerized mapping may be epidemiologically sophisticated but it is politically naive – to put it mildly – in the way it is being carried forward. It is very unlikely that the 'public' will form new coalitions in order to lobby for better child development on the basis of these maps, especially since the most important issue in this conceptualization is compensatory interventions for those children who are falling behind. There is no overarching concept of child rights or entitlement. There is no view about early childhood services and how they might be delivered. There is a very conventional view of what kind of early childhood intervention works modelled on DAP. Crucially this mapping endeavour does not see government actions at any level, local, provincial or federal, as being part of the data that should be monitored. There is no mention of the national data on ECEC which the OECD considers necessary for the delivery of services (see below). It is left open for the government to make its contribution, if any. So it is no surprise that the Unicef/IRC rating on early childhood for Canada 10 years after the EDI system was introduced in British Columbia still designated Canada with a score of 1 out of 10 for child well-being.

The main reason for discussing the mapping system here is the hold it has gained internationally. It is used now in a variety of countries, because it seems to be a sophisticated epidemiological instrument focused on young children. The mapping is taken seriously by Unesco. It was reviewed in the UK as part of a package of measures by the National Institute for Health and Clinical Excellence (NICE). The authors of the EDI system have launched a 'global hub' and they are key contributors to the World Health Organization (WHO) group of experts lobbying for better early child development – they are also linked to the WHO group who published in *The Lancet* (discussed in Chapter 10). Transposed into a WHO document, the intention of community mapping is:

- To demonstrate which environments matter most for children. This includes environments from the most intimate (family) to the most remote (global).
- To review which environmental configurations are optimal for ECD, including aspects of environments that are economic, social, and physical in nature.
- To determine the 'contingency relationships' that connect the broader socioeconomic context of society to the quality of nurturing in intimate environments such as families and communities.
- To highlight opportunities to foster nurturant conditions for children at multiple levels of society (from family-level action to national and global governmental action) and by multiple means (i.e. through programmatic implementation, to 'child-centred' social and economic policy development).[7]

Reliance on population sweeps like this is indicative of medical-based approaches, which may be very useful in identifying disease causation and distribution. It is of much less relevance when applied to early childhood, because there is not a consensus on what the problems are or how they should be treated.

But good data are necessary, even if the claims made for it are exaggerated. Most countries have national statistical agencies which routinely collect data – through household surveys, census returns and so on – on population, households, education uptake, social policy and so on. As the OECD *Starting Strong II* reported, these data sets were not set up to advance ECEC policy and provision – for example the age groupings are not applicable, and statistics about children are not disaggregated from their families. In most countries there are informational gaps concerning children under 3 years.[8] There are also problems concerning ISCED International Standard Classification of Education – used as the basis for the OECD *Education at a Glance* statistics which are the best known of all comparative education statistics. The category of 'pre-primary education' is described as 'the initial stage of organized instruction' and is not sub-categorized. Very different systems are lumped together or excluded altogether – which distorts international comparisons of take-up and expenditure on ECEC services. The OECD *Starting Strong* report suggests that all countries should develop a specific national database for early childhood services, which would focus on the key issues of demand, supply, equitable access and quality. It would include data on children under 3. Importantly, in those countries with mixed economies and a substantial number of for-profit providers, it would have

> reliable figures on public and private subsidies towards young children, disaggregated to cover key elements of expenditure, child-staff expenditure on the various ECEC types; expenditure on maternity and parental leave; expenditure on child allowances and other transfers towards families with young children, including cash benefits, tax credits and employer contributions to cover childcare expenses.[9]

These kind of financial data are especially hard to come by. For example, in 2009 a report by the Daycare Trust highlighted the difficulties of making estimates about expenditure on early childhood services in England.[10] Making policy decisions without adequate financial data is something of a dereliction of duty, especially by a government who have set out to promote early childhood services. Ideally the data would be collected *and made easily accessible* to everyone concerned.

The new EU-SILC (statistics on income and living conditions) data will offer some new comparative data, which does include childcare. EU-SILC is a multipurpose instrument, designed to further EU action on social inclusion. It mainly focuses on income and employment; detailed income components are collected mainly at personal level although a few components are included in the household part. In addition, information on social exclusion, housing conditions, education and health is obtained. It includes data about childcare use and disaggregated family income, poverty levels and employment – although not child-disaggregated data. Every year both cross-sectional and longitudinal (over a four-year period) data is obtained. This means there are common guidelines and procedures for collecting information across Europe, the results of which are relatively easy to access online.[11] It has been used for example to inform the 2009 survey on women's employment and childcare across Europe.[12]

So an essential aspect of monitoring quality is to have good data sets, routinely and regularly collected, and easily accessible, which can be used for comparative purposes both within and across countries

Another means of obtaining contextual data is through specific research projects, using a variety of qualitative and/or quantitative techniques. Such projects may well provide new insights, especially if they are rigorously and systematically carried out.[13] While there is always a place for blue skies research on new and unconsidered topics, what is most necessary is to introduce research and frameworks and sustained investment to support long-term policy goals. In the UK the national and devolved governments, with their insistence on evidence-based policy, have been exemplary. It is difficult to think of any other country where the government has commissioned and published – and made accessible – so much research in early childhood. As well as basic annual data about the demand for and the take-up of services, and the basic operation of the services, almost every new initiative or programme also has its research evaluation. Sure Start, Neighbourhood Nurseries, Children's Centres, and many other initiatives have had comprehensive monitoring and research.[14] Even if the results are inconclusive, or point to inconsistencies in the policies – or fail to take the private for-profit sector adequately into account – the information is publicly available. Government websites provide extremely useful sources of data, available at the click of a mouse!

In addition to research monitoring specific initiatives, there are population based research projects which, alongside other indicators, also track how policies impact on families. The best known of these large-scale projects is the Millennium Cohort study in the UK which is following up 19,000 children born in the year 2000.[15] It is possible to cross-reference the data from the study with the results of some of the specific policy-based studies.

The problem with much of this UK-based research, and research from the USA and other countries, is that it cannot be used for comparative purposes outside the country of origin without caveats. As I pointed out in the Introduction to this book, much research is inadvertently parochial, in that it assumes the models of early education and care that are being investigated are international and universal rather than country specific. When we undertook a systematic review of the impact of attempts to 'integrate' early education and care, the review immediately ran into the problem of what integration actually meant. Did it mean integration of welfare-based care and education for disadvantaged children, or the integration of care for working mothers with education provision, or all of these things, and under what conditions? What was particularly striking is that researchers invariably did not spell out these essential components but assumed that their particular definition would be widely understood by whoever was reading the article.[16] Systematic reviews which are a kind of meta-literature search, reviewing the research evidence according to agreed protocols, is very time consuming, but an invaluable method of teasing out the details and comparing the methodologies of particular research topics.[17]

The OECD report also points out that:

> Some caution also needs to be exercised in using research from another context, country or culture. An example often cited is that of developmental psychology which, through tracing the development and maturation of young children at different ages, made a valuable contribution to early childhood education practice . . . However inferences from the research often went beyond the actual findings.[18]

Non-English-speaking countries are at a particular disadvantage in promoting, or even comparing their research with others. There is considerable French, German, Italian, Nordic and Spanish literature, as well as material from transitional countries. All this is potentially very valuable material, and its existence should at the very least be acknowledged. There are certain topics, for example approaches to diversity and bilingualism or multilingualism and migration, or to children with a disability, that would benefit from comparative scrutiny.

While much of this government-framed research relies on standardized measuring instruments and sophisticated sampling procedures, not all of it does. The Young Lives project discussed in Chapter 10, uses both qualitative and quantitative data, and in particular uses children's own narratives about their situation.[19] Increasingly case studies, ethnographic methods, visual ethnography and video material, and focus groups are being used to supplement more standard measurements. The Sure Start programme in the UK, for instance, allowed local projects to commission their own research, which also fed into the wider programme of evaluation.[20]

So one set of measures of quality draws on information from the collection of basic data about the general situation of families, their diversity, and the neighbourhoods they live in. A second set of measures concerns the policy context in which services operate, the types of demand for and take-up of services, and the broad evaluation of government initiatives to deal with particular policy issues. Increasingly there is sophisticated comparative research, although this depends on comparable data being obtainable from each country, for instance whether poverty is measured in the same way, or whether nursery education is costed in a comparable fashion.

As Unesco points out, it is very much harder to obtain regular and reliable data in poor countries.[21] Most countries manage some kind of census returns, and there is usually some kind of household panel data. Education ministries usually have some kind of education monitoring and information systems (EMIS), giving pupil numbers, attendance figures by gender, dropout rates and so on. The data collected about early education is problematic because of the ISCED definitional criteria (see above). Generally information about early childhood services is very scanty, especially where there is a large private sector. Figures, if they exist, are often gross approximations, or doctored.[22]

Yet the context has to be thoroughly understood as a basis for judging the quality of services themselves. Data may be variable and be garnered from many sources, or they may be narrowly informative but accurate. The one imperative is to make the results available in as open a manner as possible. Only that way can scrutiny take place. Fortunately the Internet and World Wide Web has transformed the way in which information has been made available. In most rich countries at least, it is no longer necessary to have access to university libraries or apply to government ministries to be well informed. Conversely there is no longer an excuse for ignorance of what exists!

Measuring services

The question which dogs all attempts to measure services is whether to use standardized measures which can be used for comparative purposes, or to rely on self-evaluative methods which can be used for the development of individual projects. For some people these approaches stand in direct contradiction to one another; standardization represents an unacceptable straightjacket. Many of the postmodern critiques of early childhood services consider this to be the case. Hillevi Lenz Taguchi, a Swedish postmodernist, argues that such standardization denies the very nature of childhood, and children's potential for 'becoming'

> Our focus as teachers should *not* be with what we think is the right or correct thing to do in relation to such norms or truths and being fixated with learning goals and outcomes.[23]

Although she considers open-ended teacher–child relationships to be a matter of primacy in educational practice, a matter of 'ethics and justice in education', this view takes little cognizance of wider contextual issues, of the inherited cultural values and local circumstances and wider policies which shape the provision of services. It is as if the teachers operate in a vacuum, where everything can be created anew. Perhaps there are a few – a very few – places where such autonomy and new born awareness is possible, but it seems unlikely. It is even less likely within the school system.

This debate over standardization has reached a particular impasse in the USA with President George W. Bush's legislation 'No Child Left Behind.' This legislation, passed in 2001, required all children to reach certain designated literacy and numeracy standards set by their state. A relatively small amount of money was made available to help failing schools achieve the targets, but schools faced severe penalties if they failed to meet the targets. This legislation has provoked mixed reactions. On the one hand, its adherents say that it has forced schools to take the failure of pupils seriously and prioritize their needs. Its critics say that it has made schools little more than testing machines, and does not begin to address the real needs of poor children in an economically and racially divided society. The debate about outcome-based education in the USA is similar in England, with standard assessment tests (SATS) and league tables, where the poorest results tend to be in the poorest areas – but there are enough exceptions to the rule for politicians to unashamedly argue that more effort on the part of teachers can make a real difference to results. Outcomes-based education has most support in those countries where there is considerable inequality, and such education measures are used to track and try to address poor educational performance – as an alternative to, or a distraction from, addressing wider inequalities. Finland (which according to the OECD PISA 'Education at a Glance' indicators is the country that has the best education results at age 16 for literacy, numeracy and science) is by contrast a very egalitarian country, where standardized testing is of little importance, indeed perceived as harmful for children.[24]

Although it is more difficult to test younger children's attainments, not least because their preschool experiences may have been very different, this outcomes-based education has knock-on effects. It means for example that early childhood education and care are frequently judged in retrospect by the outcomes of children when they get to school. Longitudinal retrospective assessment using school outcome measures is a standard way of judging the utility and effectiveness of preschool provision. The much cited EPPE and Sure Start projects in the UK rely on retrospective data. It is also a way of assessing the effectiveness of various kinds of preschool experience in the also much-cited NICHD longitudinal project in the USA where 1364 children are being followed up through infancy into adulthood.[25]

From one political perspective, preschool experience is only economically worth having if children subsequently perform better at school. The question which policy-makers address is whether preschooling is truly foundational or whether the kind of experiences young children would anyway receive, with their mothers or carers, does the job as well as any more formalized arrangement, in which case there is no point in paying for preschool. But as we saw in Chapter 3, there are many arguments for supporting early education and care, as well as many ways of measuring it besides better school results. Generally the retrospective data suggest that high quality (better trained staff, better ratios) preschool experiences do lead to better school results, with two caveats. First, poor children do worse, and living in poverty almost always suppresses achievement, however good the quality of the provision. Second, quality matters all the way through schooling; good early childhood experiences may be foundational but they are not an insulation against subsequent bad experiences or an inoculation against poor circumstances. Retrospective measurement, like any other form of measurement, has its uses, as part of a spectrum of monitoring and evaluation. But it is not the only measure and it is not conclusive.

As well as retrospective measures judged on school performance, there are standardized measures for rating nurseries in the here and now. The best known is the Early Childhood Environmental Rating Scale (ECERS).

ECERS is described as 'an imaginative and sturdy tool for research, self-audit and assessment . . . a conceptual template.'[26] It was devised by Thelma Harms and Richard Clifford in the USA, and was first published in 1980. It has been revised several times. The current version ECERS-R was refined after prolonged discussions and feedback from practitioners and researchers. It has been adapted for use in translation, and modified to take account of settings in different countries. The principle of the rating scale has now been extended and there is now a Family Day Care Rating Scale, an Infant/Toddler Environment Rating Scale (ITERS) and School-Age Care Environment Rating Scale (SACERS). There are some foreign language versions, for example the Tamil Early Childhood Rating Scale (TECERS), which have not merely been translated but adapted to reflect local circumstances.[27]

There is an ongoing working paper on the ECERS website about the reliability and viability of the scales.[28] Generally the scale is reliable – different observers come up with similar ratings across settings and over time, and there are few redundant items.

The ECERS-R scale consists of 43 items organized into seven subscales:

- Space and Furnishings
- Personal Care Routines
- Language-Reasoning
- Activities
- Interactions
- Program Structure
- Parents and Staff.

There is also an English version, the ECERS-E. This was designed to reflect the requirements of the English National Early Childhood Curriculum for the Foundation Stage. In this version there are four new subscales to assess the quality of curricular provision in those domains that aim to foster academic development – Literacy, Mathematics, Science and Diversity.[29]

All these scales are administered by trained observers. Along with scales come training programmes, videos, inter-reliability lists and other supplementary materials. The claims made for the ECERS industry are not modest. It offers 'a meaningful, stable and reliable measure of global quality'.[30] In fact ECERS was mainly trialled in the USA, and ECERS-E, as the authors explain, in particular was linked to the accreditation system of NAEYC. This reflects the tensions of the childcare market in the USA. It is an expression of the concerns about quality that dominate the US literature: a need to establish a bottom line for some very bad provision, and an extreme variability in what exists. It also reflects a particular view of early childhood practice, where the material environment is important and there is a particular style of interaction between adults and children which values verbalization of activities very highly. It does not, for example, regard music or dance or artistic output or physical activity of any significance, and it does not inquire into accessibility or management practices or employee conditions.

ECERS then is a reliable standardized instrument for use where there are variable standards and a concern about poor performance in a mainly private market. It is of little or less use where provision is generally of a high standard, and where practitioners are concerned to make good provision even better. It cannot measure innovation. In those kinds of circumstances, more sophisticated research instruments are needed. Where standards *are* consistently high, self-evaluative processes may make more sense.

It is also of less use where ideas about what constitutes good provision are rather different, and its use in poor countries would be highly problematic, although, as noted above, there are instances where it is used. As can be seen from Table 11.1, there are different tools in use, although they too mostly also originate from the USA.

In summary, standardized assessments tools represent a lot of systematic and useful work on the part of researchers. They offer a relatively rigorous means of comparison between settings, and ways of ranking them. But their strength is also their weakness; standardized assessments are a closed system of evaluation. There is no possibility of thinking outside of the box. Such assessment tools can measure only what was preordained.

There are also many, many tools for self-evaluation and self-reflection. OfSTED, the English inspection agency, provide a self-evaluation tool, to accompany the Foundation Stage activities. Many countries also recommend evaluation tools at a national or local level.

Investigating early childhood students, Laura McFarland and her colleagues grouped students into those who initially overinflate their abilities, those who initially underinflate their abilities, and those who evaluate themselves consistently.[31] That is a neat summary of the problem with self-assessment. Self-evaluation may have the advantage of being extremely relevant to those undergoing it, but perceptions are often distorted. People do not willingly admit to bad practice, and

Table 11.1 International instruments for assessing ECEC quality

Name of assessment tool	Major categories (indicators)	Purpose	Countries where instrument has been developed/used
Early Childhood Environmental Rating Scale	Space and furnishings (8) Personal care routines (6) Language reasoning (4) Activities (10) Interaction (5) Programme structure (4) Parents and staff (6)	Research and programme improvement. Now used as a qualification criterion for some programmes	USA, UK, also Caribbean countries
International Step by Step Association Programme and Teacher standards	*Programme standards:* • Teacher–child interactions (4) • Family participation (9) • Planning a child-centred programme (5) • Strategies for meaningful learning (4) • Learning environment (3) • Health and safety (4) *Teacher standards:* • Individualization (4) • Learning environment (3) • Family participation (6) • Teacher strategies for meaningful learning (5) • Planning and assessment (7) • Professional development (4)	Planning and Accreditation for Step by Step programme	29 countries in the Russia Federation, Central Asia and Eastern Europe

Association for Childhood Education International Self-Assessment Tool	Environment and physical space (17) Curriculum content and pedagogy (39) Education and caregivers (13) Young children and special needs (24) Partnership with families and communities (5)	USA based self-assessment instrument	Used in 26 countries including Botswana, Chile, China, Ecuador, Japan, Kenya, Mexico, Nigeria, USA
IEA (International Association for the Evaluation of Educational Achievement) Pre-primary project	Observation system focusing on three domains: • Management of time – group structures, pacting of activities • Child activities – verbalization, child–child activities etc. • Adult behaviour – directive teaching, degree of involvement, listening	USA based research instrument (pre-primary instruments developed in collaboration with High Scope)	17 countries: Belgium, China, Finland, Germany, Greece, Hong Kong, Indonesia, Ireland, Italy, Nigeria, Poland, Portugal, Romania, Slovenia, Spain, Thailand, USA
Programme assessment tool, SCF-UK	• Professional practice (clear aims, protection policy, care plan, reviews, continuum of care) • Personal care (health, nutrition, recreation, privacy, sense of identity, controls and sanctions, voicing opinions) • Caregivers (4) • Resources (accessible, health promoting) • Administration (recordkeeping, confidentiality, accountability)	Planning and improvement tool for staff development Advocacy and policy development tool	6 countries: Ethiopia, Congo, Northern Sudan, Rwanda, Somalia, Tanzania

Source: Table 8.2 in Unesco (2007) *Strong Foundations: Early Childhood Education and Care: EFA Global Monitoring Report*

conversely, may be reticent or see themselves as boasting, in describing their good practice. For example, in my book *Comparing Nurseries* I describe a nursery that was by any standards a problematic place; there was high staff absenteeism; new or temporary staff were not introduced to the children and frequently did not know their names; many of the staff shouted at the children; there was an obsession with cleanliness, and twice a day the children were herded into the large bare hall, and all toys and activities that the children had been using were shelved so that the rooms could be cleaned with disinfectant. Yet in their weekly self-evaluation sessions the staff seemed to be unaware of the effect of these practices on the children. They had good examples to follow since they were located in a region where other nurseries had achieved very high standards indeed, and their co-ordinators met and exchanged views with others but no internal discussion seemed to make a difference.[32]

Margaret Carr, working in New Zealand has tried to schematize models of evaluating children's progress and classroom assessment. In Table 11.2 I present an adaptation of her model.[33] The *Learning Stories* she describes cross the boundary between assessment of children and self-evaluation of practice. She argues that assessment it is a four-stage process, describing a child's *learning stories* (in terms of the New Zealand Te Whariki curriculum), documenting them, discussing the documentation with others, and deciding how to take the work forward.

Implicit in the idea of quality is that we take stock of what we are doing. 'Taking Stock' is a frequently used title in discussions of quality. The Childcare Exchange, the US-based site information exchange site, for example, has a CD

Table 11.2 Models of assessment

Assumptions	Standard assessment	Innovative assessment
Purpose	To check against skills required for school	Enhance learning
Outcome	Fragmented and context free list of school orientated skills	Learning dispositions, children ready, able and willing to learn
Focus for Intervention	Deficit model of child, make sure missing items on checklist are remedied	Credit model of child, recognize existing dispositions and enhance them
Validity	Objective assessment	Interpreted observations, discussed agreements
Progress	Child has hierarchy of necessary skills	Child has increasingly complex participation in activities
Procedures of value to practitioners	Checklist, surveillance by external agencies	Learning stories for children, families, other staff and for staff appraisal

Source: Adapted from Margaret Carr (2001) *Assessment in Early Childhood Settings: Learning Stories*

with the title *Taking Stock: Tools and Strategies for Evaluating Programs, Directors, Teachers and Children*. This contains 64 articles on the topic of evaluation including the following:

- Do You Have a Healthy Organization?
- Need a Barometer for Assessing the Climate of Your Center?
- Signs Your Organization is Growing Too Fast.
- Nine Questions for the Dedicated Board Member: An Exchange Evaluation Instrument.
- Is Your Center Secure? 20 Questions You Need to Ask.[34]

The articles range from programme evaluation, director evaluation to child observation and child assessment. A rather less ebullient booklet *Taking Stock: Assessing and Improving Early Childhood Learning and Program Quality* was the result of a taskforce led by Sharon Kagan at Columbia University. She and her eminent colleagues pointed to the structural, conceptual, technical and resource challenges of developing measuring and assessment tools for the fragmented and under-resourced system in the USA. The Task Force, in contrast to the popular version cited above, demanded the highest standard of reliability and validity.

> States should assure that all child and program assessments are valid and reliable, meet high psychometric standards, and are well suited for their intended purpose. Data analysis and reporting methods should incorporate state-of-the-art methods to accurately and fairly document the performance of programs, including, where feasible, information from assessments of children and program quality together.[35]

The Task Force make the point that any assessment or measuring cannot take place in a vacuum; quality evaluations take place in the context of an understanding of context and quality systems of early education and care. The goals and organization of early childhood services must be made clear for assessment to be meaningful, otherwise there is no way of making comparisons or measuring standards.

There is also an Indian version of stock-taking: *Taking Stock: Developing Indicators for Analysing Costs and Benefits of Early Childhood Education and Care*. This booklet was the outcome of workshops organized by Project Access, an India-wide project of the M.S. Swaminathan Foundation, funded by the Bernard van Leer Foundation. This also pointed to the need to

- Understand and redefine multidimensional concepts for developing indicators

- List the possibilities for developing and refining costing tools
- Discuss methodological exercises for a possible costing exercise at micro-level
- Recommend the need for cost analysis at macro-level.

Here, calculating costs is part of the evaluation, but the selection of indicators was wide ranging, including programme indicators, child indicators, women and family related indicators and qualitative indicators. The tools included participatory tools which are now commonplace in poor countries, but rarely used elsewhere: resource mapping; community/household maps/daily routine diagrams/wealth ranking/time lines and other more local participatory tools such as 'Chapati diagrams'. The recommendations were more inclusive and more radical than would be possible in the relatively compartmentalized European versions of evaluation.[36]

Measuring children

If measuring contexts and settings is problematic, measuring children is a minefield. Many countries have teacher-based tools, where teachers are asked to rate pupils' performance on a range of variables – like the EDI above. There are also many specialized tests which mostly are administered by trained experts – usually psychologists. The World Bank provide a comprehensive checklist of 32 child assessment tests in current use and a résumé of the kinds of situations where they have been used.[37] These include well-known and long-standing tests including the Bayley Scales of Infant Development, the Infant-Toddler Socio-Emotional Assessment (ITSEA), the Peabody Picture Vocabulary Test, the Stanford-Binet Intelligence Test and the Wechsler Preschool and Primary Scales of Intelligence. The checklist does include cautions about the generalizability of the tests developed in rich countries, and the specificity of the tests. It recommends researchers not to put all their eggs in one basket but to use several tests for more reliable results.

There are even chemical tests for anxiety in children. Molecular levels of the stress hormone cortisol are measured by researchers as an indicator of children's ability to settle into nurseries. The hormone is said to be stimulated by uncertainty, 'with unpredictable uncontrollable events that require full alert readiness and mental anticipation'.[38] This measurement is regarded by some – mainly medically orientated researchers – as a more reliable indicator than any psychological indicator for young children.

These tests are mainly intended for diagnosis of children whose behaviour is problematic, but the *Lancet* article cited in Chapter 9 recommended their widespread use in evaluations in poor countries. Their argument is that the tests need to be used to demonstrate the success or failure of early childhood interventions. It is on this basis the World Bank publishes its list. However, some commentators argue that tests of ability are inevitably culturally biased, even if they have been used and compared across societies.[39,40]

The question is, as Margaret Carr asks, whether measuring children would tell you very much about the contexts of the children, or how their learning might be encouraged in anything other than the most simplistic way. It also raises questions about how disability is recognized and addressed, a very controversial issue which I have not dealt with in this book.

Measuring up

I have discussed some of the ideas about measuring quality. At each level there is a myriad of quality tools, but any tool requires that you know what you are doing and why you are doing it. On the other hand, there is no evading measurement and assessment. Accountability matters, to children, to parents, to staff, to politicians, to each other, and to the taxpayer who pays towards the service (even if it is a fraction of a fraction of the cost of the service or the whole of it). But accountability flows from more general questions about rationales and goals, about the aims and objectives of the services and the way they are organized. It should be possible to ask whether a system measures up at a national or an international level as well as asking whether the nursery round the corner is any good, and if the children in it are doing well.

Notes

1 Porter, T. (1995) *Trust in Numbers: The Pursuit of Objectivity in Science and Public Life*. Princeton, NJ: Princeton University Press, p. 230.
2 MacClure, M. (2005) 'Clarity bordering on stupidity.' *Educational Policy* 20(4): 393–416.
3 Dawes, A., Bray, R. and van der Merwe, A. (2007) *Monitoring Child Well-Being: A South African Rights Based Approach*. Stockholm: Save the Children Sweden and Cape Town: Human Sciences Research Council (HSRC) Press.
4 Schroeder, J., Harvey, J., Razaz-Rahmati, N., Corless, G., Negreiros, J., Ford, L., Kershaw, P., Anderson, L., Wiens, M., Vaghri, Z., Stefanowicz, A., Irwin, L.G. and Hertzman, C. (2009). *Creating Communities for Young Children: A Toolkit for Change*. Vancouver, BC: Human Early Learning Partnership. Available at www. earlylearning.ubc.ca
5 Human Early Learning Partnership (2008) *Early Development Instrument*. Vancouver, BC: University of British Columbia. The quotation is from the cover page. Available at www.earlylearning.ubc.ca/research/initiatives/early-development-instrument/
6 Schroeder et al., *Creating Communities for Young Children*, p. 52.

7 Irwin, L., Siddiqui, A. and Hertzman, C. (2007) *Early Child Development: A Powerful Equalizer*. Geneva: World Health Organization, p. 7.

8 OECD (2006) *Starting Strong II: Early Childhood Education and Care*. Paris: OECD.

9 OECD, *Starting Strong II*, p. 180.

10 Goddard, K. and Knights, E. (2009) *Quality Costs: Paying for Early Childhood Education and Care*. London: Daycare Trust.

11 See http://epp.eurostat.ec.europa.eu/portal/page/portal/living_conditions_and_ social_protection/introduction/income_social_inclusion_living_conditions

12 Plantenga, J. and Remery, C. (2009) *The Provision of Childcare Services: A Comparative Review of 30 European Countries*. Brussels: European Commission Directorate-General for Employment, Social Affairs and Equal Opportunities G1 Unit.

13 The work of the Centre for Equity and Innovation in Early Childhood at the University of Melbourne (Australia) offers an interesting example of government-funded qualitative research, postmodern in orientation, which has led to a substantial programme of work on relationships between aborigine and non-aborigine communities in Australia. See e.g. MacNaughton, G. and Davis, K. (2001) 'Beyond "othering": Rethinking approaches to teaching young Anglo-Australian children about indigenous Australians.' *Contemporary Issues in Early Childhood* 2(1): 83–93.

14 For a full list of commissioned research, see the Department for Education's website at www.education.gov.uk

15 The Millennium Cohort Study is carried out by the Centre for Longitudinal Studies, Institute of Education, University of London: see www.cls.ioe.ac.uk/ studies.asp?section=000100020001

16 Penn, H., Barreau, S., Butterworth, L., Lloyd, E., Moyles, J., Potter, S. and Sayeed, R. (2004) 'What is the impact of out-of-home integrated care and education settings on children aged 0–6 and their parents?' In *Research Evidence in Education Library*. London: EPPI-Centre, Social Science Research Unit, Institute of Education, University of London.

17 Penn, H. and Lloyd, E. (2006) 'Using systematic reviews to investigate research in early childhood.' *Journal of Early Childhood Research* 4(3): 311–330.
Penn, H. and Lloyd, E. (2007) 'Richness or rigour? A discussion of systematic reviews and evidence based policy in early childhood.' *Contemporary Issues in Early Childhood* (8)1: 3–18.

18 OECD, *Starting Strong II*, p. 189.

19 See www.younglives.org.uk/research-methodology-data/young-lives-data

20 Anning, A. and Ball, M. (2007) 'Living with Sure Start: Human experience of an early intervention programme.' In J. Belsky, J. Barnes and E. Melhuish (eds) *The National Evaluation of Sure Start*. Bristol: Policy Press.

21 Unesco (2007) *Strong Foundations: Early Childhood Education and Care. EFA Global Monitoring Report 2007*. Paris. Unesco. Available at http://unesdoc.unesco.org/ images/0014/001477/147794E.pdf

22 In the centrally planned economies of the former Soviet Union, it was common practice to alter figures to conform with targets.

23 Lenz Taguchi, H. (2010) 'Rethinking pedagogical practices.' In N. Yelland (ed.) *Contemporary Perspectives on Early Childhood Education*. Maidenhead: Open University Press, p. 30.

24 Fredriksson, P. (2006) *What is So Special about Education in Finland? An Outsider's View*. Uppsala Institute for Labour Market Policy Evaluation. Paper for EU Presidency Conference 28–29 September, Helsinki.

25 NICHD Early Child Care Research Network (2003) 'The NICHD Study of Early Child Care: Contexts of development and developmental outcomes over the first seven years of life.' In J. Brooks-Gunn, A.S. Fuligni and L.J. Berlin (eds) *Early Child Development in the 21st Century*. New York: Teachers College Press, pp. 181–201.

26 Sylva, K., Siraj-Blatchford, I. and Taggart, B. (2006) *Assessing Quality in the Early Years Early Childhood Environment Rating Scale Extension (ECERS-E): Four Curricular Subscales*. Stoke-on-Trent: Trentham, p. 9.

27 Swaminathan, M. (2000) *Quality Matters: Understanding the Relationship between Quality of Early Childhood Education and Learning Competencies of Children*. Chennai, India: M.S. Swaminathan Research Foundation.

28 Clifford, R., Reszka, S. and Rossbach, H. (2010) *Reliability and Validity of the Early Childhood Environment Rating Scale*: see www.fpg.unc.edu/~ecers/ReliabilityEcers. pdf

29 Sylva et al., *Assessing Quality in the Early Years Early Childhood Environment Rating Scale Extension (ECERS-E)*.

30 Clifford et al., *Reliability and Validity of the Early Childhood Environment Rating Scale*.

31 McFarland, L., Saunders, R. and Allen, S. (2009) 'Reflective practice and self-evaluation in learning positive guidance: Experiences of early childhood practicum students.' *Early Childhood Education Journal* 36(6): 1082–3301.

32 Penn, H (1999) *Comparing Nurseries*. London: Paul Chapman.

33 Carr, M. (2001) *Assessment in Early Childhood Settings: Learning Stories*. London: Sage, p. 3, Table 1.1.

34 See https://secure.ccie.com/catalog/product_info.php?products_id=5400127

35 Foundation for Child Development, Pew Charitable Trust and Joyce Foundation (2005) *Taking Stock: Assessing and Improving Early Childhood Learning and Program Quality. The Report of the National Early Childhood Accountability Task Force*. New York: Columbia University Press. The quotation is from p. 5.

36 Swaminathan, M. (ed.) (2000) *Taking Stock: Developing Indicators for Analysing Costs and Benefits of Early Childhood Education and Care Report of a Brain Storming Workshop organized by Project Access*. Proceedings no. 35. Chennai, India: M.S. Swaminathan Foundation.

37 Fernald, L., Kariger, P., Eagle, P. and Raikes, A. (2009) *Examining Early Child Development in Low Income Countries: A Toolkit for the Assessment of Children in the First Five Years of Life*. Washington, DC: World Bank. Available at http://sitere-

sources.worldbank.org/INTCY/Resources/395766-187899515414/Examining_
ECD_Toolkit_FULL.pdf

38 Flinn, M. and Leone, D. (2009) 'Alloparental care and the ontogeny of glucocor-
ticoid stress response among stepchildren.' In G. Bentley and R. Mace (eds)
*Substitute Parents: Biological and Social Perspectives on Alloparenting in Human
Societies*. Oxford: Berghahn, p. 268.

39 Greenfield, P. (1997) 'You can't take it with you: Why ability assessments don't
cross cultures.' *American Psychologist* 52(10): 1115–1124.

40 Serpell, R. (2000) 'Intelligence and culture.' In R.J. Sternberg (ed.) *Handbook of
Intelligence*. Cambridge: Cambridge University Press, pp. 549–577.

12 The quality chain

In this book I have tried to review ideas about quality in early education and care services. I have covered a lot of ground – international means more than just a few 'foreign' examples – and some of my accounts, I know, are very scanty. They also range very widely. If I had had more time, more money and more space, I perhaps could have done a better job. So my arguments have generally and necessarily been rather broad ones. I have argued that governments frame quality in early childhood services, by what they do, and have done over time, and by what they have omitted to do. This framing is undertaken within wider social and economic frameworks. There is not only tremendous variation in this policy making, but also enduring continuities.

Different countries have different histories and cultural traditions and no two are alike, although countries can be clustered together. The similarity of policy approaches and attitudes in English-speaking neo-liberal countries is a clear example of policy overlaps. The social democratic clustering of the Nordic countries is another. These are well-known socio-political groupings across a wide range of issues.

Most of my arguments and examples have been at an international or national level. I have argued that it is possible to trace the reasons why governments have set up and financed early childhood education and care and those reasons bear close examination. This is because the *values or rationales* are sometimes – or even often – contradictory and inconsistent and fail to lead to the outcomes which are intended. No government is entirely rational and consistent in its actions. What makes sense in one era may no longer be relevant in another. No rationale or policy is without its ambiguities, but sometimes the rationales seem particularly flawed and demonstrate 'policy stickiness'.

I have also tried to show that the *processes* by which governments try to implement their rationales for early childhood education and care, the policies they put in place, and their attempts at implementation also warrant investigation. Some ways of implementing policies are more effective than others. Some policies unfortunately amount to no more than rhetoric, because the work has not been done – or the money spent – to implement them. As the OECD points out, there is a list for good governance. What matters also is an understanding of how early childhood services are nested in a wider set of social concerns over education, health, poverty and attempts to reconcile work and family life. Early childhood services cannot be effective or of high quality as an isolated policy, but are part of a wider social picture. To achieve high-quality ECEC services requires adequate legislation, target setting, regard for human resources and the means of ensuring access for the most disadvantaged children, in a system which is subject to continuous monitoring and review and which has funding fit for purpose.

Some policies, especially in countries with neo-liberal traditions, are crucially undermined because they rely on the private sector to deliver them. Then the need for regulation becomes paramount, with paradoxical consequences, confirming standards at the same time as depressing them. Regulation is also expensive. Keeping a check on everyone requires its own costly apparatus.

International comparisons, based on internationally agreed criteria, have suggested that some countries do a lot better than others in providing ECEC services, even allowing for very different circumstances. It is not easy to directly compare one country with another in respect of ECEC services, although there is much in the way of overlap.

This book is an attempt to set the balance right, to explain how the institutions of early education and care are very much shaped at a macro-level, by what governments do and do not do, and how society is. Contexts matter, locally, nationally and internationally – we cannot have a comprehensive picture of quality without them.

In an ideal world, where the government does all that is required of it to ensure childcare and education services work (there are a very few governments who do) and at the same time welcomes autonomy, what then makes a difference between nurseries?

I have deliberately focused on macro issues, but this is to the detriment of micro issues. My justification is that discussions of quality are usually the other way around, very detailed expositions of aspects of practice. For instance, do lentils and macaroni count as natural objects in the science curriculum,[1] or do nettles in the outside space of a nursery constitute a health hazard?[2] There are of course some very serious aspects of practice which I have not discussed at all – the biggest omission is what happens on a daily basis to the one in six children who for reasons of health or other circumstances are extremely vulnerable, even if their vulnerability is temporary rather than permanent. We know that vulnerability, although it is spread across the social spectrum, is amplified by poverty. But, assuming vulnerable children get admitted to some kind of early education or care, how are they and their parents treated? How are other children taught to care for them with consideration? Or in the words of the Swedish curriculum, how is solidarity fostered with the weakest and most vulnerable? This issue is in a way a linchpin of good practice – and humanity – in any system of care and education. It warrants much more focus and well-informed discussion than I can give it here. It is an even bigger issue for good practice in countries where there are many children living with HIV/AIDS and other endemic diseases.

Despite my emphasis on the macro, I do not think for a moment that we should lose sight of the fact that the minutiae matter for children. A single day for a child is made up of many small activities, encounters and changes of pace, traditionally within a small familiar group. Being in an education or care setting is a rude shock to the system. The socio-biologist, Joachim Bensel (another cortisol man) puts it like this:

> Many types of non-maternal care in industrial societies confront children with a 'cage situation' in which they involuntarily land and over which they have no control. Their wish for 'return as needed' to their primary attachment figure cannot be fulfilled. The wish is intense when the adaptation fails, the quality of care is limited, the new caregiving person is not accepted as a secure base, and the other children cannot be used by an inhibited and fearful child as a social attraction and are perceived as a threat. For these children in such a care-taking setting, the separation distress is high and certainly not conducive to development. On the other side are children who are securely enough attached to be cared for under conditions which let them use an alternative social platform free of fear, which makes it possible for them to gain valuable experiences which they would not be offered at home.[3]

For socio-biologists, human infants, like infants of other primates, are 'parent clingers', that is adapted to spending their earliest childhood in close contact with their caregivers, requiring rich tactile stimulation in order to be reassured of the presence of those caregivers. In developed countries, the tactile stimulation has been replaced to an extent by verbal stimulation. Children are no longer routinely carried on the back, and it is no longer acceptable for them to sleep with others. The familiar caretakers, mothers, aunts, sisters, cousins and grannies in a large family group, have been replaced by mothers alone, or by mothers with some support from fathers. Socio-biologically speaking, many, if not most, experiences for young children, at home or in a nursery, are 'unnatural'. Conceptually early childhood is an invention, one which is not very well padded out.

Children are of course supremely adaptable, but there is surprisingly little discussion about how they learn to cope with group life, or what permutations of group life are possible, or how group life and home life are aligned.

Psychologists have researched this, but in a limited way. For example, in 2003 a special edition of the prestigious journal *Child Development* was devoted to research in daycare, but although closely focused on children's experiences (using impeccable scientific methodologies), most of the articles ignored macro events and treated the nurseries as an unalterable phenomenon, rather than as the product – especially in the ultra-commercial USA – of a very particular system of early education and care.[4] The trick in arriving at descriptions and definitions of quality is to combine macro and micro evidence, and it is a very hard task indeed.

So to summarize my arguments, the arrangements we make for children are, relatively speaking, new and experimental, even if they are commonly regarded as established. These arrangements vary considerably between countries, so that it is necessary to be very cautious about generalizing from one situation to another. Researchers from any one country cannot claim to be identifying some kind of global norm for children's experiences, although there is some kind of consensus and evidence bank of accumulated observations and measurement. The quality chain between the intimate details of practice and societal values is long and unstraight but always there.

Children, even the smallest children, are not ciphers or widgets, or manipulable figures on a business plan, or footnotes to a public policy document. Anyone who has young children or grandchildren wants to see them recognized and encouraged for what they are – robust, competent and active people who have a stake in society, just as it has a stake in them. They should not be warehoused, or over-instructed or marginalized, for all their resilience and vulnerability. As well as their mothers and other family members, they require skilful and sympathetic people to care for and educate them in places and spaces where they can be fully physical, be doers as well as learners.

But definitions, investigations, descriptions, and analysis – and rhetoric – are not enough. The classic question is how to improve quality and keep on improving it. UNICEF/IRC has provided a crude ranking, and if there are other data to suggest poor outcomes, then perhaps those of us who live in countries with a weak record have an advocacy job to do. Why should children and their families do worse in our own country? If the evidence is clear, do we have some kind of obligation to draw on it – unslavishly – as policy makers, practitioners, academics, or as parents? There are many different points at which one can try to exert pressure on the quality chain: relationships with young children; having conversations about, reviewing and reflecting on daily practice; improving administrative procedures; designing better policies; influencing political processes; measuring outcomes; analysing trends, training those who work with children so that they can be both pragmatic and self-critical. The big picture matters, and we need to know about it in order to understand what is happening, even if, at any one time, our links in the chain are of the smallest and most intricate kind.

ideas for exploring

Notes

1 There is a discussion for example in the ECERS-E instrument to measure quality of education provided in a setting, about whether the use of lentils and maca-roni in classroom activities can be construed as a scientific or as an artistic activity.

2 I have visited a nursery where the manager found some nettles in a corner of the garden, and immediately sent in a report form asking her organization to send a handyman to remove them on grounds of health and safety!

3 Bensel, J. (2009) 'Separation stress in early childhood.' In G. Bentley and R. Mace (eds) *Substitute Parents: Biological and Social Perspectives on Alloparenting.* Oxford: Berghahn, p. 300.

4 The special edition is *Child Development* 2003(4): 969–1825.

Index

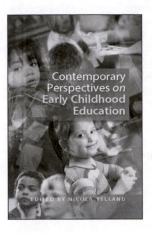

CONTEMPORARY PERSPECTIVES ON EARLY CHILDHOOD EDUCATION

Nicola Yelland (Editor)

978-0-335-23787-6 (Paperback)
2010

eBook also available

This book considers and interrogates a range of new and critical issues in contemporary early childhood education. It discusses both fundamental and emerging topics in the field, and presents them in the context of reflective and contemporary frameworks.

Bringing together leading experts whose work is at the cutting edge of contemporary early childhood education theory and research across the world, this book considers the care and education of young children from a global perspective and deals with issues and groups of children or families that are often marginalized.

This edited collection is essential reading for anyone studying or working in early childhood education.

www.openup.co.uk

OPEN UNIVERSITY PRESS
McGraw - Hill Education